READINGS & CASE STUDIES IN *Mediation*

Bruce C. McKinney
Jerry Bagnell
University of North Carolina—Wilmington

KENDALL/HUNT PUBLISHING COMPANY
4050 Westmark Drive   Dubuque, Iowa 52002

Cover image © JupiterImages Corporation

Copyright © 2007 by Bruce C. McKinney and Jerry Bagnell

ISBN 13: 978-0-7575-3964-0
ISBN 10: 0-7575-3964-5

Kendall/Hunt Publishing Company has the exclusive rights to reproduce this work, to prepare derivative works from this work, to publicly distribute this work, to publicly perform this work and to publicly display this work.

All rights reserved. No part of this publication may be reproduced, stored in a retrieval system, or transmitted, in any form or by any means, electronic, mechanical, photocopying, recording, or otherwise, without the prior written permission of the copyright owner.

Printed in the United States of America

10 9 8 7 6 5 4 3 2 1

This book is dedicated to our friends and colleagues who have inspired us by their example and their dedication to the profession of mediation, and to our wives—Jess and Amy—who inspire us to be better at everything we do.

Contents

About the Contributors   vii

1   **Introduction**   1
      Bruce C. McKinney
      Jerry Bagnell

2   **Divorce Mediation**   7
      Jerry Bagnell

3   **Mediating Employment and Workplace Disputes**   29
      Merri L. Hanson

4   **Mediating Staff Disputes at a Large State University**   45
      Jessica Katz Jameson

5   **Developing Peer Mediation Programs for Today's Students**   59
      Kirsten B. Atkinson
      Kimberly Lucas

6	**The Movement of Mediation in Social Helping Fields** Kirsten B. Atkinson	69
7	**Environmental Mediation: A Primer** Tina Nabatchi Michael E. Keller	81
8	**Mediation in Crisis Situations** Tina Jaeckle	103
9	**Mediation in Juvenile Victim/Offender Conferencing** Andrea Bodtker	117
10	**Mediating Disputes Involving Youth Gangs** Bruce C. McKinney	131
11	**Faith-Based Disputes and Mediation Intervention** William D. Kimsey Sallye S. Trobaugh	145
12	**Mediation-Arbitration in Dispute Resolution** Christine A. Coates	161
13	**Transformative Mediation: Purpose Drives Practice** Lisa Blomgren Bingham Cynthia J. Hallberlin Denise A. Walker	177
14	**Conclusion** Jerry Bagnell Bruce C. McKinney	191

About the Contributors

Bruce C. McKinney teaches courses in mediation and conflict resolution and has served as a community and divorce mediator. He received his graduate degrees (M.A., Ph.D.) in speech communication from The Pennsylvania State University, and is a faculty member in the Department of Communication Studies at The University of North Carolina Wilmington. He is co-author of *Mediator Communication Competencies: Problem Solving and Transformative Practices* 5th edition. He has taught business executives conflict resolution and negotiating skills for the Center for Systems Development at Vietnam National University in Hanoi and for Royal Education Ltd., in Ho Chi Minh City, Vietnam.

Jerry Bagnell has been a mediator and trainer since 1979. He has a Master of Education from the University of Delaware and a Master of Social Work from the University of Georgia. Jerry was designated as a Mentor and Certified Mediator by the Supreme Court of Virginia from 1994-2001. He was an Advanced Practitioner Member of the Association for Conflict Resolution, Co-chair of the Ethics Committee, and Co-chair of the Crisis Intervention Section. Jerry currently teaches courses in Negotiation as well as Mediation and Conflict Management at the University of North Carolina Wilmington.

Kirsten Bailey Atkinson has been mediating and facilitating since 1993 and is the current Executive Director of the Community Mediation Center of Cape Fear (North Carolina). She holds Masters Degree from Columbia College in Conflict Resolution. Ms. Atkinson conducts mediation, facilitation and training, at the state, national and international communities, and has held leadership roles with the North Carolina Mediation Network, including State Board president and served on the National Association of Community Mediation Board in Washington, DC.

Lisa Blomgren Bingham is the Keller-Runden Professor of Public Service and Director of the Indiana Conflict Resolution Institute (ICRI) at Indiana University's

School of Public and Environmental Affairs, Bloomington, Indiana. A graduate of Smith College and the University of Connecticut School of Law, Bingham has authored over fifty articles and book chapters. She has received research awards from the Association for Conflict Resolution, the American Bar Association Section of Dispute Resolution, International Association for Conflict Management, and Section of Environmental and Natural Resource Administration of the American Society of Public Administration.

Andrea M. Bodtker received her BA (1989) and MA (1992) in Communication at the University of California, Santa Barbara, and completed her doctoral coursework (1999) at Temple University. She has co-authored and published scholarly articles, book chapters and research reports on all aspects of communication, conflict and emotion. She has been a trained mediator since 1989, and more recently began specializing in Victim-Offender Mediation (VOM), both as a volunteer mediator and as a researcher focusing on emotional components of VOM.

Christine A. Coates holds advanced degrees in education and law, and is an experienced family law attorney, now emphasizes ADR in domestic relations. A mediator since 1984, Christie is a frequent and popular national speaker and trainer in conflict resolution. She is adjunct professor of mediation at the University of Colorado School of Law and teaches at the Institute for Advanced Dispute Resolution. She has received honors for her work as a mediator, lawyer and child advocate. Christie's dispute resolution experience is extensive, having served as a neutral in such areas of conflict as civil litigation, personal injury, commercial, debtor-creditor, divorce and child custody, non-divorce family issues, organization, government, and education.

Cynthia J. Hallberlin is the Chief Ethics and Compliance Officer with U.S. Foodservice. In this role, she is responsible for creating an ethical culture for over 28,000 employees in 82 divisions across the United States. She is responsible for the enforcement of the Code of Conduct, investigations of fraud and financial misconduct, the third-party hotline under Sarbanes-Oxley, all non-financial compliance programs, corporate social responsibility and ethics and compliance training. Before entering the private sector, she was an attorney for 19 years at the U.S. Postal Service where she was the creator and national program manager of REDRESS™, the world's largest EEO mediation program.

Merri L. Hanson is the Director of Peninsula Mediation & ADR in Williamsburg and Hampton, Virginia. Prior to establishing Peninsula Mediation & ADR in 1991, Ms. Hanson taught a variety of communication and conflict management courses at colleges and universities in California and Virginia in both full-time and adjunct capacities. She established the Isle of Wight Victim's Services Program for the Virginia Department of Criminal Justice Services Her education achievements include a Bachelor of Arts in Speech Communication, a Master of Arts in Communication and Conflict Management, and post-graduate work in organizational psychology.

Tina Jaeckle is a Licensed Clinical Social Worker, a Diplomat in the American Academy of Experts in Traumatic Stress, a Board Certified Expert in Crisis Response, and a Florida Supreme Court Certified Family and Dependency Mediator and Primary Trainer. Tina is an Assistant Professor in the Social and Behavioral Sciences at Flagler College, St. Augustine, Florida and is a Ph.D. candidate in Conflict Analysis and Resolution from Nova Southeastern University.

Jessica Katz Jameson is an Associate Professor of Communication at North Carolina State University where she teaches courses in organizational communication, public relations, conflict management, and nonprofit leadership. Her research focuses on organizational conflict management and she has published articles in *Negotiation Journal,* the *International Journal of Conflict Management, Conflict Resolution Quarterly,* the *Western Journal of Communication,* and the *Journal of Health Communication.* Professor Jameson is a mediator for NC State's employee mediation program and she previously assisted with the development of a campus peer mediation program at Temple University as well as mediation training for university administrators and ombudspersons.

Michael Keller is an Assistant Dean at the Indiana University School of Law - Bloomington. He received his Master of Public Affairs with a concentration in Environmental Policy and Natural Resource Management from the School of Public and Environmental Affairs at Indiana University. His special interests include energy policy issues particularly as they pertain to the environment and alternative energy options.

William D. Kimsey is a Professor of Communication at JMU and he received his Ph.D. from Southern Illinois University. He is a certified mediator for the Commonwealth of Virginia. He teaches courses in communication, conflict resolution, and research methods. He is the co-author of CONFLICTALK, an instrument used for measuring conflict styles of elementary, middle and high school students and he is co-author of *Mediator Communication Competencies: Problem Solving and Transformative Practices* 5th edition. He has published articles on communication and conflict in a variety of journals including *Communication Monographs, Conflict Resolution Quarterly, Canadian Journal of Peace Studies,* and the *Asian Profile.*

Kim Lucas has been an educator for most of her life before turning to mediation nearly five years ago. She is currently working on her Masters in Conflict Resolution and runs the district court program at the local mediation center (Community Mediation Center of Cape Fear). She has three children and a husband and resides in Wilmington, North Carolina.

Tina Nabatchi is a doctoral candidate in the Public Affairs program at the Indiana University-Bloomington School of Public and Environmental Affairs and the research coordinator for the Indiana Conflict Resolution Institute. Her research interests include public management, public policy, and law, particularly in relation to conflict resolution, deliberative democracy, and sustainable development administration.

Sallye S. Trobaugh is the owner of Mediation Associates, LLC and a Broker Associate for ERA Kline and May Realty in Harrisonburg, Virginia. She has served as a mediator in domestic and business disputes for over twenty years. She is a licensed Real Estate Broker, licensed Virginia Real Estate Instructor, Certified Residential Broker, a Certified Ethics Instructor, Education Director for ERA Kline and May Realty, and is a trainer in real estate negotiation, mediation, and problem solving facilitation. She has published in *Conflict Resolution Quarterly*.

Denise A. Walker is a Deputy Attorney General for the State of Indiana specializing in environmental litigation. She is a graduate of Kansas State University, and holds a Masters in Public Affairs from the Indiana University School of Public and Environmental Affairs, and a juris doctor from the Indiana University School of Law.

Chapter 1

Introduction

Bruce C. McKinney
Jerry Bagnell

One of the editors uses scenes from the Arts and Entertainment (A&E) network program *Airline* in his class, for it provides excellent examples of how and how not to manage conflict. To those of you who teach conflict and have not seen this program, it would not be a bad idea to view at least one episode, for it provides a virtual cornucopia of examples of conflict and how people react to it. The show follows employees of Southwest Airlines around (e.g., gate attendants, reservation personnel, cabin crew, etc.) and documents the different types of conflicts these people encounter daily and how the Southwest employees respond to these conflicts.

Southwest should be given credit for they have obviously let A&E air whatever they please—sometimes the Southwest employees shine, sometimes they do not. A typical dispute that seems to come up time and time again occurs when passengers attempt to board their flights in various degrees of intoxication. Southwest has a strict policy that, for safety reasons, intoxicated passengers are denied boarding their aircraft—truly an example of an expressed struggle of incompatible goals in which one party interferes with another party's desire to achieve its goal.

When passengers are denied boarding by Southwest employees, the common refrain from the intoxicated passengers (and passengers in many other disputes with Southwest) is "I am going to sue Southwest!" This is probably a good microcosm of how Americans view conflict—a litigious problem that demands some type of pursuit in the court system.

Sadly, this writer has never seen a disgruntled passenger demand "I want a mediator!" And it is extremely doubtful if there will ever be a popular television show called "LA Mediator."

Perhaps mediation is the Rodney Dangerfield of dispute resolution in the U.S.—it gets no respect. However, with a steady increase in the number of books published advocating mediation, and the steady growth of universities offering courses in mediation, perhaps one day mediation will get the respect it deserves.

The purpose of this book is to provide an educational resource for those who teach and practice mediation, and to provide readers with an understanding of the wide range of disputes that can be resolved through mediation. All authors were given general guidelines to follow, though not all chapters exactly reflect each other with respect to structure. However, all authors wrote their chapters with the idea of not writing a scholarly chapter, rather a practical chapter that a mediation practitioner could refer to if he or she had to mediate a type of dispute covered in one of the chapters in this book.

There are a plethora of books on the market that discuss the "how tos" of mediation, this is not the purpose of this book. We have attempted to provide a text which covers both traditional mediation practices, such as peer and divorce mediation, and other types of mediation not usually covered in mediation texts, such as gang and faith-based mediation.

These chapters are written from the perspective of "What do practitioners and educators need to know about this type of mediation?" As a further resource, each chapter also presents a case study and role play covering the type of mediation presented in the chapters. Some case studies involve intricate, complex issues (e.g., environmental mediation), while others present case studies that are less complex (e.g., peer mediation). All authors have extensive experience as mediators or scholars whose main area of interest has been in the area of mediation and conflict management—some authors may be have both.

What follows are twelve chapters covering mediation for a variety of conflicts. While there are types of disputes that are covered in several chapters (e.g., workplace disputes), each presents how mediation can be used in resolving these disputes from several different perspectives. In fact, several different models of mediation are discussed throughout this book. Some authors advocate the use of transformative mediation, while others follow the traditional problem-solving model. It is hoped that the reader will discern that there is no one best model of mediation, but that mediation can be viewed as an eclectic approach to resolving disputes in a manner that, in many cases, is preferable to litigation.

While this book is not only for educators, we hope that those teaching mediation can use this book to demonstrate to his or her class that mediation can only be understood through a broad spectrum of philosophies and practices. The case studies and role plays are intended to emphasize the use of mediation for a wide variety of disputes that educators may use in their classrooms.

The next chapter focuses on divorce mediation, and would be a good chapter for anyone considering entering this field. It describes all of the intricacies of divorce mediation which set it apart from other forms of mediation (e.g., domestic violence, bankruptcy, estates, etc.), and the type of training needed to become a divorce mediator.

Chapter three describes mediation in an arena that has been the in the media for a number of violent acts—the workplace. Clearly, workplace mediation is a much more viable response than violence. Because of the daily interaction between coworkers, sooner or later conflicts will exist in the workplace. And, like the peat fire analogy the author uses, some conflicts, like peat fires, burn for years before they ever surface and spike when least expected. Probably the most useful aspect of this chapter for anyone trying to convince a superior of the need for workplace mediation is the explanation of the financial cost of conflict.

Chapter four examines mediation of staff disputes at a large state university in North Carolina. While mediation programs have been available for students and faculty at universities since the early 1980s, for some reason schools have not provided the same resource for staff members. The author describes one of the biggest problems for implementing staff mediation programs at universities—publicizing and getting staff members to use mediation as a vehicle for resolving or at least managing their conflicts. The author describes other obstacles encountered when developing a mediation services for staff members and potential ways around these problems.

The positive results of implementing peer mediation programs in schools have been well-documented in *Mediation Quarterly* and its replacement *Conflict Resolution Quarterly,* and chapter five discusses the basics of implementing a peer mediation program. It also presents the reader with a variety of conflict resolution models which should be useful for any school considering implementing a peer mediation program.

Chapter six presents mediation in an arena that is one of the fastest growing but perhaps least researched area of mediation—mediation in the social helping fields, specifically within the contexts of departments of social services (DSS) and special education. The author discusses how mediation within these two contexts has been employed in North Carolina and the success and promise of these programs.

As this book is being written, Al Gore's film "An Inconvenient Truth" is receiving a lot of attention for its dire predictions of global warming. Though mediation has not been championed for this cause, there is a growing importance associated with environmental mediation, the focus of chapter seven. Situations in which the environment is threatened are ill-suited to the lengthy process of litigation—by the time a decision is reached, the damage to the environment might already have been done. In order to expedite the resolution of environmental disputes, the authors present a compelling case for mediation for the resolution of such disputes.

In chapter eight, divorce and family mediation is revisited, but from a completely different perspective from chapter two. Because divorce mediations have such a great potential for the expression of troubled emotions, the mediator would be wise to have some type of instruction in crisis intervention. This chapter examines how one can determine when a dispute has evolved into a crisis, the negative implications that this type of change can have, and what specific communicative behaviors may be employed to effectively deal with crisis situations.

The United States currently has more people in its prisons than any other country. Unfortunately the term "correctional institution" is a misnomer—"criminal training facility" would be a more accurate term based on the recidivism rate in the United States. Chapter nine addresses a form of mediation which has had some promise with respect to reducing the rate of recidivism—victim offender conferencing or (aka victim/offender mediation). The author discusses the advantages of such programs not only for victims but for offenders as well, and how this type of mediation can empower victims and give them a greater understanding of their victimization.

Gang disputes can produce potentially deadly encounters when members from rival gangs have no outlet for resolving their dispute except for violence or the use of law enforcement. Chapter ten examines why traditional responses to gangs in schools (e.g., metal detectors, security officers) have not always proved effective in reducing or, more importantly, preventing gang violence. Suggestions for mediating gang disputes are presented, with a focus on why mediation could be used to prevent gang violence before it occurs. The author also describes why many of the traditional ground rules in mediation must be drastically altered in mediation of gang disputes.

When thinking of conflict, people do not usually immediately envision conflicts that grow out of faith or spiritual practices. However, that is the focus of chapter eleven. The authors provide a framework for understanding faith-based conflicts and how these disputes can be resolved through mediation. A seven-phase model of conflict of faith-based disputes is presented which mediators can use to determine if faith-based conflicts could be resolved through mediation or another form of alternative dispute resolution.

The hybrid process of mediation-arbitration (MedArb) is presented in chapter twelve. The author traces the history of MedArb, and discusses why, in some instances, MedArb is preferable to either mediation or arbitration. MedArb is also compared to the process of litigation, and why MedArb might be a more practical way of resolving disputes than traditional litigation. Some of the unique challenges that a MedArb model presents are discussed.

Chapter thirteen presents the case for transformative mediation that was first presented twelve years ago in Bush and Folger's (1994) *The Promise of Mediation*. Specifically, the authors present how transformative mediation has been used to resolve complaints of discrimination within the United States Postal Service over a ten-year period, and the success of this program. Transformative mediation is compared to evaluative and facilitative mediation, and the Ten Hallmarks of Transformative mediation are presented. Additionally, the authors examine some of the criticisms of the transformative model and its limitations.

The writers of the chapters in this text all believe in the potential mediation has for the resolution of disputes in a variety of situations. It is hoped that the reader will gain a better understanding of not only the practice of mediation, but the flexibility mediation offers as a method of dispute resolution. If those goals are accomplished, this book has been a worthy endeavor.

Chapter 2

Divorce Mediation

Jerry Bagnell

The yellow pages have more listings for marriage counselors than divorce mediators. It is more popular to encourage success than to admit anything less. Proponents of divorce mediation tout the process as a kinder, gentler way for parties to uncouple than litigation. Although mediation can be far less damaging to individuals going through a divorce, the process is one that can challenge the practitioner, making him or her into a referee in what can be a struggle characterized by anger, denigration, and emotional extremes.

Most couples who choose mediation do so because they want to avoid litigation, either they realize it will exacerbate any anger they are feeling or because they know the adversarial process always concludes with a winner and a loser. For individuals who want to uncouple but not destroy the other party, mediation was an ideal solution.

Divorce mediation can be conducted in several settings. Court-referred cases are a good place for new mediators to begin their practice. Because cases are referred to the mediator, there is no need to do any marketing. Cases are normally held in the courthouse so an outside office is not required. Screening to determine if the case is appropriate for mediation is often done by court personnel. Some courts have an individual who manages their mediation cases, does the screening, prepares agreements from mediators' notes, and keep records.

Cases normally involve disputes about custody, visitation, and child support. Couples may be unmarried. Often the disputes involve post-divorce or other non-compliance matters. Parties are usually unrepresented by attorneys, and most have not consulted with attorneys to obtain any legal advice.

Another setting for divorce mediators is as an independent contractor for an agency or organization. Again, this is a good place for new mediators to start. Cases are referred by the agency and meeting facilities are provided. Screening to determine if the case is appropriate for mediation is done by the mediators. Mediators will be expected to provide all the necessary forms needed. Since the mediators are independent contractors, they will need to have their own malpractice insurance. Parties pay an hourly fee to the agency and the agency pays the mediators a portion of that fee. The scope of cases can be as simple as court-referred cases or as complex as a comprehensive divorce, with issues ranging from custody, visitation, child and spousal support, to distribution of property. Parties are represented by attorneys or have consulted with attorneys before or during mediation.

A third setting is private practice. It may be a solo practice or a corporation. My practice in Virginia was a corporation with a full-time office manager. Our mediators, other than me, were independent contractors referred to as "mediation associates." They represented a number of professions: attorneys, psychologists, nurses, educators, realtors, financial planners, and social workers. We routinely used teams of co-mediators, some of whom were fully qualified mediators. Some teams consisted of a mediation associate and a mediator in training referred to as a "mediation intern."

DIVORCE AND MEDIATION

The adversarial court system works well when a judge can determine the guilt, innocence or liability of an individual based upon a presentation and evaluation of factual evidence. While there is some consideration of evidence in divorce proceedings, such as whether or not adultery has occurred, there are no specific criteria for determining the best interests of children or the distribution of property.

Although divorcing couples come to court expecting a judge to render a fair decision, they frequently discover that the judge must render a decision that is legal. Neither party may perceive that decision as fair; and even though judges have the authority to make decisions about custody and visitation, the best they can do may not satisfy either parent. Mediation gives the parents an opportunity to use their personal knowledge of their children to determine what is in their best interest.

When couples in mediation argue about the value of the marital home, one party may comment about making all the drapes in the home while the other states that he planted every rose bush in the back yard. A court doesn't consider these subjective criteria, but for some parties they are more important than whether the home is appraised for one dollar amount or another.

Mediation allows parties to consider the subjective value of their assets while a court considers the objective value. Laws vary from state to state. Community property, equitable distribution, or "kitchen sink" standards, depending upon state law, define how the court divides a couple's property, but only the couple knows how they value their assets. A husband digging up prize rose bushes at 2:00 a.m. and escaping with them in his pickup truck illustrates that the dollar value of the shrubs was not the husband's criterion for their value.

There is also the issue of whether property is marital or separate. Was it inherited or was it a gift? All of these considerations have legal ramifications that separating and divorcing couples may not be aware of or may consider unfair. In mediation, the parties themselves decide how to divide their assets using standards that they define.

INFORMATION ON DIVORCE MEDIATION

Some explanations of the divorce mediation process have been so well written that they have become classics. The following summarizes portions of an article by Joan B. Kelly, a past-president of the Academy of Family Mediators (now ACR), that appeared in the first edition of *Mediation Quarterly* in 1983.

> The explicit goal of divorce mediation is negotiating a settlement of issues identified by clients and the mediator as germane to the dispute. Central to this goal is the principle that the settlement should be mutually beneficial and agreeable to both parties. Mediation promises its clients a specific end product—a negotiated settlement. If this end product cannot be obtained, the mediation terminates. If the mediation is successful, the visible result is a written agreement (Memorandum of Understanding). . . . Mediation begins with an initial contracting session, which has clear content and a structure that causes the expectations of both mediator and clients to be verbalized. Mediators explain the nature of the process, the desired end results, and the expectation for full disclosure, confidentiality—except mandated reporting of child abuse—and independent lawyer review at the end of the process. Clients sign a Contract for Mediation covering these points, fees, and an agreement not to subpoena the mediator to testify on the behalf of either client if the mediation breaks down. Clients understand what they are contracting for and the procedure and intent. Clients and mediators have also agreed on their participation in the process and on the desired end result. . . . The role of divorce mediators is very active. They educate clients regarding information needed for settlement, clarify and organize data,

> facilitate discussion and cooperative communications, structure sessions so tasks can proceed, manage conflict, refer clients out for expert information or advice, help clients weight the consequences, conduct negotiations, and produce a Memorandum of Understanding. Mediators do not make decisions for the couple but facilitate the client's own decision-making process. The relationship to the clients is one of impartiality and balance, working actively with each client throughout the process to develop a fair and equitable agreement. . . . Competent mediators possess knowledge of budgetary needs, spousal and child support considerations, various types of assets and methods of valuing them, and common monetary practices (pp. 33-34).

For years this writer has shared the concern of many practitioners for divorces or separations that involve children. That concern is explained by Bob Emery (1994) as follows:

> Mediation is a useful tool for helping parents to renegotiate their relationship. Mediation is of value because it encourages parents to cooperate—a distinct contrast to the traditional method of adversary settlement. Perhaps the greatest benefit of mediation, however, is that it helps parents to redefine new boundaries in their relationships. These boundaries are defined explicitly by the specific and detailed terms of a mediated agreement and implicitly through the process of negotiation that occurs in mediation (pp. vii-vii).

Of course, divorce mediation is not always a workable way for two partners to uncouple. If there is an imminent danger of abuse, whether physical or psychological, a person cannot be a willing participant. Since one of the principles underlying mediation is voluntariness, a person who feels intimidated or coerced or who is in fear of bodily harm, cannot give their informed consent to participate. It is important to recognize that how the person feels subjectively is more significant than how the situation appears objectively to the mediator. Since there can be a history of violence, how a person feels about that when they are deciding to participate in mediation is what is relevant.

Some organizations and individuals believe that mediation is not appropriate if there has been violence in a relationship. Many of the clients I've had over the years have acknowledged that they were victims of psychological or physical violence in the past, but still wanted to use mediation to divorce rather than litigate. In fact, a process such as mediation, which is based upon self-determination, can do more to empower a victim of domestic violence than protracted litigation in which an overzealous advocate might decide to make strong suggestions about how the person should proceed.

Because domestic violence is a possibility in every marriage or parenting relationship, I always screened for the presence of domestic violence with the goal of either ruling it out or determining what effect it would have on the voluntary and uncoerced participation of either or both parties. Mediation is appropriate when the parties volunteer to participate and their individual decisions to participate are not based upon intimidation or coercion. It is also important to determine if the parties are able to participate. Arguments abound about whether it is the mediator's role to determine if the parties are competent, if there is a balance of power and knowledge, and so on.

A mediator's primary consideration in determining the suitability of parties to participate in the process is governed by the maxim, "Do no harm." Of course that is the mantra of any professional service provider, but assessing the probability of the parties being harmed during or after mediation is not something that can be learned in a training session. A mediator must be realistic about his or her ability to handle the myriad of situations that can occur during divorce mediation whether they are in session or between sessions. A mediator cannot learn at the expense—financial, psychological or physical—of the parties to the mediation.

A realistic assessment of whether or not mediation is appropriate for a couple should include a consideration of the following principles underlying the mediation process: voluntariness, informed consent, confidentiality, and self-determination. All of these considerations are subjective and depend upon how the parties perceive their ability, not just how the mediator perceives that ability. A mediator must also consider if either party might not be acting in good faith. No checklist can assure the mediator that the process is appropriate for the parties so it is important to be vigilant throughout the process.

EXPERIENCE NEEDED FOR DIVORCE MEDIATION

Most divorce mediators have at least an undergraduate education. Some have graduate and postgraduate degrees in law, psychotherapy, education, business administration, and other professional areas. Many transition into divorce mediation from other professions rather than become divorce mediators as their initial professional endeavor.

Some colleges and universities as well as law schools offer courses in mediation. These courses usually are general in nature and do not address all of the specific skills required to become a competent divorce mediator.

Most divorce mediators take a forty-hour course in family mediation. The majority of these courses are presented by nationally known trainers who are members of organizations such as the Association for Conflict Resolution

(ACR) or the Association of Family and Conciliation Courts (AFCC). Some courses may be sponsored by state mediation organizations. In either case, these courses by themselves do not qualify individuals to become divorce mediators. The trainers who present these courses routinely make that point to persons attending the course. They also tell them that completing the course does not provide any guarantee that clients will flock to the offices of those who complete the course.

Most states require that divorce mediators take a course in that portion of state law that applies to mediation, the judicial system, and divorce. Topics may also include grounds for divorce, custody and visitation, child and spousal support, and distribution of property. There is usually a requirement that divorce mediators attend an annual update of this training. Some states require training in screening for and dealing with domestic violence in the context of mediation as well as a course on ethical issues in mediation.

Following training, divorce mediators should obtain supervised experience to be able to receive referrals from a court or to acquire a professional designation. The labels for such designations vary by state and may be called certification, accreditation, or some similar term. However, in most states mediators are not required to be licensed as other professionals such as attorneys or therapists are.

Interns at my practice in Virginia had the following requirements for certification as a Juvenile and Domestic Relations District Court Mediator:

> Observation of at least two complete domestic relations family mediation cases with a certified mediator and supervised co-mediation of at least five complete domestic relations family mediation cases with a certified mediator.

If they wanted to increase their certification to Circuit Court-Family Mediator so they could receive referrals for cases involving spousal support and distribution of property, there were additional requirements:

> Observation of at least two (one if already certified as a Juvenile and Domestic Relations District Court Mediator) complete Circuit Court-Family mediation cases with a certified mediator and supervised co-mediation of at least ten hours of family mediation including five (two if already certified as a Juvenile and Domestic Relations District Court Mediator) Circuit Court-Family mediation cases with a certified mediator.

Many of our interns recognized that these requirements were only entry level experience and continued to co-mediate with our associates to prepare themselves for independent practice and also obtained training in a variety of divorce related subjects such as:

- Managing Angry Parties
- Recognizing and Reporting Child Abuse and Neglect
- Basic Crisis Negotiation Skills
- Calculating Child Support
- The Effects of Domestic Violence on Children
- Spousal Support
- Bankruptcy
- Estates, Trusts and Taxes
- Developmental and Psychological Impact of Divorce on Children
- Identifying and Preventing Violence in Separation and Divorce
- Pension Benefits in Divorce
- Property Classification Issues
- Estates, Wills, and Implications for Mediation
- Active Listening
- Agreement Writing

Most national and state organizations provide their members with a title or designation in addition to those obtained from the state in which mediators practice. For example, mediators who meet the requirements for certification or similar state-regulated status as a divorce mediator and have a sufficient numbers of hours of practice can be designated as an Advanced Practitioner Member by the Association for Conflict Resolution (ACR).

Mediators certified or who have a similar designation from the state in which they practice usually have requirements for continuing education and must obtain a certain number of hours annually. Mediation organizations often have similar requirements for their members.

Preparation for Divorce Mediation

There is so much more to preparation than training, certification, and additional continuing education classes. In order to be successful, you have to be known for your skill, not just be a familiar face in the community.

Membership in national and state mediation organizations provides opportunities for additional training both as a student and a presenter. Presenting training to your peers is one way to establish your credibility.

Ironically, I found that even though I was a psychotherapist by profession of origin and a member of organizations with other therapists, I received very few referrals from therapists. Attorneys that worked in our practice reported the same cross-professional situation. They received very few referrals from other attorneys. One experienced attorney in our practice theorized that professionals don't like to admit to their peers that they can't handle a case they are working on and have to refer it to someone else. Whatever the reason for this enigma, I accepted the fact that I had to look at a variety of professionals to obtain referrals.

Consider networking with financial advisors, especially if you do divorces that involved property and financial assets. It can provide you with opportunities to learn about the financial aspects of divorce and can also produce referrals.

Consider joining the bar association both at the local, state, and national level. Most of my referrals came from judges and attorneys. It is important to network with your referral sources and establish credibility by presenting training about mediation. It is also very helpful to establish relationships with one or more attorneys who can advise you on the legal aspects of divorce. You can ask them to review memoranda for you and even refer clients to separate and independent attorneys to create whatever legal documents might be necessary to implement the terms of an agreement reached by the parties to a separation or divorce.

When establishing credibility with judges, it is important to have an identity and a role that is clear. Market yourself as a divorce mediator, not a mediator of every possible type of dispute. Attorneys specialize in particular types of cases. Judges want to refer cases to experts in those areas. A judge once told me that some mediators confused him. He explained that a mediator might appear in his court on a Monday as an expert witness or a custody evaluator testifying that Mrs. Jones was a better parent than Mr. Jones. Then, on Tuesday that same mediator would expect the judge to refer a case to him because he was fair and impartial. The judge said it was also difficult to determine what services someone actually offered. Were they a therapist or a mediator? Lesson learned. If you want to be a divorce mediator, don't offer other services that blur the boundaries of your practice. If mediation is an additional aspect of your menu of professional services, you may be perceived as a part-time mediator. Most potential clients and referral sources look for full-time professionals assuming they are more qualified than someone that does mediation as a sideline.

An exception to offering other services is parent education. Most states mandate that parties filing an action involving custody, visitation, or support of children attend classes on the effects of separation and divorce on children. Presenters for these classes have an opportunity to demonstrate their knowledge and credibility for groups of as many as 30 or 40 parents in one session.

When establishing a practice, if you want to be more than a solo practitioner, have a number of mediators from a variety of professions as independent contractors. That gives you the ability to assemble mediation teams with complimentary skills such as law and therapy or financial planning and education. As your practice grows, hire an administrative assistant or office manager. You want to be available to mediate and network rather than tied up doing routine paperwork.

Accept the fact that it may take a year or more before you have a sufficient number of cases to pay the bills. If you have adequately prepared and are known for your expertise and ethical and professional behavior, you can be successful as a divorce mediator.

TYPICAL AND UNIQUE PROBLEMS OF DIVORCE MEDIATION

Problems or typical areas of difficulty unique to divorce mediation occur with mediators themselves and also with the parties to mediation that are separating or divorcing.

A history of or the potential for domestic violence is a factor in every case when parties are separating or divorcing. Some protocol or procedure for screening is essential. The screening should be ongoing throughout the mediation. An example of such a process is discussed in the case study that follows.

Since divorce mediation is not an entry level profession, many mediators can blur their role as a mediator with that of their profession of origin. Therapist mediators may become too concerned with the social functioning of their clients or employ strategies to improve their relationship with regard to parenting.

Attorney mediators may tend to be more directive and may make suggestions that border on giving legal advice. Their knowledge of the law can enable them to answer clients' questions about legal issues rather than referring the clients to separate and independent attorneys. There is a tendency for clients to perceive attorney mediators as somehow more qualified than those with backgrounds in other professions. While they may know more about the law than non-attorneys, their skills as a mediator are not necessarily related to their legal expertise. One of our mediation associates was an attorney who used to say that the only guarantee you have when you hire an attorney is that he or she is licensed to practice law, not that he or she is competent. Of course the same situation applies to many other professionals.

Whether the divorce mediator is an attorney or not, giving legal advice is never appropriate. Attorney mediators can be sanctioned for dual representation. Non-attorney mediators can be accused of and may be prosecuted for the unauthorized practice of law.

Regardless of their profession of origin, divorce mediators must maintain their focus on encouraging client self-determination, avoid making suggestions and giving advice, and make appropriate referrals even when they know the answers or possible solutions to situations separating and divorcing parties may encounter.

Divorce mediators are often mandated reporters of child abuse and neglect. Frequently parents will accuse each other of behaviors that constitute abuse or neglect. Mediators may be faced with the dilemma of differentiating between what may be accusations that are unfounded and those that they suspect are accurate and place children in jeopardy. Most mediators advise their clients of the mediator's responsibility to report suspicion of child abuse or neglect, or suspicion of bodily harm or violence to another person. Such language usually appears in the contract for mediation signed by the mediator and the clients.

Mediators also have ethical considerations that may not be readily apparent. For example, they may not unnecessarily prolong mediation if the parties are not making progress. While there is no magic number of sessions that it will take to mediate a separation or divorce, when the process goes on for more than five or six two-hour sessions, mediators must consider whether to continue trying to facilitate a resolution or possibly terminate the mediation and make appropriate referrals.

One strategy for enhancing the efficiency of divorce mediation is to accept the fact that parties are dealing with highly emotional issues and need time to think about their options and gather information. As a rule, I scheduled sessions at least two weeks apart so that the parties could have enough time to gather information needed to make reasoned decisions. Also as a practical matter, few couples have the financial ability to pay for sessions that are scheduled too close together. Spacing sessions out over a period of weeks enables the parties to deal with financial as well as emotional considerations.

Another consideration for divorce mediators is referred to in most states as "substantial full disclosure." In Virginia, the parties agree in their contract for mediation to "provide substantial full disclosure of all relevant property and financial information necessary to reach a just agreement." They acknowledge in their contract that, "failure to do so may result in the agreement or any order incorporating or resulting from such agreement being vacated by the court."

A challenge for the divorce mediator is to ask questions that will not only encourage substantial full disclosure, but also provide a level of confidence that such disclosure has occurred. In cases involving self-employed clients or those in which one party handles all financial matters, it is essential to make sure that all relevant information has been disclosed.

Typical and unique problems from the clients' perspective are also quite common in divorce mediation. One of the most pervasive is Parental Alienation Syndrome (PAS), defined by Richard Gardner (1989) as, "a disturbance in which children are preoccupied with condemnation and criticism of a parent that is unjustified and/or exaggerated (p. 226)." Gardner posits that, indications of PAS are seen in about 90% of children that are involved in lengthy custody litigation.

Some problems experienced with clients are a normal part of the stress of separation and divorce. Anger is quite common. If you are uncomfortable dealing with angry parties who can berate each other with a litany of profanity, you don't want to be a divorce mediator. Besides having clear ground rules that are explained in your contract with the parties, there are several ways to control their behavior.

Interruptions can be handled by using a technique I call "Telling, Telling, and Retelling." It works like this: The mediator specifies a short time, e.g., no more than two-minutes, for one party; let's say "John," to explain some specific aspect of the problem to be resolved. The second party, "Mary," is told to listen carefully because at the end of that two minute period, she will have the opportunity to summarize what "John" said by providing a verbal summary to him. "Mary" is not permitted to take notes because the statement will be a short one with limited content.

"John" is told to listen carefully to "Mary's" paraphrased summary. The mediator then asks John, "Did she get it right?" If "John's" answer is, "No," the mediator tells "John" to tell "Mary" again. "Mary" paraphrases for "John" and he "retells" what he originally said until he is able to agree that "Mary" can tell him what he said. This doesn't mean she understands or agrees with "John." It merely means that she can restate what "John" said. The mediator then reverses the roles of the parties and continues the process.

The purpose of this intervention is to teach parties, by means of an imposed consequence, to listen to what another party is saying rather than prepare an answer, interrupt, or present an argument to the contrary. Each time a party has to repeat the telling and retelling, they will probably change their statement somewhat based on what has been retold to them by the other party. Each restatement should be clearer than the previous one. "Telling, Telling, and Retelling" can be effective when parties are angry or are not paying attention to what the other party is saying.

I also used a continuum of interventions for managing angry parties:

Mild:

a. Carefully empathize with parties and normalize feelings
b. Interrupt with questions
c. Remind them of the ground rules they agreed to accept, e.g., not interrupting
d. Explain how disruptive behavior distracts you from listening

Moderate:

a. The Anger Two-Step: Acknowledge their anger and move on
b. Pause and summarize facts while acknowledging feelings
c. Take a short break or use a caucus to explore interests and clarify concerns
d. Impose an agreed to consequence such as "Telling, Telling, and Retelling."

Serious:

a. Give short, specific commands to interrupt the parties
b. Take a long break, e.g. over lunch
c. Postpone the session and reschedule
d. Terminate mediation and make appropriate reports or referrals

Lack of knowledge about the legal and financial aspects of divorce is common. Sometimes parties may say that they have been told something by their attorneys that the mediator knows is not correct. It is often impossible to determine if the parties misunderstood what they were told or if they are merely saying the information came from their attorneys. Since the mediator cannot advise, referrals to attorneys, financial advisors, or other professionals are appropriate to resolve any such issues.

Controlling power imbalances and differences in knowledge can also be a problem. Common interventions include: using questions effectively, establishing ground rules about the length of time each party may speak, and referrals to other professionals to balance knowledge.

Many separating and divorcing couples have preconceived ideas about the process that are simply not correct. These ideas may come from the media or from others who have separated or divorced. Emphasize that everyone's experience is different and what is important is that the parties you are working with should consider what they want and need for their particular circumstances. The influence of family members, friends, or a new significant other can influence parties to make decisions in a session or change their minds about agreements reached in prior sessions.

Frequently parents will refer to their children as "my son" or "my daughter." An effective intervention is to suggest using the children's names since when a parent calls a child, they don't say, "Come here, my daughter." They would say, "Come here, Sally."

One of the most problematic situations in a separation or divorce is either party's new significant other. Often that person may be blamed for the break-up of the relationship. One party may have established a relationship with someone new following the separation. In either case, when there are children involved, one parent may want to establish a parenting plan that precludes any contact between the new partner and the other parent. While judges vary in their opinions about exposing children to new partners, the situation can be handled by the mediator by explaining that children whose parents are separating are often confused about the situation and expecting them to accept a new adult in the life of either parent is not realistic.

When facilitating the construction of parenting plans, safety of the parents and children must be considered. Sometimes the mediator may be able to ask questions so that parents become aware of safety considerations. In other cases, attorneys reviewing memoranda or preparing orders for the court may recommend the inclusion of some of the constraints that follow. When divorce mediators and attorneys have a good working relationship, judges expect that parenting plans will contain provisions regarding the safety of parents and their children.

Detailed and specific plans are in the best interest of children and their parents. Courts prefer them, because just like activity-based parenting plans, they are easy to interpret and enforce. Vague terms such as "reasonable visitation," "by mutual agreement," and "shared time or responsibility" are not specific enough to be clearly enforced. They afford an abused parent and children little or no protection from an abuser who may interpret the terms in a manner that permits the abuser to gain access to the abused parent by means of contact with the children. Parenting plans may minimize any physical contact between parents.

Joint legal custody requires a balance of decision-making power and is usually not appropriate in cases in which threats, intimidation, and coercion are present. Plans calling for picking up and dropping off the children at the home of either parent should be avoided. Transition activities such as one parent dropping the children off at school or at an extracurricular activity and the other parent picking them up should be considered.

Plans calling for the payment of child or spousal support in cash or by direct contact should be avoided. Joint meetings of the parents such as school conferences, children's sports, and social events should also be avoided. The abuser should be required to contact the school, not the other parent, to obtain report cards or any information regarding school activities.

The abused parent should have all necessary ID cards and forms to obtain medical coverage or treatment for the children without having to contact the abuser. Any co-payments, if they are to be paid by the abuser, should be paid directly to the doctor, dentist, or medical facility.

Parenting plans should include a provision that requires the abuser to notify the other parent and the school or daycare in writing in advance of any planned visit. Children should not be permitted to take keys for the abused parent's home with them when visiting the abuser. Requirements for therapy involving both parents and the children or both parents should be carefully considered and scheduled only when no other alternative is available.

While divorce mediators are limited in how much they can influence their clients, safety must be the primary consideration when preparing any parenting plan. The skillful use of questions to call parents' attention to provisions that affect safety is essential.

CONCLUDING COMMENTS

Divorce mediation can be a very different process depending upon the setting in which it is conducted. Court cases can be short and relatively simple. Private practice cases can be lengthy and quite complicated. In either setting, challenges include dealing with a possible intense level of anger and behavior that is anything but civil.

The intricacies of separation and divorce call for skills on the part of the mediator that are much greater than knowledge of just the mediation process. Divorce mediators must know the law that applies to such cases, not so they can advise, but so they will not unknowingly facilitate an agreement that would not be acceptable to the court. It also goes without saying that if separate and independent attorneys review memoranda prepared by mediators that are replete with errors, the credibility of the mediators will certainly be suspect. Mediators without credibility will not get referrals from attorneys whose clients cannot expect competence during the process of mediation.

The amount of training and experience required to be a competent divorce mediator means that choosing this field involves quite some time to develop professionally between initial training and succeeding as a practitioner. Divorce mediation cases produce outcomes that have long range implications for parents and children. Even when children are not involved, issues resolved hastily by mediators whose goal is agreement between the parties can result in less than pleasant consequences for the mediators. Mediators cannot afford, literally, to learn at the expense of clients. Malpractice insurance is a must since parties who may be appreciative at the time an agreement is reached can become very angry at mediators when the parties realize the long-term implications of agreements facilitated by the mediators. Of course, divorce attorneys are no less likely to have disgruntled clients, but not all mediation clients sing the praises of their mediators in the months following the conclusion of mediation.

If you believe that you can make a difference in people's lives by helping them reach a greater understanding and appreciation for each other's points of view, mediation may be a way for you to achieve that goal. Success in mediation means that the parties know and appreciate each other's interests. This doesn't mean that they will agree. They have the opportunity to do so but the choice is theirs. Mediators who advertise success based on the percentage of cases where agreements are reached are missing the point. When mediation is a success, that success is defined by the parties.

Especially when working with separating or divorcing couples, it is important to recognize that they came to mediation because they were not able to resolve issues themselves. That doesn't mean they want someone to resolve the issues for them, although they may ask mediators to do that. Divorce mediators must respect the right of their clients to make decisions that may be quite different than what the mediator might decide. If you want to make decisions for others, mediation is not the profession you should choose. If you want to help others reach mutually agreeable decisions by facilitating discussions without attempting to influence the outcome, mediation may be a way to do that. If you want to do that at a time in people's lives when their decision making is impaired by the emotional aspects of separation or divorce, divorce mediation is a profession you might consider.

Case Study: The Divorce of Mary and John

Prior to meeting with a couple, they were screened individually by phone to determine any history of domestic violence, the potential for domestic violence to recur, and the effect any history or recent incidents might have on either party's ability to participate voluntarily, in an informed manner, and without coercion or intimidation. Routinely women were screened first and then the men were usually screened at a different time and/or on a different day. If the telephone screening indicated that a more in-depth screening would be necessary, our protocol was to schedule separate and individual face-to-face sessions. That rarely occurred.

A letter confirming the appointment was sent to each client explaining that sessions would be two hours in length, the fee structure, the name of the co-mediator, and that a mediation intern might be present to take notes. Some practitioners believe that the parties have to agree for anyone to be present other than the mediator. We routinely used a co-mediator team and a recorder. Whether the case was in the court or private practice setting, we never had an instance of the parties objecting to the presence of a mediation team. Our rationale was similar to that of a doctor scheduled to perform surgery. Patients don't get to decide how many people the doctor chooses to assist him.

Prior to the arrival of the parties, the mediation team spent thirty minutes or so discussing information about the parties such as whether or not they had children, or if they did, their gender and ages. We also decided who would be responsible for taking the lead with various portions of the mediation.

John Doe, 35, and Mary Doe, 28, were married in 1996. They separated on June 15, 2006, and are now living separate and apart from each other, but have not yet filed for divorce. Mary acknowledged that the reason for their separation is she had an affair with her boss that the boss' wife discovered it. The boss fired Mary in an attempt to repair the relationship with his wife.

John is now living in an apartment near the school where he is a sixth-grade teacher. Mary still lives in the marital home. Mary is now unemployed. John and Mary have two children: Steven, 7 and Diane, 5.

Although divorces can include a consideration of child and spousal support as well as distribution of property and allocation of debts, this case study will only consider the initial mediation session.

We began the session by reading the Contract for Co-Mediation aloud, interjecting explanations of terms when appropriate and pausing to answer questions. Clients seemed to appreciate our taking time to explain what they could expect in detail rather than just rushing into something that they had never experienced.

Occasionally, parties brought attorneys to sessions. When the parties told us that in advance, we sent an information packet to each attorney that also included our protocol for attorney participation in mediation. The protocol was prepared by several of the attorneys that worked as mediators for our practice. Attorneys that attended mediation sessions seemed to appreciate that we had explained our expectations for them. They were used to following rules for the courts in which they appeared and none objected to the protocol we had established.

When we had finished reading the contract and answering questions, copies were circulated so that each party present had a copy with the signatures of all present for their records. The balance of advanced fees was collected and we continued with the process.

Our goal for the initial session was to focus on those issues relating to the custody of children. Some mediators prefer to begin by discussing property and then move to issues involving children. Since the focus of our practice was families with children and was advertised as such, parties expected that children would be the priority subject to be discussed.

Frequently parents had preconceived ideas about custody and visitation. Many of these ideas were incorrect. Some parents began by saying they wanted "full custody," meaning that they wanted total control over the children. Others wanted "50/50." Rather than confront either parent and tell them their information was not correct, we explained custody in simple language and answered as many questions as necessary before moving on to what options each parent wanted. It proved to be more effective to determine their underlying interests before asking for their positions.

Legal custody was explained as "decision making." Decisions might include education, medical treatment, religious training, and manner of discipline. We explained that these decisions could be made by one parent or by both after discussing the situations. If one parent were to consider the other's thoughts and feelings concerning important decisions for the children but then have complete and final authority to make decisions in any of these matters, that was "sole legal custody" as defined by law in Virginia. Another option that we referred to as the decision-making aspect of "shared parenting," was that decisions would be made jointly by both parents. This was called "joint legal custody" in Virginia. Different states may have different labels. Our point was to explain that custody was about decision making and that it was not a total package that included visitation and child support.

We then explained visitation by using the term "parenting." Since raising children has to do with so many considerations other than who they will be with at any given time, parenting was a far more inclusive and appropriate label. The process we used we called "Activity-Based Parenting."

An Activity-Based Parenting Plan is a detailed and specific plan prepared by parents for supervising the activities of their children. It includes more than the traditional visitation schedule and explains how the parents will share responsibility for maintaining the children's daily routine. It focuses on the best interests of the children despite any inconvenience to either or both parents. It does not consider which parent has legal or physical custody because those factors deal with how significant decisions are made for the children and where the children have their primary residence. Those factors are parents' business. An Activity-Based Parenting Plan makes the children the priority and does not make one parent more "powerful" than the other because of legal or physical custody.

One concept upon which the Activity-Based Parenting Plan is based is called "social capital." It consists of all those factors that have an influence on the best interests of children that are not directly related to their parents. Those factors include extended family, peer groups, familiar neighborhood surroundings, living arrangements, sports and extracurricular activities, etc.–in short any positive aspect of the children's lives other than parents that affects the children's best interests.

The Activity-Based Parenting Plan is a logical outgrowth of "social capital" and is constructed by using the child's activities and routine as the basis. The underlying philosophy is that as a child grows older, except for time spent sleeping, he or she usually spends more time away from home than at home. The assumption is that the best interests of the child are served by following a plan or schedule that is least disruptive for the child and changes his or her daily routine as little as possible.

We asked the parents to tell us what the children did each day from the time they got up in the morning until they went to bed at night. Obviously, this varies from child to child and even within families based on the age of the children. Research has shown that age is the most significant factor to consider when determining a child's best interests with respect to activities and contact with parents.

It becomes obvious that children have to be treated as individuals and that the Activity-Based Parenting Plan for one child in a family could be very different from that of his or her brother or sister. Hopefully, this will give a thump on the head to all those attorneys, mediators, and judges that treat the children as a unit and lump their visitation together based on the parents' schedules. We also hope this will bring an end to standardized visitation schedules characterized by such parent-oriented concepts as "alternating weekends and major holidays." Parenting is not supposed to be an easy task for the parents and a difficult experience for the children. Let's stop and consider what *each* child is doing on the weekend!

Another concept in Activity-Based Parenting is "parental availability," a period of time each parent is available to supervise the activities of the children. It is the basis for determining "periods of responsibility." The amount of time the children spend with either parent is not the primary consideration. If the Activity-Based Parenting Plan is truly in the children's best interest, the time spent with either parent does not have to be equal and the "periods of responsibility" for each parent could be reversed with little or no impact on the children.

Children benefit from the supervision and active participation of both parents. Schedules that provide one parent with twenty-six days of supervision per month and the other with four when that parent is only responsible for alternate weekends are not in a child's best interest. They are an example of one parent trying to exercise more control over the children and limit the children's time with the other parent.

Simply stated, once we know what the children's schedules are, we ask parents how they plan to share the responsibility for providing supervision. Rather than a particular weekend being "Dad's weekend," when using an Activity-Based Parenting Plan, it means that Dad is responsible for the children on a particular weekend. He can discharge that responsibility in three ways: personally, use a sitter or a family member, or ask the other parent to assume responsibility. The other parent has the option of saying, "Yes" or "No." Because the other parent is "off-duty," he or she is not required to provide supervision since it is the first parent's "period of responsibility." Parents tend to look at the Activity-Based Parenting Plan as the schedule for the children and "periods of responsibility" as a schedule that tells them who is on duty and what their rotating shifts look like. This makes the parents equally responsible for the shift when they are on duty and avoids the labels of custodial and non-custodial parent.

This helps parents look at caring for children in a different way than who would "have the minor children" for what period of time or what day or weekend. We wanted parents to place the best interests of their children ahead of any considerations of control by either parent. Activity-Based Parenting is a very different concept than alternating weekends.

Another concept of Activity-Based Parenting is "transition activities" - events such as school, sports, scouts, lessons, etc. that provide a child with the opportunity to transition from one parent to another by participating in an activity that enhances or reinforces the child's "social capital." The idea is that one parent would drop the child off for the activity and the other parent would pick the child up. This also permits parents to spend time with children during the school week, but still have the child sleep in the same home throughout the school week if that will assure a better focus on schoolwork. In situations where direct contact between parents has exposed the children to parental conflict, "transition activities" provide a way for the children to escape being caught in a crossfire between feuding parents.

Activity-Based Parenting considers parental responsibilities as opposed to parental rights. When there is harmony in a relationship between parents, there may still be disagreements between them as to who will be responsible for taking a child to ballet or soccer or who will be available to care for them on any given evening. Our goal was to encourage parents to accept that children have a routine that is not defined in terms such as "Mom's weekend" or "Dad's weekend." Rather, for example, we focused on who would be responsible for caring for the children on a given weekend. Our emphasis was on the reality that the children have two homes, the concepts of which are explained by Isolina Ricci (1997) in "Mom's House, Dad's House."

Using the Activity-Based Parenting concepts of "periods of responsibility," "social capital" and "transition activities," parents were able to prepare a parenting plan very different than the stereotypical visitation schedule where children might be treated as objects passed back and forth between parents. Parents agreed that Activity-Based Parenting was much more like what they had been doing to supervise the daily lives of their children. Judges in the courts we worked with also liked the concept because it clearly defined which parent was responsible for which children at any given time. Many judges told us that post-divorce compliance issues with respect to parenting were reduced and fewer parents returned to court with disputes about what was "reasonable" or "mutually agreeable."

The ultimate outcome of considering the children's "social capital" instead of the "parent's rights;" basing a parenting plan of the activities and routine of the children instead of the parents' schedules; and describing the time each parent has with the children as a "period of responsibility" rather than a visitation schedule, is that the emphasis shifts to the children and the relationship between the parents becomes far more business-like. They can truly make the best interests of their children "job one" and conduct business with each other in a civil and respectful manner taking turns supervising the children in accordance with the daily routine the children recognize as the world they live in.

John and Mary told us that the children were living with Mary in the marital home and that they wanted that arrangement to continue. Despite the feelings each had because of the affair and Mary being fired, neither parent wanted to disrupt the children's routine. They also agreed that they would continue to make any decisions about the children jointly as they always had.

Steven played soccer for his school team. They had practice on Tuesday afternoon after school and played games against other school teams on Saturday mornings. Diane had piano lessons on Wednesday afternoon after school and had ballet class on Thursday from 6:00 until 7:00 pm.

John and Mary liked the concept of Activity-Based Parenting because it was very similar to how they had been parenting before they separated. They agreed that John would be responsible for taking Steven to soccer practice and that he would remain overnight with John who would be responsible for taking him to school the following morning. Whenever Steven had a game on Saturday, John would be responsible for taking him. If the game occurred on a weekend that was John's period of responsibility, Steven and Diane would live with John beginning when school was dismissed on Friday and spend the remainder of the weekend with their father. John would be responsible for taking both children to school on Monday morning.

Mary accepted responsibility for taking Diane to piano lessons and ballet classes. The parents agreed that, with the exception of Steven on Tuesday, the children would live with their mother during each week school was in session.

Despite the initial tone of agreement between parents, an argument began when we discussed the Thanksgiving holiday. The tradition had been that Steven's mother would come to spend that entire period with the children and their parents at the marital home. Mary told us that since the time that grandma became aware of the affair and Mary's being fired from her job, she became very hostile toward Mary and had encouraged John to divorce her.

Mary made it quite clear that she did not want to continue the Thanksgiving tradition since she knew that John's mother might cause a scene in front of the children that would spoil the entire holiday. Since this would be the first Thanksgiving since the separation, both parents agreed that John would be responsible for the children and take them to their grandmother's. Mary acknowledged that she would get a break since she wouldn't have to prepare the meal. She said she would have dinner with a woman from the choir at church with whom she had a close friendship.

John agreed that the family would spend Christmas together acknowledging that his mother was also included in that tradition, but stating that he and Mary would think about that holiday and have a decision during the next mediation session.

Essentially parenting for the remainder of the year would be based upon alternating responsibility for weekends and major holidays. The tradition for the children's birthdays was to have a party at Chuck E. Cheese or a similar location and invite all the children's friends. Both parents would attend as they always had.

Since John's schedule was based on the school year, he had summers free and could be responsible for the children when Mary began a new job. The parents agreed that would be the plan unless Mary's work schedule made it possible for her to spend more time with the children. The unique aspect of this plan was that the children would live in the marital home at night and John would be responsible for them during the days of summer.

John and Mary agreed to return in two weeks to complete their parenting plan and to discuss financial and property issues. Until then, they agreed each would continue to drive the car they had routinely used and that John would pay the credit card account both used for purchasing gas.

When John and Mary departed, the mediation team spent approximately thirty minutes processing what had occurred during the two-hour session. The senior mediator would begin by asking the recorder, usually a mediation intern, what was different than what he or she expected. The intern then queried both mediators to determine, for example, why certain questions were asked and what the mediators expected when the parties responded. The goal of a processing session was for all members of the mediation team to discuss the progress and substance of mediation while it was still fresh in their minds. The final aspect of processing was to prepare a brief written plan for the next session to be discussed when the team met prior to beginning that session.

QUESTIONS FOR DISCUSSION

1. What are the pros and cons of using a mediation team rather than a single mediator?
2. How did the parents' focus on their children facilitate preparing a parenting plan?
3. How might unresolved issues or issues not discussed affect the next mediation session?
4. Suppose after the mediation session, John discussed with his mother what he and Mary agreed to?
5. Things seemed to be fairly amicable for a couple where an extramarital affair occurred. Should the mediators have asked about that?

Role Play: The Divorce of Mary and John

John and Mary have returned for their second mediation session. It has been two weeks since they last met with the mediation team.

John wants to maintain the tradition of going to his mother's home to celebrate Christmas Day. The tradition was for the children go to sleep in their own beds at home, wake up and find presents under the tree and then go to Grandma's. Grandma would prepare a Christmas dinner. Everyone would remain overnight and return home the next day.

Mary says she will not go to Grandma's and wants the children to spend Christmas with her and John as they had previously agreed. John acknowledges that was the agreement, but didn't realize that meant excluding his mother.

INFORMATION FOR MARY

You believe that you and John might have been able to stay together and work things out if it hadn't been for all of the interference from his mother. She has been a meddling old busy body since you were first married. She never wanted to come to your home because you drank and smoked. You refrained from doing either when she came for Thanksgiving, but always resented having to do so. Imagine the old lady trying to tell you what to do in your own home!

You know that the children will enjoy spending Christmas Day with their father, but since that has always been at Grandma's, they will probably be upset about not going there. You want to do what is best for the children, but don't want to ruin your holidays by including Grandma. John's mother hasn't called you even once since the separation to find out how you and the children are doing. She did send a gift for Diane's birthday, but mailed it to John. You have retained an attorney and are prepared to file for sole custody if John won't accept your position and resolve the issue in mediation.

INFORMATION FOR JOHN

You want to maintain the tradition of going to your mother's home to celebrate Christmas Day together as a family. Mary says she will not go to your mother's because when you and Mary separated, your mother told Mary she never wanted to see her again since she had ruined everything for you and her grandchildren.

You considered trying to reconcile with Mary to keep your family together but the pressure from your mother to divorce her is overwhelming. Your mother doesn't drink or smoke, something Mary does that your mother has always disapproved of. Your mother has lectured you many times about the children being exposed to second-hand smoke.

You want to spend Christmas Day with the children at your mother's, but Mary says if you really want to be with the children, you can spend the day with them in their home. She insists that you agreed to spend Christmas with her and the children but didn't mention that would be at your mother's. Since that is where you have always spent Christmas Day with the children, what else could she have thought you both agreed to?

Mary doesn't know that your mother has also been sending you $1,000 a month since Mary lost her job. You didn't realize how that might be used as leverage against you by your mother but she has mentioned how she would stop helping out if you disappoint her. You are between a rock and a hard place. If you spend Christmas Day with Mary and the children, your mother will be furious. If you insist on taking the children to your mother's, Mary has threatened to take you to court and ask the judge to order that the children be with her in their home.

REFERENCES

Emery, R. E. (1994). *Renegotiating Family Relationships: Divorce, Child Custody, and Mediation.* New York: Guilford.

Gardner, R. A. (1989). *Family Evaluation in Child Custody Mediation, Arbitration, and Litigation.* New Jersey: Creative Therapeutics.

Kelly, J. B. (1983). Mediation and Psychotherapy: Distinguishing the differences. *Mediation Quarterly,* 1, 33-44.

Ricci, I. (1997). *Mom's House, Dad's House.* New York: Simon & Schuster.

Chapter 3

Mediating Employment and Workplace Disputes

Merri L. Hanson

It is before dawn and the mediator has begun her commute to a federal worksite several hours away to conduct a 6- to 8-hour workplace mediation. Within a condensed period of roughly a day, a skilled employment mediator facilitates an opportunity for dispute resolution at some level of the parties' choosing—settlement, resolution, and/or satisfaction. Many experts say that mediation of workplace problems simply accelerates a settlement process that would otherwise take months or even years. In fact, mediation provides the opportunity for so much more than mere settlement of a pending legal claim—it also holds the opportunity for the substantive resolution of myriad causes of conflict and the satisfaction of underlying interests for both employers and employees.

In planning for today's case, the mediator assesses the basics: how many parties, how many representatives, how many and what types of issues, and what value will the mediator bring to this mediation. While each workplace mediation is unique, it follows common themes. The mediator welcomes the opportunity to facilitate dialog, negotiation, and constructive problem solving and knows that participants will likely feel more hopeful and relaxed at the end of the session than they do at the beginning. Workplace mediators are keenly aware that they are privileged to serve in a capacity that makes a practical difference in the day-to-day lives and overall satisfaction of employers and employees.

Today's dispute is another claim of employment discrimination—non-selection on the basis of age and race. And beneath that legal claim lies a complicated web of communication needs, chances for relational improvement, desires for opportunity, and a craving for recognition. There is an energizing improvisational element to the session that they create together. It is a Gestalt experience—much more than the sum of its parts. The mediator will bring to bear far more than the minutes spent in case preparation; the mediator will bring all that she knows and believes about human nature, human needs, human relationships, human communication, problem solving, negotiations, cultures, groups, organizational structures and dynamics, employment law, discrimination law, disabilities law, leadership, and motivation. At the end of the day the parties will make decisions that impact their futures.

Workplace conflict is typically ongoing, episodic, and pervasive. Perhaps the best analogy of workplace conflict is that of the "peat fire." Take, for instance, the peat fires of the San Joaquin delta region of central California. This immense delta region south of Sacramento is comprised of hundreds of square miles of rivers, streams, and peat bogs and has persistent and pervasive peat fires that burn for years. Peat fires occur as a result of a lightening strike or some man-made cause of fire out in the delta that goes unchecked. These fires often burn for some time before firefighters attempt to extinguish them. As a result, the fire travels underground and smolders in the rich vegetable matter for many miles and many years. It is not unusual, for example, to read about a new spike on a line of fire that has been burning for twelve years and surfaced 1.7 miles due east from its last spike nine months ago. Like these peat fires, we tend to avoid immediate resolution of the conflicts we experience in the workplace. As a result, our problems smolder unresolved and become compounded over time. We don't know when the next spike will occur; we just know that it will.

MEDIATING DISPUTES IN THE WORKPLACE

It is the complex relational nature of most workplace or employment disputes that makes them particularly well-suited to facilitative or transformative methods of mediation. Most pre-retirement adults spend more of their waking hours with people at work than with the family members they choose and cherish. We have profound needs for accomplishment, satisfaction, recognition, and harmony and suffer to varying degrees when relationships and events block the satisfaction of these needs, and so do our employers.

In a broad sense, employers have taken a variety of informal and formal approaches to managing and resolving conflict. Informal approaches include a wide range of processes such as simple problem-solving conversations, face-to-face negotiations, facilitation, ombuds, and mediation. Informal approaches aim to preserve relationships and resources, and resolve problems at the earliest practicable level. Formal approaches are typically reactive to some legal claim or complaint and include costly, time-consuming processes like arbitration and administrative hearings to adjudicate rights and authority. One of the clearest distinctions between informal and formal dispute resolution processes is that informal procedures require consensual decision making by the parties, and formal procedures result in imposed decision making by a third party.

In order to promote appropriate conflict management and dispute resolution in the workplace, many business and governmental agencies are adopting better preventative and early conflict resolution approaches for improving and sustaining workplace relationships. Facilitative and transformative models of mediation have been particularly effective for improving communication and workplace relationships. In both of these models of mediation, the focus of resolution is at the level of underlying interests (i.e., needs) of the parties rather than mere negotiation of the terms of settlement of legal claims—although this may also occur. Unlike traditional formal systems for dispute resolution that adjudicate a winner and a loser, mediation fosters resolutions that address the underlying sources of conflict–breakdowns in relationships (Levine, 1998).

MITIGATING THE COST OF CONFLICT

One indicator of how important harmonious workplace relationships are is the cost associated with workplace stress as a byproduct of a conflict-fraught workplace environment. An Unscheduled Absence Survey in The Journal of Occupational and Environmental Medicine (1999) reported that health care costs are nearly 50 percent greater for employees who report high levels of stress due to workplace conflict. One would think that employers would be motivated to take proactive steps to reduce such stress.

What are the costs associated with the breakdown of important employment relationships? Numerous studies attempt to define and quantify the costs of workplace and employment conflict. Such costs are typically categorized as:

Direct Costs: fees of lawyers and other professionals, settlement payouts, etc;

Productivity Costs: value of lost time; the opportunity cost of what those involved would otherwise be producing;

Continuity Costs: loss of ongoing relationships including the "community" they embody;

Emotional Costs: pain of focusing on and being held hostage by our emotions (Levine, 1998).

Consider for a moment just the direct costs of an EEO complaint filed against Department of the Air Force, outlined by stage of complaint in 1999 US Dollars (General Services Administration, 2002):

Pre Complaint	$ 822.78
Counseling	1,360.03
Filed Formal	787.08
Investigation	3,213.44
Post Investigation with Resolution	2,231.12
Proposed Disposition	2,854.90
Final Agency Decision Without Hearing	1,521.00
Hearing	6,041.20
Final Agency Decision after EEOC Hearing	2,281.50
SUBTOTAL:	$ 21,113.05

Note that these figures only cover a portion of the direct costs associated with the processing of an EEO complaint; they do not include costs of settlement or direct costs paid for lawyers and other professionals or the cost of appeal, productivity costs, continuity costs, or emotional costs. Neither are such costs unique to the U. S. Air Force, but instead typical of costs experienced by federal agencies in general. Similar cost analyses are also available for unfair labor practice claims, tort claims, contract disputes, etc.

In the private sector, back in 1986, the Rand Corporation estimated that it cost $100,000 to defend a wrongful termination suit—just for costs of defense! It is further estimated by Fortune 500 senior human resources executives that at least 20 percent of their time is spent in litigation activities, and that 30 percent of the typical manager's time is spent dealing with conflict (Ford & Barnes-Slater, 2002).

Not only is conflict big business, it is clearly costly to any employer, no matter how you quantify the costs. Cost avoidance has clearly been the primary driver behind the proliferation of employment and workplace ADR programs and initiatives.

DISPUTE RESOLUTION IN EMPLOYMENT AND THE WORKPLACE

In 2004, *Conflict Resolution Quarterly* published a series of reports on work that were funded during the previous decade by the Hewlett Foundation. As part of this compendium of reports about the state of various dispute resolution contexts, Bingham (2004) authored the most comprehensive review of employment mediation to date. For an in-depth review, Bingham's article is a must read. This current chapter on employment and workplace mediation is not intended to duplicate Bingham's work, but to broaden the context to include the mediation of workplace disputes and a practitioner's perspective.

Disputes that occur in workplace and employment settings tend to fall into two broad categories: 1) disputes about rights (law), and 2) disputes about interests (needs). In addition, there is also a distinction between "employment disputes" and "workplace disputes"—employment typically referring to rights-based disputes and law-based actions (e.g. discrimination complaints, termination of employment, etc.), and workplace typically referring to interest-based disputes that have not been construed as being rights-based (e.g. roles and responsibilities, career advancement, etc.). Both categories of dispute resolution focus on some level of problem solving—e.g. solving legal problems or solving relational problems.

It is important to note that although a dispute may be construed as either rights-based or interests-based, most disputes characterized as rights-based are in fact interest-based. This is largely due to the means of dispute resolution that employees have available to them that have traditionally been either completely informal (conversations) or completely formal (fact finding, hearings, etc.). Hence, in order to access some form of dispute resolution, employees have had little choice but to construe their disputes as meeting whatever level of formality is required to access a rights- or law-based dispute resolution process. Indicative of this phenomenon is the large number of EEO filings of claims of discrimination, few of which ultimately meet the legal threshold of discrimination but many of which are resolved in the interest-based process of mediation. In FY 2005 there were 75,428 EEOC complaints filed (http://www.eeoc.gov/index.html). This represents a decrease from FY 2004 filing of 79,432 complaints and FY 2003 filing of 81,293 complaints. Most employment and workplace mediators will tell you that the majority of discrimination cases they mediate are more about perceptions, relationships, and communication and not about bona fide acts of discrimination.

Rights/law-based employment disputes are typically characterized as EEO/civil rights complaints, wrongful discharge, whistleblower complaints, wage and hour violations and other conditions of employment, or unfair labor practice complaints, occupational safety violations, contract disputes, union grievances, etc. (Bingham, 2004).

Interest-based workplace disputes frequently present as generalized communication and relationship problems about roles and responsibilities/duties, authority and decision making, appropriate and inappropriate conduct, etc.

The way that a dispute is construed is further influenced by whether the dispute arises from an existing, ongoing employment relationship or one that has been terminated. If the employment relationship has been terminated, the dispute will generally be construed as formal and rights-/law-based, and settlement of the pending legal claim becomes the only focus of the mediation.

What are the impact of formality and the imposition of a rights/legal frame on the methods of disputes resolution and problem solving? First, formality provides a narrower sense of scope and an alternative process for redress should the mediation not result in a resolution. If the parties do not reach consensual resolution, they can always resort to the formal process for a third-party decision. Informal, interest-based disputes often find negotiation in mediation as the only hope for redress. What can they do if they don't reach resolution? Informal, interest-based disputes can also be so unfocused in scope as to be difficult to resolve. For instance, how do parties resolve a problem that is ultimately about disliking one another? The exception to this problem of scope seems to be the dispute that is based upon a unique episode that provides clear focus rather than a lengthy conflict history between employees who have had many unproductive outcomes to prior conflict episodes and have difficulty defining the specific problems that need to be resolved.

It should, therefore, not be surprising that resolution rates for disputes that are construed as rights/law based are higher than resolution rates for seemingly simpler workplace problems.

PRIVATE AND PUBLIC SECTOR PARADIGMS

Private and public/governmental sectors have thus far taken rather different paths in the resolution of workplace disputes. The federal sector has clearly led the way with programmatic approaches to dispute resolution and the use of mediation for all workplace and employment disputes. The Administrative Dispute Resolution Act–ADRA (1990 and 1996) requires all federal agencies to develop alternative means of dispute resolution for resolving all disputes at the earliest practicable level and time (R. J. Evans, 1998). "Alternative" refers to informal and non-adversarial processes that don't result in an imposed third-party decision. As a result, federal agencies are far ahead of their state and private counterparts in institutionalizing the use of ADR, particularly mediation, for all manner of formal and informal workplace and employment disputes. As previously noted, such programmatic approaches are largely driven by proven cost savings to federal agencies.

State agencies have been slower to follow suit when it comes to the resolution of employment disputes for state workers. While state courts have long used mediation to resolve a variety of civil and criminal suits, fewer states have adopted state equivalents of the ADRA requiring programmatic approaches to employment dispute resolution. For instance, in 2003 Virginia implemented the Virginia ADRA that requires all state agencies to develop alternative means of dispute resolution procedures within the administrative structures of the agency.[1] In addition, some states have dispute resolution programs for resolving employment disputes involving state workers.[2]

In contrast, the private sector has been slow to develop programmatic approaches to the resolution of employment or workplace disputes. Private sector

Readings and Case Studies in Mediation

by Bruce C. McKinney and Jerry Bagnell, is a collection of readings by mediation scholars and practitioners on a variety of topics in mediation, such as employment mediation, divorce mediation, peer mediation, social service mediation, etc. Included in each chapter is a case study and role play that is written to highlight the principles put forth in each chapter. **Readings and Case Studies in Mediation** does not need to be read sequentially, and chapters are all stand alone documents. All authors have extensive experience in teaching and practicing mediation, and in some cases chapter authors have experience in both fields.

Chapters Include:

- Divorce Mediation
- Mediating Employment and Workplace Disputes
- Mediating Staff Disputes at a Large State University
- Developing Peer Mediation Programs for Today's Students
- The Movement of Mediation in Social Helping Fields
- Environmental Mediation: A Primer
- Mediation in Crisis Situations
- Mediation in Juvenile Victim/Offender Conferencing
- Mediating Disputes Involving Youth Gangs
- Faith-Based Disputes and Mediation Intervention
- Mediation-Arbitration in Dispute Resolution
- Transformative Mediation: Purpose Drives Practice

Readings and Case Studies in Mediation can be used as either a primary text in a mediation class or as a supplemental text in a conflict management class. Your students will gain a better understanding of not only the practice of mediation, but the flexibility mediation offers as a method of dispute resolution.

For more information visit our website – www.kendallhunt.com
or call
Brianne Racer at **(919) 510-0160**
or email
bracer@kendallhunt.com

KENDALL/HUNT PUBLISHING COMPANY
4050 Westmark Drive P.O. Box 1840
Dubuque   Iowa   52004-1840

handling of employment disputes remains largely reactive and defensive, or driven by external agencies like the EEOC. The two predominant approaches to employer and employee rights—"employment at will" or "right to work"—provide very different presumptions regarding employee rights and employer responsibilities, and hence, on the interest of either side in resolving disputes informally rather than formally. In 1997, a study of general and litigation counsel of Fortune 1000 companies reported that 87 percent had used mediation and 80 percent had used arbitration in the previous three years (Bingham 2004; Lipisky, Seeber, & Fincher, 2003). Only 19 percent reported broad use of mediation; 43 percent cited occasional use. The majority of cases involved rights rather than interests. Less than 40 percent of these companies had policies favoring the use of ADR. Finally, there is a tendency of private employers to adopt arbitration as a means of employment dispute resolution to avoid individual employment rights litigation (Colvin, 2003).

Federal agencies have affirmatively adopted programmatic approaches to employment and workplace dispute resolution that are preventative, provide opportunities for early resolution, as well as traditional means for formal resolution of disputes. State agencies are increasingly developing opportunities for the informal, early resolution of disputes as well as ongoing access to formal dispute resolution procedures. The private sector, however, remains largely reactive and defensive in handling workplace and employment disputes.

MODELS OF MEDIATION IN EMPLOYMENT OR THE WORKPLACE

Employment and workplace mediation is somewhat unique in that it provides one of the few contexts for programmatic approaches to dispute resolution. The structure of organizations and the rights and responsibilities they have for their constituent members make programmatic approaches to dispute resolution possible in ways that are not possible in the public at large. Dispute systems design has, hence, become popular in such contexts. In the simplest sense, dispute systems design assesses the nature of conflict in the organization, the structure and culture of the organization, employer and employer needs, organizational mission, etc. and develops informal and formal mechanisms for conflict management, resolution, and problem solving (Constantino & Merchant, 1996).

EXPERIENCE NEEDED TO MEDIATE DISPUTES IN THE WORKPLACE

The training needed to effectively mediate employment and workplace disputes depends largely upon the dispute issues and complexity (including but not limited to number of parties involved), context of the mediation, and programmatic requirements such as use of a particular model of mediation (e.g. facilitative or transformative). Some mediators have clear preferences or limitations regarding use of particular mediation models; others are trained in multiple models of mediation and feel comfortable using a model that may be required by a program (such as USPS's Redress program that requires the use of a transformative model of mediation) (Bingham, 1997). Such programmatic requirements limit mediator freedom and some mediators do not want to be constrained in this way. In order to be a broadly effective mediator in employment and workplace contexts, a mediator must be able to demonstrate flexibility and agility in the use of a variety of models of mediation while fulfilling their ethical and contractual duties to the programs they serve.

In addition to mediation process training, effective employment and workplace mediators also need training in organizational, group, intercultural, and interpersonal communication; organizational development; employment law; discrimination law; disabilities law; negotiation; conflict resolution; and dispute resolution program requirements. Employment and workplace disputes are complex and multi-layered and require a depth of knowledge and workplace experience that is unlike any other mediation context.

Finally, there are additional requirements for mediator success in the employment context involving personal capacities that are not easily learned. Lang and Taylor describe these additional competencies as one's "Constellation of Theories" (Lang & Taylor, 2000). Each mediator has a set of beliefs, values, and theories that serve as the basis for the facilitation of problem solving. In addition to the depth and breadth of a mediator's "Constellation of Theories," effective mediators have personal capacities that include the ability to sustain focus and energy throughout lengthy sessions (sometimes in excess of six to eight hours), and performance skills that keep participants engaged and motivated.

PREPARATION FOR WORKPLACE MEDIATION

Unlike some evaluative forms of dispute resolution where the mediator needs to read pre-mediation briefs and evidence, employment and workplace mediation require seemingly little in the way of case preparation.

The mediator may or may not have convening duties (scheduling with the parties, obtaining a mediation location, ensuring access to facilities if they are secure, educating the parties about mediation and how to prepare, fostering positive commitment to the process, etc.). In most programmatic contexts, an internal employee performs most if not all of these convening activities.

In employment and workplace mediation, the mediator's role is largely limited to the period of the mediation conference itself and there is typically little pre-mediation or post-mediation engagement. Again, it is not so much what the mediator does to get prepared for a particular case as it is the depth of relevant education and experience that the mediator brings to bear upon the mediation. In situations where mediators are not familiar with relevant law or regulations, required model of mediation, party complexity, etc. this again becomes a matter for education and training. If a mediator does not clearly have the necessary knowledge or skill for a particular mediation, the mediator is ethically bound to decline or withdraw as soon as this is known.[3] Co-mediation and mentoring with a mediator who does have the necessary knowledge and skill is also a good way to develop mediator competency.

One key distinction between mediator styles in the employment context is the extent to which they use joint session and caucus (separate sessions). Most facilitative and transformative mediators prefer joint session and caucus as necessary. This is because the parties themselves are the decisions makers—not the mediator. The parties are the ones who need to learn information and share perspectives, and this is typically best accomplished in joint discussion. Caucus is particularly helpful in the employment and workplace context for the facilitation of reality testing and the development of ideas (options) for resolution. Caucus is used heavily in more evaluative models of employment mediation to facilitate the negotiation of settlement offers.

Employment and workplace mediation programs also have paperwork requirements that need to be understood and carefully followed. Such paperwork typically includes forms about participants and issues, confidentiality agreements, settlement agreement templates, and exit evaluations or assessments.

TYPICAL AND UNIQUE PROBLEMS ASSOCIATED WITH WORKPLACE MEDIATION

Typical problems associated with employment and workplace mediation include: 1) inadequate case convening, 2) inadequate party education and preparation (e.g. failure to bring important case documents and information), 3) not having the necessary parties at the table, 4) programmatic constraints that do not meet the needs of the particular dispute, and 5) disruptive third parties.

Inadequate case convening can result in party no-shows as well as inadequate party preparation and the absence of the necessary decision makers. The quality of case convening has a huge impact on the success of the mediation itself. The importance of the convener role cannot be understated. In a well-convened case, all parties know what to expect in the mediation, how the process will work, what to bring, how to prepare, the value of bringing a representative for support and advice, other process options should resolution not be reached, and realistic expectations for resolution.

Who needs to participate is not as simple a question as it might seem. Typically those who need to participate are people who have direct knowledge of the events in question (e.g. employee and supervisor), people with decision-making authority (e.g. employee, supervisor, upper-level manager), and people with important subject matter knowledge to provide advice and support (e.g. representatives including attorneys and labor/employee relations personnel, union advisors, human resources advisors, personal advisors, etc.).

Programmatic constraints often impact the scope of resolution that can be reached, or a mismatch between a programmatically required model of mediation, the nature of the problem to be resolved, and the capacities of the parties—For instance, resolving relational issues with an evaluative model of mediation may not satisfy the parties needs for problem resolution at an interpersonal level (e.g. focus would be on settlement and resolution of legal issues). Likewise, a party who has strong adversarial communication skills may make it difficult for a fragile party to feel listened to and valued in a facilitative mediation.

Both the case convener and the mediator can play preventative and remedial roles in handling these typical challenges to the successful resolution of employment and workplace mediation cases.

Case Study: Carla and Joe Mediating in the Shadow of the Americans with Disabilities Act (ADA)

The dispute in this case is set in a government/federal shipyard context. It involves a limited number of employees and varied issues including disability rights in the context of federal employment. Read the following case study individually and then work in small groups of three to five to answer the questions at the end of the case.

Joe Jones has worked at the shipyard for seventeen years in a variety of positions within materials handling. Joe is widely viewed as an effective and popular supervisor. His stated goal is to have a workplace where people arrive on time, work productively, and leave at the end of the day with a smile on their faces.

Joe was recently moved into a supervisory position in a different section of materials handling as a result of a reorganization and consolidation of departments. It has been six months since the move, and Joe is so frustrated with several of his employees that he is actually considering early retirement; he just can't seem to get that smile back at the end of the day with this lot he now has to supervise!

One employee in particular, Carla, is giving him an especially difficult time. Carla was also relocated in the reorganization. Unofficial word is that no one would put up with her behavior, so management placed her under Joe's supervision. Joe believes that Carla was assigned to him because he is the only African-American manager and not part of the "good old boys" network.

Figuring out how to deal with Carla's behavior has been quite a challenge. While her performance evaluations have been satisfactory in the past, she displays wild mood swings and alienates other employees with whom she must work. Last month she "went off" on an upper-level manager, and when Joe wrote a letter of reprimand as a step in progressive discipline, he wound up as the subject of an EEO complaint! Carla alleges that Joe is harassing her because of her disability (bi-polar disorder).

Joe has been informed that Carla elected to use Department of Navy's mediation process as a way to resolve her EEO complaint. Naturally, Joe is concerned about being tagged as a manager who would discriminate against an employee, and wants to set matters straight.

At the mediation conference Carla and a union representative are present. In addition to Joe (the first level supervisor), the agency sends a labor relations representative to provide advice for Joe and assist with drafting of the settlement agreement, if one is reached.

During the mediation Carla explained how frustrated she has been in coping with all of the changes brought on by reorganization. She loved her former job as manager of the industrial clothing and uniform store and misses the autonomy she had in that position. It seems that Carla can better manage her psychiatric disability when she functions more autonomously and doesn't have to interact with numerous other employees in order to get her job done. She really wants the letter of reprimand removed from her personnel file, and believes that the agency set her up for problems when they relocated her.

Joe is surprised when he learns that this is not the first time that Carla has used EEO as a mechanism for resolving problems regarding her disability. Joe is also surprised to learn that Carla's union representative provides helpful continuity regarding the history of Carla's attempts to deal with her work performance, various requests for "accommodation," and conflicts with fellow employees and supervisors.

In a past EEO complaint, Carla sought an accommodation from the shipyard on flexible work hours and independent work. The shipyard resolved that dispute with Carla during the informal stage, and Carla's work performance improved with these accommodations. Everything seemed agreeable to Carla until the reorganization happened and her work assignment and hours were changed.

Joe was completely unaware of Carla's previous request for accommodation. The mediator facilitates a discussion between Joe and Carla that allows them to express their mutual concerns regarding performance, appropriate workplace behavior, productivity, and Carla's request for accommodation. The mediator then caucuses with Carla and her representative.

In a caucus with Joe and the labor relations representative, the mediator facilitates a discussion regarding what a "reasonable accommodation" might be—whether flexible work hours are allowable in Joe's division, and other concerns that Joe has about supervising a "fragile" employee. He continues to feel like he has to handle her with "kid gloves," and wants guidance regarding how an accommodation squares with his supervisory responsibilities to Carla as well as other employees. Joe and the labor relations representative formulate options for resolution that they believe meet the shipyard's interests and Joe's concerns as Carla's supervisor while also meeting key concerns that Carla raised.

When the parties reconvene after the caucuses, they discuss their respective proposals for resolving the dispute between them. It quickly becomes clear that there is significant overlap in their proposals, and the mediator facilitates the generation of sufficient detail to ensure that their agreement is actionable.

As a result of the mediation, Joe feels better prepared to supervise Carla and he understands disabilities accommodation issues far better than he did before. The mediation wasn't as painful as he had feared. In fact, Joe is frustrated with management himself. Joe recently had a knee replacement and management seems to keep putting off his request for handicapped parking. Maybe mediation could be used to resolve his concerns, too!

QUESTIONS FOR DISCUSSION

1. What are the roles of the various parties in the mediation?
   a. Mediator
   b. Complainant
   c. Complainant's Representative
   d. Manager
   e. Other Agency Representatives
2. Who were the decision-makers in the mediation?
3. What were the surface positions/ demands of each of the sides in this dispute?
4. What were the underlying needs and interests of each of the sides in this dispute?
5. What did each side gain in the mediation? What did each side give up?
6. What skills and knowledge did the mediator need to facilitate effectively in this situation?

Role Play: The Accounting Department

INFORMATION FOR DEBBIE MULLEY

You have been working in the accounting department for over a year now. You generally like your job and have spent your whole career with the same company. However, a year ago you were severely disappointed when Carmen Beltran was hired as a supervisor because you really wanted this position. Carmen was hired from outside the department, and you think this was a mistake because you have much more knowledge about the workings of your department. What really upsets you is when Carmen speaks Spanish with another Hispanic co-worker, Maria Hernandez. You don't know if they are discussing work-related issues or if they are talking about you, and this is really starting to bother you. Recently Art Gonzalez was given a big bonus when he was selected employee of the year. He was hired by Carmen, and he has only been in the department for ten months. How could someone so new to the organization become employee of the year after only ten months of work! You finally went to Carmen to complain about this situation, but she only told you to "grow up" and work harder. You are thinking of filing an EEO complaint on the basis of racial discrimination because you feel that Carmen and Art were given preferential treatment because they are Hispanic. The EEOC counselor in your company has asked to try to mediate this dispute before you take any further action.

INFORMATION FOR CARMEN BELTRAN

You have enjoyed your supervisory position over the past year, and feel that you are doing an exceptional job. You have a good feeling for who will make a good employee and who won't. You feel that when you hired Art Gonzalez, you made an exceptionally good choice. And though he has been with the company for only ten months, he was awarded employee of the year and given a nice bonus. Your co-worker, Debbie Mulley always seems to be unhappy about something. She is a good worker, but she seems to get upset if you speak Spanish to any other employees. As long as you speak about work-related issues, why should this be a problem? When Art was named employee of the year Debbie got very upset and threatened to file an EEOC complaint. Your EEO counselor suggested that you and Debbie try to work your differences out through mediation. You have agreed to do so, but you don't think it is quite right that a subordinate (Debbie) has the right to take you to mediation—it is disrespectful.

SPECIAL INSTRUCTIONS FOR MEDIATOR(S):

You are the mediator for this case. It is early in the problem identification and understanding phase of the mediation. Invite the parties to each give an uninterrupted overview of the problems they wish to resolve and listen carefully for issues and interests. After the opening overviews, work with the parties to identify a list of issues that need to be resolved as well as a list of the underlying interests of each of the parties. Facilitate discussion between the parties with the goal of developing mutual understanding of the issues and of one another's underlying interests. Save ideas for resolution for a later time.

Note: adequate problem identification and understanding is the key to resolution of employment and workplace disputes, hence the instruction to mediate just this phase of the dispute and save discussions about options/alternatives for a later exercise.

It is tempting to move too quickly to solutions and thereby impede the process.

CONCLUDING COMMENTS

Another case concluded and another long day for the mediator. This case was longer than the norm (seven hours), but the parties seemed pleased with the outcome—an agreement of their own choosing. The problem-understanding phase of the mediation was particularly challenging. The agency representative wanted to focus exclusively on legal merits of the case, while the initiator wanted to resolve issues at a much deeper level. The mediator worked to facilitate the understanding of the needs of both sides and was finally able to help the parties turn the corner toward agreement.

The two-hour drive home gives the mediator plenty of time for reflection: what could she have done differently to help the parties achieve mutual understanding earlier or more effectively? How could she have better met the parties' facilitation needs? What additional research or training might equip her more adequately for future cases? Always thinking about the next case, additional ways to stretch. . .always anticipating the next opportunity to make a difference in the workplace.

NOTES

[1] Texas also has a state ADRA; according to www.policyconsensus.org six states have Administrative Branch ADR programs.

[2] According to www.policyconsensus.org there are currently fifty individual administrative Agency ADR programs (some states have multiple programs and not all states have programs); some provide specifically for the resolution of employment disputes (e.g. Virginia Department of Employment Dispute Resolution).

[3] Model Standards of Conflict for Mediators (September 2005 revised version); available at http://www.acrnet.org/pdfs/ModelStandardsofConductforMediators final05.pdf.

REFERENCES

Bingham, L. B. (1997). Mediating employment disputes: Perceptions of redress at the United States Postal Service. *Review of Public Personnel Administration, 17* (2), 20-30.

Bingham, L. B. (2004). Employment dispute resolution, *Conflict Resolution Quarterly, 22* (1-2), 145-174.

Claxton, A. J., Chawla, A. J., and Kennedy, S. (1999). Absenteeism among employees treated for depression. *Journal of Occupational and environmental medicine, 41* (7), 605-611.

Colvin, A. J. S. (2003). Institutional pressures, human resource strategies, and the rise of nonunion dispute resolution procedures. *Industrial and Labor Relations Review, 56* (3), 375-391.

Constantino, C. A., and Merchant, C. S. (1996). *Designing Conflict Management Systems: A Guide to Creating Productive and Health Organizations.* San Francisco: Jossey-Bass.

Evans, R. J. (1998). *Notes and comments: The administrative dispute resolution act of 1996.*

Ford, J., and Barnes-Slater, C. (2002). Measuring conflict: Both the hidden costs and benefits of conflict management interventions, available at www.Mediate.com.

General Services Administration (2002). The cost savings associated with the Air Force alternative dispute resolution program, Office of Equal Opportunity. *Journal of Occupational and Environmental Medicine* (1999), Unscheduled Absence Survey.

Lang, M. D., and Taylor, A. (2000). *The Making of a Mediator: Developing Artistry in Practice.* San Francisco: Jossey-Bass.

Levine, S. (1998). *Getting to Resolution: Turning Conflict into Collaboration.* NY: Reed Business Information, Inc.

Lipisky, D. B., Seeber, R. L., and Fincher, R. D. (2003). *Emerging Systems for Managing Workplace Conflict: Lessons from American Corporations for Managers and Dispute Resolution Professionals.* San Francisco: Jossey-Bass.

U.S. Equal Employment *Opportunity* Commission. (2006). Discrimination by type: facts and guidance, available at www.eeoc.gov/index.html.

Chapter 4

Mediating Staff Disputes at a Large State University

Jessica Katz Jameson

Academic institutions play an important role in modeling critical thinking, open and active exchange of ideas, and dialogue to achieve the goal of preparing students to become engaged employees and citizens. In order to create a culture that values collaborative conflict management, all parts of the university system should practice that behavior. Mediation programs that are available to administrators and staff improve the university's ability to institutionalize alternative dispute resolution practices and provide an important option for addressing staff disputes. Administrative staff members are central to academic institutions and they experience the same kinds of conflicts that are endemic to all organizations.

While campus mediation programs have proliferated since the early 1980s (Warters, 2000), services have often been made available to students and/or faculty, but not necessarily administrative staff. Higgerson (1998) defines support staff as all individuals who are not faculty appointments, generally holding secretarial, administrative, and student work positions (although they may also hold a variety of teaching, research, extension, and/or grant writing appointments). University support staff work with a wide variety of constituents, including students, faculty, department heads and deans, and other staff. Added to the challenge of the diversity of the campus population is the fact that many large, Research I Universities have an ingrained social structure among faculty (according to rank), tenure- versus non-tenure-track instructors, and staff, with support staff often at the bottom of the hierarchy. All of these aspects of the organizational climate create the preconditions for employee dissatisfaction and conflict. Because high staff turnover is frustrating for staff, students, and faculty, it is in the university's best interests to prepare for staff conflicts. There is a strong business case for mediation because universities compete to be the employer of choice for faculty and staff.

Is Mediation Appropriate for Staff Disputes?

In the landmark book on campus dispute resolution, *Mediation in the Campus Community,* Warters (2000) points out that there is often no appropriate venue for managing staff conflicts. While universities may have a grievance process, staff conflicts over issues such as equal task distribution, work habits, or communication styles are inappropriate for a formal grievance. Higgerson (1998), one of the few authors to write about staff conflict specifically, recommends that department heads and chairs follow a three-step framework for managing staff conflict: minimize conflict potential; set the tone for airing disagreements; and make managing (not resolving) conflict the goal. While Higgerson's advice is sound, the assumption that a department head should take on the role of third party can be problematic due to the power imbalances mentioned above. A mediation program that allows staff to speak with a neutral third party provides an option for airing disagreements and may result in the highest likelihood of satisfaction, relational maintenance, and improved working climate. The fact that staff conflicts may include conflict with the department head also supports the need for another conflict management alternative.

Research comparing mediation to other forms of alternative dispute resolution (such as arbitration), consistently finds that mediation leads to such outcomes as greater satisfaction with agreements (Brett, Barsness, & Goldberg, 1996), greater perceptions of fairness of the process and outcome (Blancero & Dyer, 1996; Brett, Barsness, & Goldberg, 1996; Fisher, & Keashly, 1991; Karambayya, & Brett, 1989; Shapiro, & Brett, 1993), and improved relationships with coworkers (Bush & Folger, 1994, 2005). Additional potential outcomes of mediation include increased employee empowerment and ability to manage future conflicts more independently (Bush & Folger, 1994, 2005). Further, research by Friedman, Tidd, Currall, & Tsai (2000) has shown that employees who address conflict directly and use collaborative strategies, such as mediation, have reduced levels of stress and improved perceptions of organizational climate. For all these reasons it makes sense to create or expand campus mediation programs to include conflicts among university staff.

Staff disputes are challenging because they often fall into the category of relationship conflict (Holton, 1998). These conflicts generally present as "task" conflict, such as issues of scheduling (i.e., one employee wants to come in late or leave early), performance (i.e., a staff member accuses another of not meeting expectations), or differences in perceptions of interdependence (i.e., one staff member wants to work more collaboratively than another), which can result in a tendency to treat them as simple problems to be solved. For example, a conflict between two staff members may result when one staff member refuses to help the other. On the surface, this seems like an easy conflict to resolve: the department head simply tells employees they are expected to help each other out and if they cannot they should find employment elsewhere; however, there are several flaws in this strategy. For one, control over the outcome is left in the hands of the department head without participation of the disputants. This has been found to lead to perceptions of dissatisfaction and low procedural justice (i.e., Shapiro & Brett, 1993). Two, one employee may grudgingly agree to help the other, but show his or her displeasure with the employee in other ways, resulting in conflict avoidance rather than open discussion of the conflict. Three, and most important, the underlying issue has not been discussed and therefore the conflict itself has not really been managed: the department head has dealt with a symptom, rather than a cause.

EXPERIENCE NEEDED TO MEDIATE STAFF DISPUTES

In mediation, the attitudes, beliefs, and emotions underlying an employee's behavior are likely to be revealed and create an opportunity for increased understanding and actual transformation of the conflict (Galtung, 1996). Because the majority of staff conflicts referred to mediation (in this author's experience) are relational in nature, it is important that those who mediate staff conflicts are open to a transformative style of mediation as opposed to a strict "problem-focused" style (Bush & Folger, 1994, 2005). The benefit of the transformative approach for staff conflicts lies in its focus on empowerment and recognition. By allowing parties to fully participate in as many decisions guiding the mediation process as possible, they have a greater stake in the process and are more satisfied with the final agreement. Allowing parties to talk about the issues that are most critical to them also reveals information about the staff members that they probably did not know about each other before, often leading to recognition of the other's situation that did not previously exist (the phrase "I had no idea you were going through that" is often the turning point in a mediation session).

Another important mediator skill for staff conflicts is managing power imbalances. There is an awkward irony on university campuses in that they promote critical thinking and open, participatory models of management, yet academic structures operate within a strict hierarchy. As mentioned above, staff may often perceive themselves to be the lower-power party and as such, can feel intimidated in a mediation session where the opponent is their department head, a faculty member, or another staff member with seniority or a higher pay grade. Mediators need to recognize the power dynamics at play and their potential impact on the mediation, such as a party's willingness to speak openly or the potential to accept agreements that are not in their best interests. Wiseman and Poitras (2002) recommend that mediators address the power difference up front by clarifying the differences in communication within and outside the mediation session. The mediator can explain that the mediation context requires openness and equal participation, which may be distinct from the procedures in the workplace. This can help reduce the higher-power party's fears of losing its authority, while creating a safe space for the lower-power party to share concerns. If there is resistance from either of the parties, Wiseman and Poitras recommend an exploration of why the parties agreed to mediation in the first place. This question may help remind the parties of the problem they want to resolve and help steer them toward a more collaborative, trusting, path.

THE EMPLOYEE MEDIATION PROGRAM AT NORTH CAROLINA STATE UNIVERSITY

Our employee mediation program was designed specifically for NC State employees, including EPA (exempt from personnel act, mostly faculty) and SPA (subject to personnel act, mostly administrative staff).[1] The mediators are administrators and faculty from across campus who have participated in a 40-hour mediation training from an established mediation consulting firm. We have approximately twenty-two trained mediators who serve in this capacity as part of their administrative work (i.e., human resources and Office for Equal Opportunity staff) or as university service (i.e., faculty). The benefit of having a variety of mediators is that it allows disputing parties to choose the type of person they want to mediate for them. Staff, for example, may want a faculty member to mediate as they may perceive them as neutral and someone they will not have to collaborate with professionally (or they may explicitly NOT want a faculty member to mediate, due to perceptions of power imbalance described above). In cases where faculty members are involved in a conflict with support staff, they may want to have a faculty member mediating as this will increase their comfort.

We use a co-mediation model, so generally there is one administrator and one faculty member mediating each dispute, but this allows flexibility based on the situation and party needs. We almost never assign a mediator to a case where they have had any previous interaction with a party or where they are likely to have future interaction. This is, in fact, one of the benefits of having a mediation program in a large institution, as it greatly contributes to confidentiality and the parties' willingness to participate. (Of course, being a large, state organization carries its share of limitations as well, especially in terms of resources and approvals for creating a mediation process, but that is the subject for a separate chapter. Those who are interested in creating a campus mediation program are strongly referred to the Warters book, cited previously).

Mediators in our program have different attitudes toward preparation for mediating staff disputes. Some prefer to have as much information about the case as possible and will discuss the parties' concerns with the intake officer (a member of the human resources department). Others prefer to know as little about the case as possible to reduce the chances of bias. The intake process at our institution works as follows: a staff member brings a complaint about a coworker to a department head or has called OEO or human resources. If deemed suitable for mediation (i.e., there is no obvious policy or legal violation that would require formal investigation), the party will be asked if they are interested in mediation. If that party is interested, an HR officer will contact the other party to see if they are also willing to attend a mediation session. Once both parties have agreed, the intake officer locates two mediators who are available. The lead mediator contacts the parties to set a date and time for the mediation, and then HR schedules a room in a neutral location (usually the student center or an administrative building where neither of the disputing parties works). The lead mediator does not communicate with parties individually before the mediation session (except in the event of scheduling changes).

CHALLENGES OF MEDIATING STAFF CONFLICTS

In addition to the challenges presented by power imbalances raised above, campus mediation programs face the obstacles of publicizing the process and encouraging employees to participate. While the university Web site includes information on the mediation program, it is easily lost among hundreds of pages of protocols and policies. Information provided to all new employees in orientation may also be missed due to information overload at the start of a new job. Like many other organizations, we have found that the best way to publicize the mediation program is through successful cases and word-of-mouth diffusion (Jameson, 1998). The more department heads and deans are aware of the mediation program and its successes, the more likely they are to refer their staff to the program.

Aside from the challenge of diffusion, there is also the challenge of adoption. Department heads, like other managers, may not appreciate the benefits of sending their staff to someone else, and may believe that not managing the conflict on their own will be seen by others as a sign of weakness (Jameson, 2001). This is exacerbated by the fact that academic department heads are tenured faculty and not required to attend conflict management training (in fact, while a variety of employee training programs are available to department heads and faculty, most do not take advantage of them as their evaluations and rewards are more directly connected to research productivity).

Adoption of mediation is also challenging because leaders of all types view problem solving as part of their job, and often frame staff conflicts as problems to be solved (Kolb & Sheppard, 1985). Even when department heads do recommend mediation, support staff may fear taking a problem to human resources out of a belief that it will negatively affect future performance reviews. Human Resources departments face a potential conflict of interests in that they want to be neutral in mediation, yet they are advisory to senior leadership and must revert back to "management" mode in the event mediation is unsuccessful and the conflict becomes a formal grievance (Warters, 2000). Finally, even if a staff member is comfortable with the mediation process, they may perceive it as futile in a conflict with a tenured faculty member or another employee of higher status (Jameson, 2001).

In addition to making information available about a mediation program, there are more proactive ways to spread the word about mediation. Mediators, for example, should be ambassadors for the program and should make sure support staff and faculty they work with are aware of the program and its benefits. Because many employees have never experienced mediation before, it is helpful if someone can spend some time explaining the process to reduce any fears or misconceptions (we have developed a "What to expect during your mediation" brochure to help reduce uncertainty and anxiety). Arguably one of the best ways to improve understanding of the mediation process and encourage participation is to train more employees in mediation (Jameson & Johnson, 2004). While this may not be economically feasible for large numbers of staff, as mediator attrition occurs, it may be wise to provide mediation training to more department heads and support staff to increase awareness of mediation and institutionalize the process. This not only creates a larger cadre of potential mediators, but empowers more university staff to improve their own conflict management through the internalization of mediation principles. This can obviously have a ripple effect throughout the entire campus community.

The good news is that mediation is becoming more common and accepted as an alternative form of conflict resolution. This may be in part due to the proliferation of peer mediation programs in primary education (see chapter five), resulting in a student body that often expects mediation to be part of the campus infrastructure. Our experience is that, when staff experience mediation, they appreciate the opportunity to talk to each other in a safe space, and often comment that it is the first time they were able to talk to each other in a way they felt heard and understood. While the mediation program here is too new to provide empirical evidence of an effect on the campus community, the seeds for more productive communication and conflict management have certainly been sown. The following sections include a case study that illustrates how the relationship between two staff members can be transformed through mediation and a role-play that reflects the difficulties of power imbalance in a conflict between an administrative assistant and an associate professor[2]. These examples demonstrate the potential of mediation for managing staff conflicts.

FINAL COMMENTS

Conflict is a necessary part of organizational life, and universities are no exception to the rule. In fact, the very nature of universities as complex systems made up of diverse populations suggests that conflict should be anticipated, even welcomed, as members attempt to communicate and coordinate their activities. Numerous studies have demonstrated the effectiveness of mediation as an alternative to rights-based procedures that focus on determining the "right" solution, rather than improving understanding and empowering parties to create the "best" solution for their needs. It is completely consistent with the mission of our universities to develop conflict management practices that encourage communication, dialogue, and understanding. Such processes need to be made available to all members of the campus community, with the ultimate goal of institutionalization of mediation and constructive conflict management practices.

Case Study: Roberta and Margaret

Roberta and Margaret work together in facilities management. They share an office that includes a computer and a telephone. There is a table between the two desks for the telephone, but the phone often ends up on one desk or the other depending on who used it last. Because the office space is small, Roberta and Margaret often bump into each other when they are in the office at the same time.

The office situation has created a stressful climate for Roberta and Margaret, who share supervisory duties over the housekeeping staff. While they work different shifts, their schedules overlap so that they can coordinate employee tasks. Roberta and Margaret are constantly bickering, both to each other and about each other, and they undermine each other's authority with the staff. The rest of the department is experiencing the brunt of this conflict and have individually started to complain to the director of facilities. Academic departments have also begun to complain about poor service and maintenance standards and the director recognizes that action must be taken to manage this conflict.

The director has tried to talk to Roberta and Margaret individually, but each one accuses the other of being uncooperative and neither one is willing to admit their role in this situation. For example, Roberta complains that Margaret's chair is always pushed all the way back and that she is unorganized. She also accuses Margaret of not communicating with her.

Margaret complains that Roberta is always on the phone and she keeps the phone on her desk rather than returning it to its appropriate place on the table. Margaret is also upset that even though Roberta has been working at this institution for ten years (eight years longer than her), she refuses to answer any of Margaret's questions and often snaps at her when she asks.

The director recognizes that both of these employees are valuable–they both come to work on time and, despite their problems with each other, have a good work ethic and loyalty to the organization. She calls the human resources department for advice and learns about the possibility of mediation. She approaches Roberta and Margaret and strongly recommends that they try mediation because the department can no longer run this way. Roberta and Margaret both agree to give it a shot.

The mediators assigned to this case are a faculty member and a member of the human resources department. Neither mediator has had any previous interaction with Roberta or Margaret. The mediators describe the mediation process, specifically pointing out that the goal of mediation is to help Roberta and Margaret create an agreement that will improve their working relationship. Roberta and Margaret both appear motivated to resolve their conflict so they can improve their comfort and satisfaction in the workplace.

Margaret was the one who originally requested mediation, so she is invited to speak first. She explains that she is very frustrated about their office situation and believes that the small space is the source of their problems. She confides that she has a bad back and must sit a certain distance from the computer keyboard, which means her chair is often pushed back and she knows this is a problem when Roberta is in the office. She also complains that when the phone rings, it is hard for her to get to because it is always on Roberta's desk, and out of her reach, rather than on the table between the desks, where it belongs. Margaret is also offended by the fact that Roberta is very short with her, and she is annoyed that Roberta will not answer her questions. The mediators ask Margaret a few follow-up questions to make sure she feels heard, and then they ask Roberta to share her view of the situation.

Roberta agrees that the office space is a problem. She is very frustrated about the chair, but did not realize there was a medical reason involved. She comments that she is on the phone a lot, and it is just easier to have it on her desk rather than constantly putting it back on the table when she hangs up the phone. She is upset about what she perceives as Margaret's lack of organization, which results in files not being put back where they belong, and post-it notes stuck everywhere. She claims that every time she comes into the office there is a post-it note on her computer with questions or things to do, and often she does not get messages accurately.

Roberta also cannot understand why Margaret has so many questions when she had the "same exact job" in her previous workplace, where she worked as many years as Roberta has. She perceives Margaret as lazy and a slow learner, and she does not feel it is her responsibility to get Margaret up to speed. Once again, the mediators ask a few clarification questions, and then move on to set the agenda for the mediation by asking both Roberta and Margaret what the key issues are that need to be addressed in order for them to feel better about working together.

With the mediators' help, Roberta and Margaret identify three main issues that need to be worked out: the placement of the telephone and Margaret's chair, communication with each other about what has happened during their shift, and the organization of paperwork and files. They agree to start with the issue of improving their communication with each other. The mediators ask them to come up with specific examples of times they had difficulty communicating.

Margaret tells the story of a time they had to coordinate the repair of a leaky roof and she needed to ask Roberta to help her with the task. Roberta just said "you know where the forms are, get them signed and set up the work order." Margaret was hurt by Roberta's unwillingness to help, as she had never done this at a state institution before. Margaret pointed out that while she had held a similar job before this one, it was a private construction firm and their procedures were very different, which has made learning this job very stressful.

When Margaret had finished speaking, the mediators noticed a significant difference in Roberta's physical appearance and tone of voice. Roberta had clearly heard something new, which was confirmed when she said "I really had no idea that things were so different where you worked before. When you got this job, I assumed you knew all the procedures. When you asked me questions, I thought you were just lazy and wanted me to do the work for you, now I understand why you had questions. It must have been really hard for you this past couple of years."

At this point, all eyes were on Margaret, who said "you have no idea how much it means to me just to hear you say that you understand why it was hard for me." Margaret was a bit teary-eyed at this point, so a mediator jumped in and complimented the two for their good work listening to each other and pointed out that they had already made some real progress. At that point, the parties talked some more about specifics regarding how they might improve their day-to-day communication with each other and how to organize the office files.

After twenty minutes or so of working out those details, a mediator said, "Okay, we have addressed the issues of improving your communication and organizing the office, now we need to talk about the telephone and the chair." Roberta and Margaret both looked at the mediators quizzically and laughed. Roberta said "The telephone? The chair? Who cares about that? That's not important, we've worked out our differences and those things don't even matter now." They agreed that nothing about the telephone or chair needed to be included in the agreement, that those were "little" things that were bothering them because of these larger misunderstandings they had. They both felt that their relationship was different now, and looked forward to returning to the office and a more cooperative, less stressful climate.

QUESTIONS FOR DISCUSSION

1. Should the facilities director have intervened in this conflict <u>before</u> complaints started coming in? (What signs might there have been that a conflict was brewing?)
2. What assumptions did Roberta and Margaret make about each other's intentions prior to mediation? What aspects of the <u>situation</u> may have led to a climate conducive to conflict?
3. What are the underlying interests or issues that helped explain Roberta and Margaret's behavior prior to mediation?
4. What was the role of empowerment and recognition in the transformation of Roberta and Margaret's relationship? What other beneficial outcomes might result from successful mediation?

Role Play: The Professor and the Secretary

The Margaret/Roberta scenario illustrates that by paying attention to empowerment and recognition, relationships can be transformed and mediation can lead to effective long-term agreements (Bush & Folger, 1994, 2005). Mediation is more challenging when there are significant power differences between disputing parties because the need for openness and participation stands in contradiction to the hierarchy of the typical academic institutional structure. The following role-play between an administrative assistant and an associate professor illustrates these challenges.

SCENARIO

The following role-play describes a conflict between Joanna, an administrative assistant, and Dr. Scorch, a tenured faculty member in the department of art and design. While this is not a case between two support staff, it is indicative of a typical campus conflict and illustrates the challenges unique to university settings. When enacting this role-play, parties should be instructed to reflect carefully on the underlying interests of the parties, as well as the role of perceptions, power, values, and emotions that are central to each disputant. Mediators should be prepared to confront these concerns to achieve empowerment and recognition for both parties and develop an agreement that will have long-term effectiveness.[3]

INFORMATION FOR JOANNA JACOBS

Joanna is an administrative assistant in the department of art and design in a Research I institution. She has been employed there for eighteen months and because she has a BA degree and is a good writer, many faculty have asked for her help preparing grant proposals as well as other teaching and research-related documents. Other administrative staff members in the department serve very specific technical duties such as scheduling, accounting, or student records, according to their skill sets and job descriptions. Joanna's main job is to support the department head, but the department head encourages her to work with faculty in order to provide faculty support and give Joanna more challenging tasks consistent with her level of education and abilities. Joanna likes doing this kind of work, although she often feels pulled in many directions due to the large number of faculty who come to her for assistance.

She has become increasingly uncomfortable with Dr. Scorch's behavior, but has made a concerted effort to accept this behavior. She does not like his communication style, and feels that she is on the receiving end of a lot of his aggression. She knows that Dr. Scorch is well-liked by the department and dean. She is nearing her second annual review, and has finally decided to talk to the department head about the stress that Dr. Scorch is causing her and boundaries that she feels need to be made when it comes to doing projects for the faculty.

When the department head asks her if she is having any specific problems, she tells him that Dr. Scorch is creating an uncomfortable environment for her. The department head tells her that this is "just part of Scorch's personality," and that she should not take it personally. However, she maintains that she has a hard time dealing with his communication style.

The next day Scorch approached her and apologized for his behavior and told her not to take it personally. She thanked him and told him she came from a family in which yelling was not allowed, and that made it very hard to adapt to his communicative style. He told her that she would get used to him and "his bark is worse than his bite," and he meant her no ill will.

However, several weeks later Joanna is in her office when Dr. Scorch storms in and yells "Where is my damn proposal?" She finally tells the department head that she can no longer work with Dr. Scorch. Because the department head does not want to lose such a valuable employee, he tells her to try the campus mediation services.

INFORMATION FOR DR. RICHARD SCORCH

Dr. Scorch is an associate professor who has been in the department of art and design for ten years. He is generally liked by his students and is popular with the department head and dean because of the amount of sponsored research (grant money) he generates for the department. Dr. Scorch is an active researcher and relies heavily on the office staff for support. He has become particularly dependent on Joanna because of her organizational and writing skills. Due to the pressure of grant deadlines, Dr. Scorch is often in a panic and can be found running through the office talking out loud to himself or barking orders at others. At times, Dr. Scorch becomes loud and aggressive. Most of the faculty laugh off Scorch's behavior and attribute it to his "Type A" personality. He generally calms down and returns to his normal, jovial self by the end of the day, but not before wreaking havoc on those he is directly working with.

NOTES

[1] Readers interested in viewing the mediation policy are referred to: http://www.ncsu.edu/policies/employment/mediation/REG05.35.1.php

[2] The case-study and role-play scenarios are based on a synthesis of actual cases. Details such as names, departments, and titles have been changed to protect any employees who may have been involved in situations like these.

[3] This role-play provides a good opportunity for students to practice mediating disputes with power differences. Mediators need to figure out how to help the parties achieve sincere understanding of each other's communication styles and interests. If that does not happen, any agreement reached is much less likely to be effective over the long term.

REFERENCES

Blancero, D., and Dyer, L. (1996). Due process for non-union employees: The influence of system characteristics on fairness perceptions. *Human Resource Management, 35*(3), 343-359.

Brett, J. M., Barsness, Z. I., and Goldberg, S. B. (1996). The effectiveness of mediation: An independent analysis of cases handled by four major service providers. *Negotiation Journal, 12*(3), 259-269.

Bush, R. A. B., and Folger, J. P. (1994). *The Promise of Mediation: Responding to Conflict through Empowerment and Recognition.* San Francisco, CA: Jossey-Bass.

Bush, R. A. B., and Folger, J. P. (2005). *The Promise of Mediation: The Transformative Approach to Conflict (Revised edition).* San Francisco, CA: Jossey-Bass.

Fisher, R. J., and Keashly, L. (1991). The potential complementarity of mediation and consultation within a contingency model of third party intervention. *Journal of Peace Research, 28*(1), 29-42.

Friedman, R. A., Tidd, S. A., Currall, S. C., and Tsai, J. C. (2000). What goes around comes around: The impact of personal conflict style on work conflict and stress. *The International Journal of Conflict Management, 11*(1), 32-55.

Galtung, J. (1996). *Peace by Peaceful Means: Peace and Conflict Development and Civilization.* Thousand Oaks, CA: Sage.

Higgerson, M. (1998). Chairs as department managers: Working with support staff. In S. A. Holton (ed.), *Mending the cracks in the ivory tower: Strategies for conflict management in higher education* (pp 46-59). Boston, MA: Anker Publishing Co.

Holton, S. A. (1998). What's it all about? Conflict in Academia. In S. A. Holton (ed.), *Mending the cracks in the ivory tower: Strategies for conflict management in higher education* (pp 1-11). Boston, MA: Anker Publishing Co.

Jameson, J. K. (1998). Diffusion of a campus innovation: Integration of a new student dispute resolution center into the university culture. *Mediation Quarterly, 16*(2) pp. 129-146.

Jameson, J. K. (2001). Employee perceptions of the availability and use of interests-, rights-, and power-based conflict management strategies. *Conflict Resolution Quarterly, 19*(2), 163-196.

Jameson, J. K., and Johnson, J. T. (2004, June). "Bridging dispute system design theory and practice: The case of Unity Hospital." Paper presented at the annual meeting of the International Association for Conflict Management, Pittsburgh, PA, June 6-9, 2004.

Karambayya, R., and Brett, J. M. (1989). Managers handling disputes: Third-party roles and perceptions of fairness. *Academy of Management Journal, 32*(4), 687-704.

Kolb, D. M., and Sheppard, B. H. (1985). Do managers mediate, or even arbitrate? *Negotiation Journal, 1*(4), 379-388.

Shapiro, D. L., and Brett, J. M. (1993). Comparing three processes underlying judgments of procedural justice: A field study of mediation and arbitration. *Journal of Personality and Social Psychology, 65*(6), 1167-1177.

Warters, W. C. (2000). *Mediation in the Campus Community: Designing and Managing Effective Programs.* San Francisco, CA: Jossey-Bass.

Wiseman, V., and Poitras, J. (2002). Mediation within a hierarchical structure: How can it be done successfully? *Conflict Resolution Quarterly, 20*(1) 51-65.

Chapter 5

Developing Peer Mediation Programs for Today's Students

Kirsten B. Atkinson
Kimberly Lucas

Peer mediation has been part of school cultures for over thirty years. Peer mediation was introduced in North Carolina schools in 1978 as part of the Orange County Dispute Settlement Center, and its implementation was a proactive approach to helping young minds develop alternative ways of resolving conflicts on the playground and in the classrooms. The program was designed to create a culture where students could take responsibility for their own problem solving. Focusing on listening skills, respect, empathy, and decision making, peer mediation programs continue to hold much promise for the future.

The implementation of peer mediation within the school environment has assisted in reducing the number of disciplinary actions and the time that teachers and administrators have to spend dealing with conflicts, and encouraged students to utilize their problem-solving skills (Diekman, 2004). The mediation process allows for discussion of a student-to-student conflict and promotes brainstorming ways to find a solution.

The modern-day school yards require a more savvy approach to the once-simple model of dealing with conflict. American high schools today can be risky places with the existence of gangs, drugs, and the record numbers of high school violence around the country. According to the U.S. Bureau of Justice, 7-9 percent of students reported being threatened, and 30 percent of students (grades 6-10) reported they were involved in moderate or frequent bullying (DeBates & Bell, 2006). In a country where divorce is prevalent, young people are not only exposed to school yard conflict but they experience conflict in the sanctity of their home. Empowering students with strategies that enable them to deal with conflict and cultural diversity increases their ability to communicate effectively and deal with future adult situations. This chapter offers the examination of a local North Carolina Peer Mediation program, as well as recommendations for techniques and curricula that readers and practitioners alike should consider when implementing modern day peer mediation programs (PMPs).

CONFLICT RESOLUTION PROGRAMS

There are essentially four strategies to implementing conflict resolution programs: (1) Process Curriculum, which focuses on implementing conflict resolution as a separate curriculum or regular lesson plan.; (2) Peer Mediation, a strategy in which select students are trained to mediate conflicts between their peers; (3) Peaceable Classrooms, which incorporate conflict resolution into the curriculum and classroom management; and (4) Peaceable Schools, which operate on the same basis as Peaceable Classrooms with a school-wide approach. Current literature on school disputes suggests that these strategies and processes are still among the most effective means of positively affecting school climate and resolving peer-to-peer conflicts (Jones, 2004). Practitioners and educators of the mediation world need to have their communities understand the lexicon of the mediation field. There are subtle differences between Conflict Resolution Education (CRE) programs which can include character education, anger management, pro-social development, social-emotional learning (SEL) and bullying PMPs. Where conflict resolution programs focus on the ethos of conflict and its resolution and can be taught in large classrooms or select smaller groups, Peer Mediation is the knowledge and application of strategies to help others resolve conflicts.

The basis of PMPs is built on elements of one or more CRE or SEL programs available. Typically, not every student is predisposed to effectively manage the resolution process for others, even if the student can understand the tenets of conflict resolution. Thus, PMPs are usually smaller in size, more intimate in nature, and often meet regularly with a school leader who heads up a program.

In both conflict resolution and peer mediation, students learn such concepts as:

* Conflict Is Normal–Conflict is neither good nor bad.
* Understanding Perspectives–We see things from different points of view.

- I-Statements–Empowering students to verbalize their feelings about a problem/conflict.
- Restatements–Restate what you heard the person say to ensure that you understand what they are saying.
- Conflict Styles–Win-Win/Assertive
  Win-Lose/Aggressive
  Lose-Win/Passive
- Active Listening–Look at the person talking and use appropriate body language.
- Open-Ended Questions–Ask questions to obtain more information.

Students participate in hands-on activities and role plays in order to maximize the learning potential. In order to reach all students, the trainings need to be fun and engaging. There are numerous choices of training curricula available and the trainer should choose that which is most suited to the mission of their respective school system and the desired intervention strategies.

In PMPs, students typically focus on strategies to effectively resolve conflicts and trainings can incorporate a 5-step process into a 26-step process depending on the curriculum one uses. After the disputants have concluded their mediation, the mediators should debrief with one another. A mediator/co-mediator can mutually reflect on the mediation experience, and make suggestions for improvement. Often, forms are made available to student mediators so that the feedback construct is consistent and easy to follow. Questions such as "What went well? What we would like to do differently in the future?" should be addressed. Afterward, the completed paperwork should be turned into the peer mediation advisor. Guidance may be needed for student mediators who consistently score low on co-mediator debriefings. Additionally, ongoing training for all Peer Mediators is essential to insure that all students are prepared for the many challenges that they are likely to face.

The implementation of peer mediation within the school environment has assisted in reducing the number of disciplinary actions, reduced the time that teachers and administrators have to spend dealing with conflicts, and encouraged students to utilize their problem-solving skills. The process allows for discussion of the conflict and promotes brainstorming ways to find a solution. The disputants choose the solution that is most suitable for their needs. This empowerment ensures that they are most likely to follow through on the agreement.

Though current literature often highlights the softer advantages of peer mediation programs, one would look to the evidence-based programs to understand the specific data available on PMPs. Two of the best resources for exploring PM programs are the SAMHSA Web site (the national center for Substance Abuse and Mental Health Programs) and the U.S. Department of Education's published report "Conflict Resolution Education: A Guide to Implementing Programs in Schools" (1996).

SAMHSA defines evidence-based programs in to three categories, "Promising," "Effective," and "Model" Programs. Model Programs are measured on integrity and utility and must meet at least a 4.0 on a scale of 5 according to the National Registry of Evidenced-Based Programs. The U.S. Department of Education's published report "Conflict Resolution Education: *A Guide to Implementing Programs in Schools*" focuses on the first comprehensive research done in the field. Depending on the local school administration's desired outcomes, emphasis, and funding, peer mediation coordinators may want to consider the following Peer Mediation curricula:

* **"Peers Making Peace Program"** (PMP) reports of 1,305 mediations involving more than 2,400 students, indicated that 1,275 or 97.7 percent resulted in successful resolution. Discipline referrals decreased by 57.7 percent in Peace Makers schools. Assaults decreased by 90.2 percent and expulsions decreased by 7.3 percent, also in Peace Makers schools (see www.paxunited.org).
* **"Fighting Fair: Dr. Martin Luther King, Jr. for Kids"** developed by the Peace Foundation, is a curriculum that incorporates conflict resolution lessons and historical struggles. Topics such as racism, prejudice, war, defusing anger, confronting fear, and speaking out against injustice are addressed. This curriculum is marketed as suitable for upper elementary and middle school students (see www.peace-ed.org).
* **"We Can Work it Out"** is developed by the National Institute for Citizenship Education in the Law and the National Crime Prevention Council. The target population is middle and high school students and for this crime prevention/legal education program (see www.streetlaw.org)
* **"Too Good for Violence"** (TGFV), another SAMHSA program, reports that training generally relieves teachers' concerns by showing the relationships between prevention programming, academic success and improved classroom behavior. Teachers observe more frequent use of social skills and prosocial behavior, improvements in student attitude, and emotional competence (see www.modelprograms.samhas.gov).
* **"Resolving Conflicts Creatively"** (RCCP) is listed as an "Effective Program" with SAMHSA–one demonstrating a consistent pattern of results, consistently positive outcomes, and one which is strongly implemented and evaluated. The research of a school system that implemented the RCCP program indicated a 71-percent decrease in physical violence in the classroom, and observed 66 percent less name calling (see www.ncrel.org).

Though there are many other resources and curricula available for PMPs, finding a PMP that both fits the school culture, capacity for implementation, and desire for statistical support is important. Some PMPs, even without a research base, have outcomes indicating decreased school violence, increased a learner-friendly academic environment, and a more learner-friendly classroom, reducing management issues.

Today, PMPs have evolved to reflect the many differences in our school environments. The language, amount of training time available, and level of administrative support have all affected how PMPs are created, sustained, and developed. It is incumbent upon modern-day peer mediation coordinators to learn from past program trends.

One change in the construct of early PMPs is the selection of students. Historically, students were chosen as peer mediators often based on grades and popularity. This group of "selected" students was based merely on factors that did not necessarily increase chances of resolution. Often students were asked to mediate for fellow peers where there was no common respect, so cases had little buy-in from disputants.

Today, we witness educators appreciating more than just grades. Locally, educational leaders invite the "average" student who demonstrates emotional intelligence[1] to come to the peer mediation table. Case assignment is based on individual mediator abilities to relate or build rapport with their peers. It has often been the experience of some trainers that students without the highest grades often make better mediators.

Another difference in modern day programs is the time allocation that school systems give for peer mediation training. Initially, peer mediation trainings began with a 20-40 hour teaching block. Often, these were week-long training seminars designed to teach students and teachers alike. A training professional from an agency such as the local mediation center would serve as an ideal trainer, bringing together "actual" mediation experience and training into the classroom. The classroom teacher should be present during the trainings, apply modifications to the classroom and assist in reinforcing the concepts that were presented throughout the training, and in addition to identifying classroom situations where mediation would be helpful.

In some models, peer mediation trainings are held after school to accommodate the teacher's busy work schedule. Students would stay after school several days in a row or use lunch and study hours to coordinate their peer mediation training with their school requirements. With the evolution of "No Child Left Behind," and the increasing pressure for teachers to achieve high test scores, it has put educators in a difficult situation.

EXPERIENCE NEEDED TO MEDIATE PEER DISPUTES

Two types of training are needed for successful mediation programs. First, training of the school staff and peer mediation program managers is required. Without training the staff, many do not understand that mediation can be appropriate for matters that were once handled by teachers and administrators. Training the staff means educating them regarding the new school culture that now embraces student accountability for cheating, bullying, name-calling and other mediation-appropriate conflicts. With proper staff education, appropriate referrals help support the program and the students that are applying the skills they have been taught.

Second, training for students must be comprehensive in nature. Students must be trained by a mediator who can model, practice, coach, and provide real-life mediation scenarios that hold students' interests and help them to explore the application of their new-found skill in a variety of arenas. Trainers with courtroom experience for example can appeal to the interests of students wanting to become attorneys; mediators with family and divorce experience can help students develop a better understanding of their own family dynamics; and mediation-trainers who have extensive school experience can help students and teachers work together collaboratively in the classroom and beyond.

PREPARATION FOR PEER MEDIATION

How do our teens prepare for becoming peer mediators in today's school climate? Students are best suited to become effective peer mediators because they know their peers and can relate to the issues they face. They can conduct the meetings from the perspective and attitudes of young people. Additionally, they can empower their peers to solve their conflicts without the presence of adults—a powerful self-esteem builder for all involved.

Once students have gone through the steps to learn how to mediate, they must be able to process the experience in a variety of ways. Some mediator-trainers have students write out their thoughts in mediation journals; other trainers allow for students to bring in real-life conflicts as a basis for role-plays. Teaching students to use their knowledge and apply it to home and personal circumstances allows for growth that extends beyond the classroom. For instance, trainers who dip into adult learner models for high school mediators (not recommended for younger peer mediators) can help students understand how their own parents enter into destructive patterns of communication. Teaching about assumptions and anger management helps student to process or disassociate themselves from ineffective communication behaviors.

IMPLEMENTATION OF THE TRAINING PROGRAM

The development of a peer mediation program requires the combined work of the school counselor/administrator and the mediation professional. The training dates would be mutually agreed on by the counselor and the trainer, generally upon initial contact. A typical training can be accomplished in twelve hours or two full school days, with refreshers to be conducted on an as needed basis.

The school counselor/administrator typically selects the students who will be trained as peer mediators. The selection is most often accomplished through student sign-ups or teacher recommendations. The counselor/administrator can then interview the students and select those who are best suited for the training. Peer mediators are role models and should be respectful and trustworthy.

Confidentiality is an important factor in peer mediation and must be stressed to all participants. If the confidence is broken, it should result in the peer mediator being removed from the program. A diversified group based on culture, gender, academics, and behaviors is desirable. A group of twelve to twenty is most desirable, as they will be separated in groups of four for role plays.

The location in which the training is to take place is also selected at the discretion of the school counselor. The desired area would be large enough for groups to conduct role plays and participate in team-building activities. Some schools prefer to conduct the peer mediation training off campus, while others have ample accommodations at the school.

It is crucial to the mediation that the peer mediators understand that they are there to facilitate the process. Mediators do not verbalize their personal opinions or impose their ideas on how to resolve the conflict. The disputants must come up with their own ideas and solutions to ensure their buy-in of the agreement. People are most likely to follow through with an agreement when they establish it themselves.

TYPICAL AND UNIQUE PROBLEMS ASSOCIATED WITH PEER MEDIATION

Perhaps the most common problem in implementing a peer mediation program is the origin under which the programs get established. For instance, some school systems use peer mediation programs as a means of disciplinary action while other use the program for social development. Misunderstanding the nature of the program can inhibit its success. Some research has demonstrated that when school staff is unclear about the program implementation, a peer mediation program is less likely to succeed (Matloff & Smith, 1999). Another problem is that there is some argument as to the developmental readiness of children to be able to resolve their own conflicts without adult intervention.

Pre- and post-testing has helped to validate the learning of the academic components; however, the application and maturity needed to assist peers in resolving conflict can be subjective and often immeasurable. Perhaps the guiding principle should be that all children should be afforded the opportunity to demonstrate the readiness and core skills and apply them in different ways, whether it is a formalized mediation or simply a conversation with an adult who can guide the young student in effective communication models.

A third problem inherent in this type of mediation has now been rectified. It used to be that students would use peer mediation to get out of class. As a means of avoiding the classroom at any expense, some students would feign a conflict and be dismissed from class in order to have it mediated. Peer mediators have been quick to identify the type of student known to do this and have assisted program managers to do a better job at intake- assessing the true nature of the conflict and its appropriateness for mediation.

Finally, the problem that has continued through the decade is the lack of time and priority for such programs. Pressure of testing and school academia forces administrators to choose basic academics over the social emotional learning programs. This either-or thinking keeps educational institutions from maximizing the benefits of mutual gain in both academic and social learning, limiting the students from becoming problem-solving citizens in a global and diverse world.

CONCLUDING COMMENTS

We should continue to examine the changing needs in the peer mediation arena. Consistently evaluating our knowledge regarding our expanding worldwide population and pursuing ongoing research will help to insure that we are reasonably informed of the changing issues that affect the adolescent population. It is through that understanding that we will be best equipped to provide them the tools they need to adequately resolve their conflicts and promote peaceful solutions.

Case Study: Developing the Peer Mediation Program

Dr. West, a high school principal has called to inquire about your peer mediation services. She states that she is not pleased with how conflict is being resolved in the school classrooms. It is her consensus that problem-solving skills are being replaced by disciplinarian actions. Thereby, instead of educating students with the skills to deal positively with conflict, they have used the approach of allowing an adult to handle it and decide on the outcome.

The majority of the staff feels that they are spending too much of their day dealing with discipline in lieu of academics. However, there are several teachers who like being the disciplinarian, and insist there are no problems in their classroom that they can't handle.

Dr. West believes that many of the students simply do not have the skills they need to communicate their conflicts, without allowing them to escalate. She has hired you to come and assist her school in developing a peer mediation program. She has also introduced you to Ms. Johnson, school counselor, who will be your primary contact person and assist you in the training.

QUESTIONS FOR DISCUSSION

1. What is the first step in determining if peer mediation is appropriate at your school?
2. How do you open up discussions with the teacher who feels that "there is no conflict in his/her classroom?" What will assist this trainer to ensure success?
3. What steps do you take with the interested students, knowing that you have 100 interested students and training available for only 25?
4. What program do you select and why?

Role Play: A Case of Perception

INFORMATION FOR MORGAN

You are in class taking a test and you feel that Amanda is looking over your shoulders—from your perspective, trying to cheat. This is not the first time you have noticed this occurring, and you are upset. You spent hours studying for this test over the weekend and were unable to go to the mall with your friends because you wanted to do well. Your friend, Caroline, told you that she hung out with Amanda at the mall on Saturday, and they went to a movie that night. This escalates your anger, because while you were home studying she was having fun. Now, when it comes time to take the test, she is trying to take your answers. How could she do this to you?

INFORMATION FOR AMANDA

During the middle of a test, Morgan suddenly turns around and yells at you. You hear her say something about cheating and looking over her shoulder. You can't believe the things that she is saying because the two of you are supposed to be friends. The test questions are written on the board in the front of the classroom, and you may have been leaning up some to read the questions on the board but that was it! You are a good student and don't need to copy someone else's answers. Morgan doesn't know this, but you have been having trouble with your eyesight and your mom has made you and appointment with an ophthalmologist. Your integrity is at stake and your friendship is in jeopardy.

NOTE

[1] Daniel Goleman's Emotional Intelligence also known as "EQ" is defined as the "capacity for recognizing our own feelings and those of others, for motivating ourselves, and for managing emotions as well in ourselves and in our relationships". *Emotional Intelligence,* New York: Bantam, 1998.

REFERENCES

Crawford, D., and Bodine, R. (1996). Conflict resolution education: A guide to implementing programs in schools, youth-serving organizations, and community and juvenile justice settings. Program Report, U.S. Department of Justice and U.S. Department of Education.

DeBates, D., and Bell, J. (2006). Peer education teams help curb school violence. *Delta Kappa Gamma Bulletin,* Summer, 72, 4.

Diekman, C. H. (2004). *Research-Based Effectiveness of the Peace Education Foundation Model.* Miami: Peace Education Foundation.

Jones, T. S. (2004). Conflict resolution education: The field, the findings, and the future. *Conflict Resolution Quarterly,* 22, 1-2, 233-267.

Kenney, D. (1998). Crime in the schools: A problem-solving approach. *National Institute of Justice Research Preview.*

Matloff, G., and Smith, S. (1999). Responding to school-wide conflict resolution–peer mediation program: Case study of middle school faculty. *Mediation Quarterly,* 17, 125-141.

Chapter 6

The Movement of Mediation in Social Helping Fields

Kirsten B. Atkinson

Social helping fields may be one of the fastest growing fields now using the mediation forum. The field of social helping encompasses a variety of roles and professionals who are concerned with the quality of life and provision of services to individuals and families. Social helping agencies include those assisting families with the devastating affects and recovery of drugs; agencies that assist parents of special needs children; in-home therapists and educators, mental health professionals and more. Perhaps the most known social helping entity is the Department of Social Services, a local organization funded through state funds to guard the safety of our most vulnerable in society: the poor, the young (Children's Protection Services or CPS), and, the feeble (adult services for elderly). For the purposes of this chapter, we will examine the special education mediations and social work mediations.

If we explore why these agencies and their "cases" are suitable for the mediation, we have only to look as deep as the human condition. In the world of social helping fields where several professionals and service agencies work with families to provide basic needs and services—never interfacing or interacting—the mediation forum allows for all professionals to be on the same page with one family. This forum of mediation has also been coined as family group conferencing; child and family team meetings; and family facilitation. In the special education forum, these meetings have been termed "Facilitated Individual Education Plan" or FIEP. The process embodies the principles of creating a safe environment for discussion and for families and their social helping professionals to design mutually agreeable steps toward clearer communication, health, independence, and service provision.

The coordination between family goals, needed services, and service-provider accountability has a unique interdependence. As each agency or stakeholder is charged with providing services set for the family's success, each agency also functions on a timeline specific to the nature of the service. For instance, the current North Carolina requirement for children who have been removed from the home is that a stable environment must be established within a year's time. This means that if the social service system needs to see mom "drug-free" for three months before it would consider reunification with the child, and the drug rehab runs for six months, there is very little room for slip ups. Interagency coordination must be balanced with the requirements for enrollment, participation, and the like.

Often, social service clients struggle with new employment issues as they learn to become self-sufficient while juggling parenthood and recovery. In structures such as a judicial system, where there is little room for collaboration, families are often set up to fail. The idea that one can isolate the many needed pathways for recovery, self-sufficiency, and restitution all at one time, leaves little room for success. With a balance of communication, effort, and transparency, the mediated forums provide a win-win for families and systems alike. Furthermore, with the discussion and agreements documented at the end of the meeting in a memorandum, many people have little argument when the agreed-upon actions are not successful. A good agreement addresses fallback plans, "what-ifs," and invites support systems (such as family members) to aid in the comprehensive solution. Many judges have stated that the personal choice of social service clients not to follow through is no longer cloaked in the excuses judges used to hear, such as, "I didn't know—I couldn't get there [transportation]" etc. Many parents of special needs children finally feel heard and understood.

To exemplify the application of mediation used within the social service forum, consider families that are involved with several social helping services such as drug rehabilitators, credit card advisors, and child protection services. Because social services deals with clients who are unable to help themselves to some degree (after all, that's how DSS gets involved especially concerning children or the elderly) the social service case manager typically assists the family in navigating the sometimes complicated waters of accessing help from the community, the schools, and other service agencies. When there are several agencies that are providing services, there is no one person coordinating the interfacing of the many service providers to the larger family. Agencies end up depending on a single family member– often the client—to coordinate activities, communicate information, and articulate barriers to retrieving services. In some cases, a close relative is pulled in to navigate the details of service management, but too often this person is as equally debilitated in resources, resiliency, knowledge, or power to generate the movement and coordination needed. A social worker may enter into the family environment recommending child care resources; a credit card advisor may be recommending taking a second job; or a third social helping professional such as a school counselor may be asking parents to look into parenting classes to eliminate the evidence of home conflict affecting a student's learning.

Too often, the combination of recommendations from the multitude of outside professionals is cumbersome and unrealistic, and often based on information that does not have the breadth of a full group information exchange. In addition, often entire family systems are struggling with multiple jobs, multiple child responsibilities and very little time or money to assist others. This goes without saying that the elderly (often the paternal/maternal grandparents) are asked to rear their grandchildren when their age and energy does not meet the demands of the youthful spirit. All of these conditions are swarming around a set of familial dysfunction that often involves the unpredictable world of drug use and its insidious claws.

As state and federal agencies jump on the mediation bandwagon, the culture of human services has begun to shift into a more user-friendly, "server-friendly" model. In this model, fewer resources are duplicated, services are adjusted to match family circumstances, knowledge is shared by both family members and service providers, and accountability is the by-product of using this group-think model.

Another example of this mediation forum's worth is from the other side of the looking glass as experience in special education mediated forums. A parent needing guidance through the school system to determine assistance for a special needs child and FAPE (Free and Appropriate Public Education) may come to depend on the expertise of the advocate who helps to guide, inform, and fight for what his or her child is entitled to. Often this parent advocate has more information and updated knowledge than the school personnel who is designated to that role. Conversely, the advocate often lacks information because the parent has handed "his or her side of the story" to the advocate, without any opportunity for clarification as when a full group convenes. Thus, this cross-system collaboration supports the old adage, "two brains are better than one," where all people come to the mediation table, voices can be heard, and new information can be learned. Confidence is regenerated, relationships are clarified, and the expense and hassle of other systems of justice (such as due process) are avoided by the early intervention of communication and clarification.

THE CURRENT STATE OF DSS MEDIATION

Before examining a case actually mediated within the two social helping fields described in this chapter, let's first examine what current literature says about mediating these types of disputes. The shift into utilizing mediation is coming from the social helping fields themselves. This chapter highlights the use of mediation in a DSS context and a special education context.

Looking for a way to limit operational costs and avoid litigation, future misunderstandings, the North Carolina Department of Health and Human Services attempted to create a program by training employed social workers at the local level to mediate/facilitate family team meetings with the county's Department of Social Services (DSS). The North Carolina Family Group Conferencing (NC-FGC) Project started in the fall of 1998 and ended in the summer of 2002. Over this four-year period, the project promoted the use of family group conferencing (FGC) through training, evaluation, and publication. This "insider-neutral" model has worked for more rural areas in North Carolina, especially areas without alternate outsourcing services. Other North Carolina DSS offices have elected to work with an "outsider-neutral" model. In this model, DSS contracts with mediation-practitioners to conduct the family team meetings. This "outsider-neutral" model affords the social worker more time to focus on case information and less on scheduling, preparing, conducting, and writing the memorandum of understanding.

Often, the outside-neutral model gives clients a truer confidence in the neutrality of the mediator/facilitator. For example, a client who has had long ties with the local social services (let's says in food stamps, and child protective services) might not feel as if the social worker's "sister facilitator" or "inside-neutral facilitator" represents full neutrality. I experienced this myself when first observing an insider-neutral model. Language such as "our agency" and "all we want for you" seeped into the facilitators dialogue which left no doubt that I was in the presence of a non-neutral setting. Furthermore, it implies that the neutral may have information not normally privy to an outside-neutral but to agency workers themselves.

Finally, the use of an outside-neutral can lead to conducting the meetings away from the social service building. The off-site mediation location has led many clients to be more receptive, have less hostility, and feel more comfortable and confident that the process itself is confidential. In both outsider and insider neutral models, stakeholders beyond the client and the social worker are invited and encouraged to attend. The meeting structure can include neighbors, friends, priests, family members, school personnel, foster parents, *guardian ad litem,* and even the social worker's supervisor. By having all parties share information and potential contributions to the resolution, all parties have a piece in the larger success. This model allows the parties' family, support professionals, and neighbors to exert accountability and hold disputants to their agreements.

Today, family team meetings have proven to be quite successful. In a local example, a program to facilitate the family team meetings began in 2004 in a collaborative effort between the Department of Social Services and the local community mediation center. In 2005, 201 cases were successfully facilitated. In 2006, the data reflects that 316 cases were referred for a family team meeting and of those 309 have been successfully closed.[1]

The overwhelming response from social workers is that the program affords families to view DSS as a truly helping agency and to see social workers in a light that supports the family and its circumstances. Families feel as if they are being heard, and their appreciation for the process is exhibited by the voluntary contribution of information, participation, and accountability.

Personal stories from social workers reflect that families are able to see the social worker as someone who is trying to help rather than exert power over their lives. The social worker "works less" trying to convince families to do things, but rather can now sit back and respond to the neutral's questions: "help me [facilitator] understand how putting [the client's] child in day care will help mom. . . ?" In this particular example, the social worker needed the child to be "socialized" and wanted daycare to be the means to that end. In exploring the family culture (mom was not from this country), the social worker found that both mom and dad were homeless and they valued family togetherness, which meant exploring different options. What was the outcome? Mom agreed to begin socialization with her toddler if it could be done in a group setting such as with church mothers in the shelter she was already in. By exploring positions (day care) and interests (socialization) by a trained facilitator, both parties came out with an agreement they could support.

In another case, it was discovered that the social worker had been misinformed about whether her client had actually attended the required pediatrician's appointment. The social worker had apparently called the doctor's office and received information that mom's appointment never happened. Because of the social worker's information (mom did not show for the appointment) the social worker came to the mediation table ready to remove the child based on medical negligence. The school counselor was present for this family team meeting and had disclosed that she had personally driven mom to the appointment that day and because the pediatrician could not find the child's folder, they were asked to come back later. The value of this information could have changed mom (and child's!) entire pathway. The accountability with a third-party neutral asking questions of all parties takes away any of the personalization that went on before.

To highlight another example, in 1999 the North Carolina Department of Public Instruction Exceptional Children's Division was mandated by the federal government to adjust the special ed program to be in compliance with the due process laws which allow parents to request mediation while filing with the courts. The Institute of Government[2] was contracted to train mediators from across North Carolina in the language and rights of parents with special needs children. Exceptional Children (EC) Division Director and former Maine attorney, Kate Neale, had the wisdom and foresight to move the mediation forum into the IEP (Individual Education Plan) development stage.

Rather than wait until a conflict and lawsuit develops, the educators, parents, parent advocates, and education specialists sit at the table in a facilitated conversation.

Often these meetings come together with years of contempt between schools and parents as each fights for the services that meet each child's needs with the FAPE[3] laws that govern the options. The data suggests that this mediation and facilitation program has been wonderfully successful and holds much promise for future use of mediation in the special education arena.

The 2005 North Carolina Special Education Year End Report states that 129 requests for Mediation were related to Due Process hearing, and that 75 mediation requests *not* related to due process hearing. This suggests that mediation is being used both *before* the litigation process and as a parallel to the litigation process. Of the thirty-six mediations related to due process hearing, twenty-three had full agreements, five had partial agreement, eight had no agreement; eight had mediations decline, and ten had their requests withdrawn (parties settled themselves). Of the seventy-five mediation requests not related to due process, thirty-five had full agreements, one had a partial agreement; four had no agreement reached, nineteen of the mediations were declined, and sixteen withdrew their request (parties settled themselves) (Public Schools of North Carolina, 2005).

In both highlighted examples (DSS and special education), the data suggests that the use of mediation within these social helping arenas and with social helping professionals have much promise for future and expanded applications.

Experience Needed to Mediate Social Helping Field Disputes

Because we are referring to two different types of social helping situations—an education context and a social work context—one can reasonably expect two different training requirements from these arenas. The initial training for special education mediators was conducted in 1998 by the North Carolina Institute of Government, and a multi-member roster is maintained today by the EC Division. Today, the group is a blend of mediation-practitioners and former special education personnel who are now trained as mediator-facilitators. Special education mediators are required to attend fifteen hours of continuing education annually. These trainings consists of group facilitation skills (typically for those less experienced in group dynamics), or trainings that focus on the "nuts & bolts" of special education (for the mediators less familiar with the special education nuances and due process procedures).

Training for the social work mediations is slightly different. Under the guidance of NC State University and Dr. Joan Pennell, training is required for both the social workers who will be participating in the Child and Family Team meetings, as well as any outside contractor employed to perform the mediations and facilitations. Of North Carolina's one hundred counties, all have had some opportunity to have their social workers participate in these initial trainings.

It should be noted that many of the mediation practitioners performing these types of mediations previously come from the social helping fields themselves. Others come from the business world, and still others from the education field. It is fair to say that from whatever background the mediator enters, the mediator has some duty to "unlearn" the assignments of his/her previous professional role, while still utilizing the knowledge base and experience to help them explore the necessary depth of these family discussions. Not unlike attorney-mediators who must resist the temptation to fuel a client's case with similar case histories, so must a mental health professional resist the temptation to assign diagnostic labels to clients.

PREPARING FOR DSS MEDIATION

Preparation for social helping mediations of this type are relatively similar to the preparation for other types of mediations in that *intake* and *building rapport* are the secret to success. If one is conducting a Family Team Meeting (FTM), it is imperative to talk with both the social worker and as many family members as is reasonable. Certainly, the newness of this North Carolina program requires that mediation-practitioners take the extra time to guide families through the introduction of the FTM process and of the role of the mediator-facilitator. Often this means defining what your role is not. For instance, as families may have had a history of service agency involvement, many assume that the mediator is "just another person in the system." It is imperative that mediation-practitioners separate themselves from the identity of the social worker and the local social work department. The immediate payoff is the trust building that occurs with the client, and that will come in handy if things get heated at the mediation table.

One intake strategy is to ask the client if the social worker has let them know that a mediator would be calling. The clients response will indicate two things: because it is standard operating procedure for social workers to let families know a mediator will be calling to set up a family team meeting, if the family says "no, I don't know who you are or why you are calling," it can indicate to the mediator that the client either (1) didn't educationally understand what the social worker had relayed to them in the first place (not uncommon), or (2) they have a bad relationship with their social worker and they either weren't listening or this is the subtle way of "letting the outside neutral know just how much I don't appreciate this social worker in my life."

In either case, the intake gives the practitioner the opportunity to explore what the client needs independent of the social worker's perceptions (or recommendations). More importantly, the intake provides an opportunity for the mediation practitioner to build rapport. Building rapport is a meaningful skill for the reflective practitioner (Atkinson, 2001). For the client, a healthy rapport with the mediator can strongly influence the outcome.

TYPICAL AND UNIQUE PROBLEMS

In both types of mediations, the intake process can be cumbersome. This is due in part to the large number of people at the table. Matching calendars, listening to personal input, and educating families about the mediator role can take many hours to coordinate.

Once the mediation begins, some mediators have been observed as slipping into their past professional roles. This is particularly common when an insider-neutral social worker mediates a case for another social worker. Organizational norms and vocabulary are quickly distinguished by clients who may already be leery of the procedure.

One remaining potential problem of this process is that no single case has the same dynamic. The learning curve for the mediation practitioner can be long and arduous. The multi-faceted face of this mediation model involves more than just mediation skills. One must be able to juggle several personal agendas at the table while maintaining rapport and capturing critical information from multiple participants. The written agreement that is reached must be legally and socially sound and yet achievable for the family.

CONCLUDING COMMENTS

Because families using social helping professionals often have a number of service providers for a single family, the mediation forum provides a cost-effective and communication-savvy means for families and service providers to create a win-win opportunity. The comprehensive exchange of information and the memorandum of understanding produced create accountability (for both client and the professional) and allow for a free flow of practical (albeit sometimes emotional) discussion. As mediation flows into the common man's language, families and businesses are finding ways in which this subtle, but helpful skill streamlines mutual understanding, creates a forum under which communication is enhanced, develops consensual goals, and allows the voice of the heart to be present.

Case Study: The Mother Who Tried Her Best

(The following case is a real-life scenario, only the names and identifying details have been changed to protect confidentiality. The author has selected a social work case study because the core knowledge of the special education language is needed to examine a case study for special education).

The Department of Social Services has asked you to conduct a family team meeting with a single mother who has been reported by the schools as having her teenage daughter skip school. The mother has had past (and negative) experiences with the Department of Social Services. Mom has five children (two still live at home with her, her mother and her grandmother) and thirteen grandchildren. No family members are knowingly involved with drugs (a common factor found in many DSS cases). Mom works a minimum wage job at a local hotel. She keeps a clean house, but has mostly "convenience foods" for the children to much on. There are no fresh fruits and vegetables to speak of. The Department of Social Services (DSS) was called in based on a school-skipping concern, but in the process of investigating the family, the DSS social worker discovers that mom is not administering the diabetes medication her daughter needs. DSS labels the case as "Medical Negligence." The social worker has asked for a family team meeting to look at the resources and information available for healthier living. Mom feels as if she has no control over her teenager, and is at her wits end, which may have more to do with the general tiredness of single parenting than the fact that her daughter, Sharelle, is actually any real trouble. Mom managed to get public assistance in getting her daughter the best diabetes portable testing unit. The daughter, Sharelle is quiet, a good student, and fairly self-reflective. She does not talk about herself or her needs at home. The maternal mother and grandmother come to the meeting for moral support but are quiet, just like they are at home. The school nurse has been asked to come to the meeting and has serious concerns about Sharelle's weight. Sharelle skips several classes a day or sometimes skips school because of her "cramps."

QUESTIONS FOR DISCUSSION

1. What information did you actually need prior to conducting the meeting?
2. How would you open up the conversation with multi-parties?
3. Did you have any preconceived notions about any of the stakeholders?
4. How or what did you explore in order to reach a resolution?

5. Should there have been less or more people there?
6. Since you are conducting this meeting at Social Services, how have you communicated your neutrality to the participants?

Role Play: The Problem of Sharelle Skipping Class

INFORMATION FOR SHARELLE:

You are a 10th grader attending an alternative school in town. You are quiet and shy, but bright. You live at home with your mother and grandmother, and have plenty of maternal figures in your life. You are a diabetic. Your medicine has recently been changed and you are unable to swallow the pills they have given you. Furthermore, the medication adjustments have caused irritable bowels so you must leave the classroom frequently. You are often gone for long periods and your teachers have publicly addressed you (which embarrassed you). Students who use the rest room after you also make fun of you. You have decided it's easier to stay at home than be ridiculed.

INFORMATION FOR SCHOOL NURSE

You have never been to a family team meeting before. Sharelle's classroom teacher was unable to make today's meeting, so you were asked by the teacher to be present for this meeting. You received a call from the facilitator confirming the time and date of the meeting. It was explained to you that the process was informal and you do not need school documentation. You bring your documents on Sharelle anyway. You do not know about her, but she is friendly towards you and the teacher that was supposed to be at the meeting. You do know Sharelle keeps skipping classes. As the school nurse, she has never been seen in your office to date.

INFORMATION FOR SHARELLE'S MOTHER

You just don't know what to do with your daughter, Sharelle. You have been called into this meeting because the school teacher reports she is skipping classes. Upon further information, you find out (at this meeting) that she has not been taking her diabetic medicine. She has the best diabetic testing equipment and you have a hard time motivating her to go to school. She often leaves for school in the morning but comes back to the home once you have left for work. You feel like DSS is being unfair to you. You were never formally educated.

INFORMATION FOR SOCIAL WORKER

You received a call from the school stating that Sharelle has been skipping school. After a home visit, you discover a fairly clean home, but lots of junk food including fried foods. You know Sharelle has diabetes and the home diet leaves much to be desired. You have requested a team meeting to get some answers and make a plan for Sharelle. The classroom teacher is unable to make the meeting and sends her friend and colleague, the school nurse, in her place.

INFORMATION FOR MATERNAL GRANDMOTHER

You spend most of your day trying to help your daughter (who works two jobs). She has raised six kids only two of which are still home: "Sharelle" the 15-year-old in question, and her younger brother, "James," an eighth grader. You were never formally educated.

NOTES

[1] Data is from the annual Community Mediation Center report to the Department of Social Services, Wilmington, North Carolina.
[2] NC Institute of Government is a teaching and consulting entity for local and state government officials. Visit www.iog.unc.edu for more information.
[3] FAPE stands for "Free and Appropriate Public Education" education laws established to protect children's educational rights.

REFERENCES

Atkinson, K. B. (2001). *Exploring the tacit knowledge of practitioner.* Unpublished Master's thesis, Columbia College, Columbia, South Carolina, USA.

North Carolina Bar Foundation, and the North Carolina Dispute Resolution Commission. (2003). Alternative dispute resolution in North Carolina: A New civil procedure.

Public Schools of North Carolina. (2005). Special education mediation program end-of-year report 7/1/04-6/30/05, see www.ncpublicschools.org.

Chapter 7

Environmental Mediation: A Primer

Tina Nabatchi
Michael E. Keller

Mediation has long been accepted as an appropriate means of resolving labor-management and community disputes, but its application to environmental conflicts is relatively recent. Although the first documented case of using mediation in an environmental conflict dates back to 1974 (Blackburn & Bruce, 1995), mediation remained an uncommon (and often impromptu) approach to resolving environmental conflicts for the next two decades. Since the mid-1990s however, legislation such as the Administrative Dispute Resolution Acts of 1990 and 1996 and the Negotiated Rulemaking Acts of 1990 and 1996, as well as the growing awareness and acceptance of the potential benefits of alternative dispute resolution (ADR) in resolving conflicts, have enabled different forms of environmental conflict resolution to become more regular and official features in environmental decision- and policy-making at all levels of government (see generally, O'Leary & Bingham, 2003).

For example, in 1999, Congress created the U.S. Institute for Environmental Conflict Resolution, an independent federal agency designed to help other federal agencies address the complex relationships and numerous disputes involving the environment and government (see: www.ecr.gov). Many state governments are following suit, using a variety of approaches to environmental dispute resolution (O'Leary, Yandle, & Moore, 1999). Local governments have also been active in applying ECR to community disputes involving environmental issues.

Environmental Conflict and Environmental Dispute Resolution

Environmental Conflict Resolution (ECR) and Environmental Dispute Resolution (EDR) refer to the application of various ADR techniques, including mediation, to environmental conflicts. Environmental conflicts involve fundamental and ongoing differences among parties concerning values and behavior as they relate to the environment (Stern & Hick, 2000). More specifically, environmental conflicts are actual or potential disputes involving issues regarding the environment, natural resources, and/or public lands. Environmental conflicts can also involve the prevention, clean-up, or consequences of water, air, or soil pollution (Emerson, Nabatchi, O'Leary, & Stephens, 2003; O'Leary, Nabatchi, & Bingham, 2004).

The range of environmental conflict is large. However, disputes can be classified as being upstream (those involving planning or policy-making), mid-stream (those involving administrative decision making) or downstream (those involving compliance and enforcement) (Emerson et al., 2003; O'Leary & Bingham, 2003; O'Leary et al., 2004). For example, upstream environmental conflicts can involve the creation and implementation of environmental, natural resource, health and safety policy, or education policies at the national, regional, state, or local level. Midstream environmental conflicts can involve administrative decisions regarding implementation or issues such as environmental permitting. Downstream environmental conflicts can involve litigation over the ways in which lands are used, the allocation or distribution of natural resources, or the siting of industrial or other large facilities, among other issues.

Environmental conflicts can also be generally categorized by the scope of the dispute (Bingham, 1986; Emerson, et al., 2003; O'Leary, Durant, Fiorino, & Weiland, 1999; O'Leary, et al., 2004). For example, a dispute can be policy-level dispute, pertaining generally to a class of resources, locations, or situations, or it can be site-specific, involving a particular natural resource, location, or situation. A policy-level dispute would be considered an upstream dispute, whereas a site-specific dispute would be considered a downstream dispute.

ECR and environmental mediation have been used successfully in a wide variety of environmental conflicts. For example, ECR has been used in land use disputes such as commercial development, housing, facility siting, and transportation; natural resource use or management issues such as fisheries, timber, and mining; water resources issues such as water quality, flood protection, and water use; air quality issues such as odor, acid rain, and air pollution; and issues related to toxics such as chemical regulation, asbestos removal, and waste clean-up policies, among others (Bingham, 1986).

WHY ENVIRONMENTAL MEDIATION?

Advocates suggest that environmental mediation (and other forms of ECR) alleviate many of the problems associated with traditional modes of environmental policy-making and dispute resolution (for an in-depth discussion, see Amy, 1987, 1990; Emerson, et al., 2003). In general, advocates of environmental mediation suggest that legislative, administrative, and judicial forums and their respective approaches to dealing with environmental controversies are often ineffective and inefficient. Moreover, they assert that these forums sustain rather than resolve disputes and act as catalysts for future conflicts.

First, participation in the legislative arena is often limited to elite groups. Participation is expensive and time consuming; many groups and individuals affected by a particular environmental decision cannot effectively participate in the legislative arena because they lack financial resources or adequate manpower to engage in lobbying. As such, the concerns and interests of many groups are not heard. Moreover, the innate controversy surrounding environmental policies often precludes a viable consensus among legislators, which results in vague and ambiguous legislation.

Second, as government agencies try to interpret and implement vague policies, controversies about specific actions or projects flare. Once again, participation is limited. Some parties are deliberately ignored or left out of processes, and some parties, even if invited to the table, lack the financial or human resources to participate effectively. Of course, most agencies, at least at the federal level, must receive public comments, or hold hearings where concerned parties can voice their preferences. However, ECR advocates suggest that these procedures only give the appearance of participation and that agencies often do not consider the comments and testimony when they make and implement decisions.

Finally, the judicial system becomes the remaining outlet for concerns and controversies about legislative and administrative decisions regarding the environment. Again, however, advocates of environmental mediation suggest that litigation is not an efficient or effective process for resolving environmental conflicts. The costs of litigation and the time required (usually months and often years) to go through various litigation processes are prohibitive to many interest groups, especially those that are small or represent local interests. Moreover, litigation can be ineffective in actually resolving the issues at stake in environmental disputes. The litigious approach is not designed to resolve differences, but rather to decide issues; the courts are frequently limited in their ability to address the substantive dimensions of environmental conflicts, and thus render decisions only on the procedural grounds (Lake, 1980). This means that many of the underlying controversies remain unresolved, increasing the possibility of future lawsuits.

POTENTIAL BENEFITS OF ENVIRONMENTAL MEDIATION

In contrast to adversarial approaches to resolving environmental conflicts, advocates suggest that environmental mediation (and other ECR techniques) is a faster, less costly, more accessible, and more durable way to resolve environmental disputes (O'Leary and Bingham, 2003; O'Leary, Durant, Fiorino, and Weiland, 1999).

Advocates assert that the negotiation techniques embraced in ECR processes such as environmental mediation have several potential advantages (see Emerson, et al., 2003; O'Leary et al., 2004). First, environmental mediation can reduce the risks associated with the uncertainty of win-all or lose-all litigation. Moreover, environmental mediation can reduce court costs, legal fees, inflationary delays, time, and other conflict-related expenses. Second, advocates suggest that the participatory nature of environmental mediation promotes more stable and efficient outcomes. Full participation by all of the interested parties facilitates effective negotiation and is a key element in producing better and more equitable environmental decisions. When all parties are at the table, there is a better chance that all the relevant issues will be raised and that the parties will be better situated to make efficient trades, produce more stable and efficient outcomes, and reach decisions that effectively address the substantive nature of the dispute. In turn, this can increase the likelihood of achieving a stable and durable agreement among parties. Third, the participatory nature of environmental mediation promotes a sense of procedural justice (for a discussion of procedural justice, see Lind & Tyler, 1988). When participants sense that they have received procedural justice, the perceived legitimacy of decisions and outcomes increases, which reduces the likelihood of future challenges to the decisions. Finally, the participatory nature of environmental mediation can also help compensate for the lack of public access to the decision-making sessions in the legislative, administrative, and judicial arenas. Folberg and Taylor (1984) nicely summarize the potential benefits of environmental mediation:

> Mediation can provide conflict resolution for environmental disputes far less expensively, in terms of time and money, than can litigation. Moreover, it can provide all participants a greater sense of satisfaction because of their active role. It allows the participants to maintain a degree of control. It allows the consideration of more creative environmental options than does litigation. Most important, mediation promotes cooperation (p. 220).

EXPERIENCE NEEDED TO BE AN ENVIRONMENTAL MEDIATOR

How does one become an environmental mediator? The potential paths to such a career are exponential; therefore, this chapter will present some general considerations in your pursuit of becoming an environmental mediator.

Start with training. Environmental mediators must have strong mediation and facilitation skills and abilities. You can gain these skills and abilities by engaging in at least two types of training: basic mediation training and environmental/public policy mediation training. Basic mediation training will provide you with a good understanding of the theory and practice of mediation. It will help you develop fungible skills and abilities that are applicable in all mediation settings. Basic mediation training is available from numerous private organizations, professional mediator associations, and community mediation centers. You should also supplement basic training with more advanced training in mediation skills. The Association for Conflict Resolution (ACR), the National Association for Community Mediation (NAFCM), and state mediator associations can help you locate training opportunities.

You should also pursue training that focuses specifically on environmental conflicts and/or other public policy disputes. These trainings will help contextualize environmental disputes and give you the skills necessary to effectively deal with the complexities of environmental mediation. The Association for Conflict Resolution (ACR) and state mediator associations can help you locate environmental and/or public policy trainings. In addition, the U.S. Institute for Environmental Conflict Resolution maintains an excellent list of environmental mediation and other ECR trainings (see www.ecr.gov).

Education is good; expertise is better. In general, environmental mediators have varied educational backgrounds; they enter the field from a number of academic disciplines such as law, public administration, public policy, urban studies, environmental studies, environmental science, planning, and the like. Environmental disputes generally involve issues that transect these fields of study (in addition to several others); therefore, in addition to the procedural skills you gain through mediation training, you also need to have substantive knowledge about the environment, public policy and administration processes, and law.

There are numerous degree programs in dispute resolution at colleges and universities across the country that can help you build this general knowledge. In addition to degree programs, there are also many semester-long courses available, such as the Program on Negotiation, associated with Harvard University, as well as certificate programs. Broader academic training can be obtained with a variety of degree options, such as planning, public administration, law, or environmental studies, and can be especially valuable when acquired from institutions with negotiation and conflict resolution classes. Mediate.com maintains a nice, if limited, list of academic programs in and related to conflict resolution (see: http://www.mediate.com/training/).

Gain experience, then gain some more. In mediation, experience counts. It is very important to get real mediation experience by taking your training out of the classroom and putting it to use in the real world. In all likelihood, you will not begin your mediation career dealing with environmental disputes. Rather, you will probably start out mediating smaller, less complex disputes in settings that are more interpersonal in nature. Mediating for a community mediation program is a great way to build basic skills and gain experience. In such a setting, you will have the opportunity to deal with one-on-one disputes, and as your skill set grows, you will also likely be able to mediate disputes that involve larger groups of people. This will provide you with the basic experience needed to mediate environmental conflicts.

Beyond basic experience in mediation, it is important to develop specific experience with environmental cases. One way to gain this experience is by working with an experienced environmental mediator, who can act as a mentor, guiding and advising you through both procedural and substantive issues. Such an 'apprenticeship' can be extremely valuable in both building your mediation skills and giving you confidence in those skills.

A final note about experience is in order. The types of disputes eligible for environmental mediation are extremely varied; therefore, it can sometimes be helpful to have a "concentration" or area of expertise with regard to the environment. For example, as you acquire training, education, and experience in environmental mediation, focus on a couple of areas in which you can build knowledge, such as a specific policy area (i.e., environmental or natural resource policy, health or safety policy, or planning) or a specific resource (i.e., air, soil, water, timber, or biological diversity).

Meet, greet, and otherwise network. Much as in any professional career, mediators must build a reputation and gain name recognition. Networking is both a skill and tool that can help make or break your career (regardless of your field). It is important to join professional associations and attend meetings. This is one of the best ways to stay on top of advances in the field and learn about (and seize!) career and other opportunities.

PREPARING FOR ENVIRONMENTAL MEDIATION

Environmental mediators must do a considerable amount of leg-work before the mediation session(s) can take place. Carpenter and Kennedy (1985) offer two pieces of advice about preparing for and managing environmental conflict: (1) "to find a good solution, you have to understand the problem," and (2) "planning a strategy can help you reach a better solution."

Conducting a conflict assessment can be extremely valuable to you in preparing for mediation. A conflict assessment provides a map of the dispute, which can be used as an evaluation tool to determine how to initiate and manage the mediation. The primary goal of a conflict assessment is to help identify the issues in controversy, the affected stakeholders, and the appropriate form(s) of ECR for handling the conflict. A first step in conducting a conflict assessment is conferring among key parties in the dispute to evaluate the causes of the conflict and to identify the entities and individuals who would be substantively affected by the outcome.

A next step is to assess the positions, interests, needs, and values of both the key parties and other potential stakeholders. Given this information, the mediator can then identify a preliminary set of relevant issues to be discussed during mediation. Other prospective stakeholders are then informed and educated about the mediation process, so the mediator can determine whether those stakeholders should participate; stakeholders can also determine whether they want to participate. Finally, the conflict assessment will point the mediator toward any procedural or substantive knowledge that will be necessary or helpful in mediating the dispute.

Once the conflict assessment is complete, the mediator should take additional steps to prepare for the mediation. For example, in her summary of the literature, O'Leary (1995) finds several general suggestions about the appropriate roles for environmental mediators. These roles indicate how mediators should both prepare for and manage the mediation process. Among the suggestions are:

1. Identify the positions and interests of all parties, and determine whether each party is willing to participate in good faith;
2. Help the parties understand and recognize the costs and benefits of mediation;
3. Help the parties prepare for negotiation by working with them to clarify their values, interests, and needs;
4. Draw attention to and deal with inequalities among the parties, especially those involving information and power; and
5. Build trust among the parties.

O'Leary's (1995) review of environmental mediation also suggests several ingredients for successful mediation. First, and perhaps most obviously, the key parties to an environmental conflict must participate in mediation for it to be successful. There is little point in trying to work toward an agreement if any key party to the dispute is unwilling or unable to participate in the mediation in good faith. Second, those participating in the mediation should have the authority to approve agreements, or at the very least, direct access to those who do have such authority for approval. Third, any written agreement must not only be acceptable to all parties, but must also be something that could realistically be implemented. It is the responsibility of the mediator to assist the parties in clearly thinking through implementation issues and identifying plans of action in various "what if" scenarios.

Issues and Problems Associated with Environmental Mediation

Certain characteristics of environmental conflicts add to their complexity, making the application of ADR techniques more difficult. Some of these characteristics include: interorganizational, as opposed to interpersonal conflicts; multiple parties; multiple forums for decision making; unequal power and resources among parties; public/political arenas for problem solving; multiple issues; and technical complexity and scientific uncertainty (see generally, O'Leary & Bingham, 2003). These characteristics are briefly discussed below.

First, unlike many others types of meditory conflicts, environmental conflicts are not interpersonal in nature; rather, they are interorganizational. Interpersonal conflict takes place between two or more people and generally involves private, individual interests and needs. Conversely, interorganizational conflict takes place between (and often within) two or more organizational entities and generally involves public or community interests.

The interorganizational nature of environmental conflicts leads to a second characteristic: multiple parties. There are a host of possible government, private, and public interests with a stake in an environmental conflict. Elected and appointed government officials at the local, county, state, and/or federal levels are usually involved in environmental conflicts since many of these conflicts arise from the formation or implementation of governmental legislation and policies. Often these government officials represent different agencies (for example the Department of the Interior and the Environmental Protection Agency), different departments or subdivisions within an agency (for example the Bureau of Land Management and the Fish and Wildlife Service within the Department of Interior), or even different branches of government (for example, officials in Congress and officials from an administrative agency such as the Department of Agriculture). Private interests also play a large role in environmental conflicts. Industry, commercial, and other business people are often involved in environmental conflicts such as those involving the siting of facilities, pollution abatement issues, or the granting of various permits. Finally, there are numerous public interests represented in environmental conflicts such as community residents, interest groups, and public interest law firms. Frequently governments and private and public parties also need and use the services of scientific, research, and technical consultants, adding to the number of stakeholders involved in the conflict.

A third characteristic of environment conflict is that it involves multiple forums for decision making. Each of the parties to the dispute will likely represent different organizations or groups, each of which will have different mechanisms for decision making, authority, and accountability. Moreover, given the breadth of potential participants, there will also likely be unequal power and resources among parties, a fourth characteristic of environmental conflict. As Susskind (1978) suggests, most environmental disputes tend to pit those who stand to gain short-term economic advantages against others who fear long-term environmental losses. It is critical that the mediator pay attention to these imbalances and inequalities to achieve a fair, balanced, and workable agreement.

Fifth, environmental conflicts inherently involve public/political arenas for problem solving. Environmental disputes are public disputes in several respects. Not only do they address issues of the proverbial "public interest," but they also tend to involve the public sector (government agencies) as parties to the dispute. Thus, environmental conflicts are often 'high profile' which can increase the reluctance of parties to move away from positional stances toward interest-based agreements.

Environmental conflicts also tend to involve multiple issues. The interconnectedness of the environment and environmental issues means that such disputes seldom involve only one environmental medium. Rather, environmental conflicts tend to transcend boundaries and involve numerous environmental concerns and issues which must be addressed simultaneously (or at least concurrently) in the mediation process. In addition to addressing environmental concerns, an environmental mediator must attend to the elements of the conflict that emerge from differences in values and worldviews, conflicting interests, and the uncertainty that surrounds various courses of action. For example, popular attitudes and political culture, technology, laws and political interests, economics, and religion especially as related to Native American culture, can help trigger and sustain environmental conflicts.

Finally, environmental conflicts inherently involve a certain amount of technical complexity and scientific uncertainty. Mediators must be sure that one side does not control the technical data necessary to understand the dispute and possible alternatives for resolution (Riesel, 1985). Indeed research suggests that misinformation or lack of information encourages and is at the root of many environmental conflicts (see for example, Carpenter & Kennedy, 1985). Regardless of how much technical data is available, environmental conflicts almost always have elements of scientific uncertainty since they typically involve decisions concerning fundamental and irreversible alterations in the physical environment (O'Leary, 1995).

As with almost any form of mediation, the best way to understand the issues and learn how to deal with them is with case studies and role plays. We turn to these next.

Case Study: Balancing Environmental and Industrial Concerns in Delaware

The following case study is adapted from a case in *States Mediating Solutions to Environmental Disputes* (Policy Consensus Initiative 1999: 2-4). This case study is one of five examples showing how states use mediation and other consensus-based processes to make environmental decisions and resolve environmental disputes. The Policy Consensus Initiative (PCI) Web site has numerous case studies about environmental mediation and mediation in other substantive contexts (see: http://www.policyconsensus.org/casestudies/index.html).

In 1971, the Delaware state legislature passed the Delaware Coastal Zone Act, a broad piece of legislation dealing with air, water and land management along almost the entire state coastline. Over the next twenty-five years, the Department of Natural Resources and Environmental Control (DNREC), the state agency with responsibility for implementation, used an informal, undefined regulation system that frequently created conflict among industrial, environmental, labor, agricultural, and governmental groups, among others. One particular area of controversy concerned the DNREC's case-by-case approach to processing permit actions. The conflict was particularly fierce among environmental groups, who asserted that the approach was inadequate in protecting the long-term health of the coastal zone, and industrial representatives, who argued that the approach helped maintain the economic viability of companies operating in the coastal zone.

The DNREC wanted to draft more formal regulations and hired the Massachusetts-based Environmental Mediation Services to assess the feasibility of using negotiated rulemaking, a consensus-based process that shares many similarities with mediation. The initial conflict assessment suggested that such a process would not work given the circumstances of the situation. A primary reason for this assessment was that industrial representatives had no incentive to participate in any ECR process: they were generally happy with the current informal regulations and could stand to lose from a negotiated agreement.

Recognizing this situation, the conflict assessment team suggested the key parties might be willing to participate in negotiations if the governor announced that "he would establish new regulations that would be substantially different from the existing, informal rules and, at the same time, stressed his preference to create those regulations through a consensus process" (Policy Consensus Initiative, 1999: 3). In 1996, Governor Tom Carper and DNREC Secretary Christophe Tulou made such an announcement and formed the Delaware Coastal Zone Regulatory Advisory Committee. The 20-member advisory committee included environmental representatives such as the Sierra Club and the Delaware Nature Society, industrial representatives such as the DuPont Corporation and Chemical Industry Council, local representatives from labor unions and the farming community, and government representatives from the DNREC.

Between the fall of 1996 and December 1997, the advisory committee held three two-day consensus-based negotiations. The sessions began with a discussion of representatives' interests and a brainstorming session to identify options to meet those interests. The next sessions focused on building a consensus-based agreement. The group worked to develop an agreement that contained a procedure for "offsets" in the permitting process. An offset allows for some environmental degradation in exchange for other environment improvements. Thus, the agreement allowed "industry the flexibility to add and change products and processes" and assured environmental groups of "continuous environmental improvements" to the coast (Policy Consensus Initiative, 1999: 3). The committee asked the DNREC to develop a set of environmental goals and indicators and to monitor the implementation of the offset policy.

In December 1997, negotiators crafted a final draft memorandum of understanding, and by March 1998, all advisory committee members, as well as the governor, signed it. Following the requirements for negotiated rulemaking, a full public comment process was held, including publication of the proposed rule and public hearings across the state. During this process, no committee members opposed the proposed regulations and many members publicly endorsed them. In April 1999, the regulations were formally adopted; they remain in force today.

QUESTIONS FOR DISCUSSION

1. Would you consider this case to be an upstream, midstream, or downstream dispute? As site-specific or policy-level conflict? Why?
2. If you were the neutral in this case, how would you have prepared?
3. What does this case suggest about the importance of conducting a conflict assessment? What do you think would have been the outcome if no conflict assessment was conducted? Why?
4. What were the likely positions and interests of the various representatives on the Delaware Coastal Zone Regulatory Advisory Committee? How did the negotiated agreement meet their respective interests?
5. What types of procedural and substantive knowledge would have been helpful to the neutral in this case?
6. How accurately does this case reflect the characteristics of environmental conflicts? How is it similar to cases in other mediation settings? How does it differ?
7. PCI (1999: 4) notes, "For the first time in the long history of Delaware's Coastal Zone Act, government, industry, environmentalists, organized labor, and agricultural interests all supported the same set of rules." What factors do you think contributed to the success of this ECR process?
8. What do you think would have happened if a consensus-based process was not used?

INTRODUCTION

Every summer, hundreds of thousands of tourists flock to Riverberg, a small Midwestern town, to enjoy its natural beauty, outdoor recreation, and the two largest water parks in the country: Aqualand and Clear Waters. Summer is the peak tourist season; more than 50 percent of the hotels and restaurants, and more than 75 percent of the stores and attractions are only open from mid-May until the end of September. Almost everyone in Riverberg and many people in the neighboring village of Tinyville are in some way dependent on money from tourism. For example, local governments count on tourists to increase the tax base to pay for schools, roads, and other municipal responsibilities. There is a cottage industry in owning cheap rentals to house the influx of summer help. Construction firms and workers depend on the continued growth of tourism so they can build more motels and attractions. Needless to say, almost everyone has a vested interest in both maintaining and increasing area tourism; however, a recent controversial proposal from Aqualand to expand its park has generated unrest among the governments of Riverberg and Tinyville, Aqualand, environmental groups, and the Hotel Owners Association. A mediator has been called in to help resolve the dispute.

BACKGROUND INFORMATION

Andy Roland is one of the city's wealthiest business executives and the "hands-on" owner of Aqualand. After twenty-five years in the business, Roland has developed a keen sense of the trends, and realizes what it takes to stay competitive. Roland wants to expand Aqualand to bring in the latest water and amusement rides and keep his edge on the competition. In addition to keeping the title of the largest water park in the country, the expansion of Aqualand (along with other tourist activities) would draw between 5-10 percent more visitors during the summer. Currently, Aqualand covers about 600 acres. The proposed expansion would require seventy-five acres of land, but Roland would like at least 100 acres for any future rides not yet in the plans. There are two primary options for expansion: Aqualand can expand into a wetland area or it can expand into a brownfield.

THE WETLANDS

Aqualand is bordered on the west by a wetlands area owned by Tinyville. The wetland is on a bird migration route and is an aviary sanctuary for many birds and is used by both visiting and local bird watchers. As a wetland, it is protected from development unless a previously drained wetland of comparable size and detail can be found, remediated back to its previous vegetative state, and flooded. The wetlands owned by Tinyville cover 150 acres and cannot be partially drained.

The only nearby site with similar conditions for wildlife is also in Tinyville and owned by Ruth Morgan, a local socialite. Morgan's land consists of twelve 40-acre parcels, four of which are developed with two of these developed sites for sale for $1.3 million each. Morgan has plans to develop the other eight lots, which in their current undeveloped state sell for $800,000 each. To offset the loss of the Tinyville wetlands, Roland would have to purchase four of Morgan's lots (160 acres) at $3.2 million ($20,000/acre). It would cost an additional $1.6 million to transplant and flood the land ($10,000/acre) for a total cost of $4.8 million. It would be more difficult to flood the other acres of Morgan's land because the two developed lots currently for sale are on low elevations and would be adversely affected by flooding.

The western edge of the wetlands borders County Trunk road. This road runs directly into the frontage road for the major freeway that brings most of the tourists to Riverberg. If Aqualand expanded into the wetlands, this road would provide a second thoroughfare to the park. Although this would help reduce congestion in Riverberg, it would also increase traffic and wear on what was otherwise a fairly quiet county road. County Trunk road is scheduled for repair in two years at a cost of approximately $430,000 (although the distance from the freeway to the proposed entrance of Aqualand would be less than half of the total segment planned for repair).

THE BROWNFIELD

The 100-acre lot to the south of Aqualand was awarded to Riverberg 17 years ago to cover back taxes after its previous owner passed away. A building on the site was used to produce leaded stain glass and jewelry. Due to inappropriate disposal practices, the site is contaminated with trichloroethane, lead, and other chemicals. It is therefore considered a brownfield. The brownfield is located in a slight depression, and lies on sand layered on clay over a solid bedrock surface. This configuration has so far prevented any seepage of toxins into the ground water or the migration of toxins to any of the neighboring properties, including Aqualand. Because of its low mobility and volume, the Environmental Protection Agency (EPA) has decided not to list the site on the National Priorities List. This has allowed Riverberg to simply monitor the site without the requirement of any expensive action; however, without the listing, the site is not eligible for federal clean-up funding under Superfund. After a preliminary assessment, the EPA provided the following acceptable measures which Riverberg could take:

1. Fencing and Monitoring. This is the current measure being taken, by Riverberg. It requires the city to maintain a six-foot-high perimeter fence, capable of keeping out trespassers, and to monitor the ground water for any migration of toxins. This measure is cheap, but does not reduce liability for the city should the hazardous waste begin to migrate. The fencing around the site is also an eyesore.
2. Capping and Monitoring. Riverberg could tear down and properly dispose of the structures on the premises, cap the site with clay, and continue monitoring for the migration of toxins. This option would cost an estimated $2 to $3 million. While capping would eliminate the eyesore, it would also mean that

Riverberg could not sell or lease the property for any commercial purpose which would entail digging into the surface of the clay. Moreover, liability at the site would not diminish, but would be shared by Riverberg and the new tenants. Finally, the city could build a park on the site, but has passed on this measure. A park would provide no revenue and this is prime real estate valued at $100,000 per acre with a tax rate of 3 cents on the dollar.

3. **Remediation.** Riverberg could also remediate the site. This two-step process involves aerating the soil to remove the volatile organic compounds (VOCs) and transporting and disposing of the waste in an approved landfill (the closest and most cost effective is a site in Tinyville). This option would remove the liability for the city (or any other owner) and the site could be zoned for any activity. However, with an estimated cost of $20 million or more, it would cause a shortfall in city revenues. Therefore, Riverberg would either have to raise taxes or find some other way to have the costs covered. Only complete remediation of this site will allow Roland to receive financing for the purchase of this property. Due to the liability hazards of brownfields, no bank would provide a loan if options 1 or 2 were followed.

SPLITTING THE PARK

Roland has suggested that a two-site Aqauland location is possible. The second site would be in Tinyville and would generate substantial tax revenue for the village. The cost of water, sewer, and electricity to the remote site would be formidable for all parties involved. No other details are available.

THE PLAYERS

Aqualand

Andy Roland is the independent, strong willed owner of Aqualand. He wants to expand Aqualand and keep the title of America's largest water park. He knows this will require a lot of capital, but thinks it is well worth the investment.

THE CITY OF RIVERBERG

Riverberg derives all of its energy needs from the Riverberg Electric Company, a city-owned, not-for-profit, hydroelectric generating plant. So far, this plant has fulfilled all of Riverberg's energy needs; however, increasing demand has stretched the generators to their capacity limits. Currently, the plant offers electricity to resident commercial customers for four cents per kilowatt hour (kWh), as compared to the five to seven cents per kWh charged by sources outside the city. Nevertheless, if demand continues to increase, the Riverberg Electric Company will be forced to charge the going rate, at least during peak hours when Aqualand derives most of its electricity, and maybe at all times. In addition, there are published reports of possible brownouts in high-demand locations throughout the state. Brownouts would cause shortages that Riverberg businesses can ill afford. One proposal for alternative energy sources is the installation of wind turbine generators at the Aqualand expansion site. Wind turbines could not be installed on the brownfield site due to Riverberg zoning restrictions; however, support from the business association could assure the removal of this rule. There are no such restrictions in Tinyville.

Riverberg realizes that this is the opportune time to make use of the brownfield site; however, it cannot afford to fund the remediation without an increase in tax revenue, likely an increase in the city room tax. In addition, Riverberg would have to supply the water and sewer lines no matter where the Aqualand expansion, because Tinyville lacks the capacity and desire to open its own treatment plants, and private wells for water and septic systems for sewage are prohibited in both Riverberg and Tinyville. Therefore, Riverberg can deter the wetlands option by charging up to double the standard water and sewer rates for lines that run out of the city—fees for water and sewer services that could amount to over $1 million annually.

THE COUNCIL OF TINYVILLE

Although Tinyville is having economic difficulties, the citizens have voted repeatedly against annexing the village to Riverberg. Any additional funds generated from the sale of land or through tax revenue would be welcome. Therefore, Tinyville wants Aqualand to split the park and expand to the alternative site. Their second choice is to drain and expand into the wetlands, and then flood parcels of the Morgan land. However, Ruth Morgan already built four houses and has eight more planned for her acreage. It is only her interest in bird watching that might make a transaction possible.

THE HOTEL OWNERS ASSOCIATION

The Hotel Owners Association, a major portion of the business association, is headed by Pat Besley. Besley owns Clear Waters, the second largest water park in Riverberg, and owns or co-owns 3 of the largest luxury hotels, with a total of 900 rooms. Although the association has no clear jurisdiction over the decision to expand Aqualand, its members comprise an influential corps of businesspeople who could make it very difficult for the city to acquire the funds necessary for schools, roads, and liability protection against the brownfield site. Riverberg has stated that the current 3-percent city room tax would need to double to help pay for the $20 million remediation of the brownfield site. This outrages the hotel association. They assert that while the current rate is lower than in similar locations, it gives the city a competitive edge when vying for tourist dollars. In addition, the association feels that the city already singles out the inn, hotels and resorts to carry the brunt of any revenue enhancement measures and that the city should look elsewhere for funding.

WHOLE WORLD FORCES (WWF)

Whole World Forces (WWF) is an environmental group that focuses on wetlands protection. Sam Atkinson, a native of the area, is the director of the organization and the owner of Turn, Turn, Turn, a company that manufactures and installs wind turbines. The company is one of the leaders in the wind energy generation industry and fits well with WWF's holistic approach to solving environmental problems. While the WWF has publicly campaigned for the plight of the wetlands, some of its members, including Atkinson, have privately marketed wind turbines and generators to Aqualand. This is an advance for both alternative energy and the WWF, since a certain percentage of Turn, Turn, Turn's profits go to the environmental organization.

Alternative energy needs for the expansion have already been noted. Atkinson proposes the installation of at least five 200kw wind turbines to offset the estimated need for energy. Each wind turbine costs $180,000 and equates to a price of 6 to 8 cents per kHz over the life of the unit based on a steady wind velocity of 10 mph. These are state-of-the-art wind generators and include all of the equipment necessary to adapt to the current systems. The installation of turbines would quell brownout worries and reduce the peak kw use for the park. The power company charges Aqualand a single annual rate based on the peak kw use during June, July, and August (e.g., if Aqualand has a peak use of 8000 kw at some point during its summer operation, Riverberg Power Company charges Aqualand for year-round service based on that rate of use). This adds up to hundreds of thousands of dollars a year. Wind turbines will reduce this peak consumption rate, and therefore has the potential to save tens of thousands of dollars per year.

THE MECHANICS OF THE MEDIATION

Representatives of Aqualand, Riverberg, Tinyville, the Hotel Owners Association, and Whole World Forces have agreed to participate in mediation to resolve the dispute over Aqualand's expansion. The parties have also agreed that if no consensus is found, four out of five affirmative votes are necessary for the approval of any agreement. There are four possible outcomes: 1) Aqualand's use of the brownfield by any legal means of acquisition, 2) the use of the wetlands under the same conditions, 3) splitting the park, or 4) no expansion. All of the outcomes must fall under the conditions prescribed in the above text, but are otherwise open to the negotiating skills of the parties. The outcomes may vary, but certain facts are irrefutable. First, the brownfield option is not possible without the support of Riverberg. Second, the wetland option is impossible without Tinyville's support. Finally, no transaction concerning the park is possible without Aqualand's satisfaction.

You are a party to this mediation and are negotiating for the best possible outcome. You will bargain for the optimal option according to your party's point of view. You must consider the cost of land acquisition, electricity costs and production, sewer and water needs, and taxes. You are the only party who knows the exact information given to you in your confidential information below. You have no obligation to share this information with any other parties and can use it to ensure the optimal outcome for you and your constituents.

CONFIDENTIAL INFORMATION FOR ANDY ROLAND, OWNER OF AQUALAND

An economic analysis by an independent consulting firm indicates that splitting the park into two sites is economically unfeasible. Therefore, you have no intention of opening a site separate from the current location. You have $10 million to spend on everything but the park construction costs. A national bank will finance $7 million; the remainder is from cash reserves. You would prefer to expand to the wetlands for a number of reasons. First, unless the brownfield site is remediated, you would not be able to erect rides because substantial excavation activities are involved. Second, the wetland site leaves open future expansion possibilities to the north and south. Finally, the wetlands allow for a park entrance from County Trunk road. You are concerned about a recent test from the well on the southwest corner of the property. A routine monitoring test showed a minute amount of an inert volatile organic compound (VOC) similar to that found at the brownfield site. It is almost impossible for the VOCs to have migrated from the brownfield site. The compounds are harmless to plant and animal life, but if the public knew about the contamination, the park could face catastrophe. No matter what happens, you must be true to your naturalist side. You have striven to take the state of the environment into consideration when making any business decisions and this opportunity is no different.

Confidential Information for Government of Riverberg

Little reduction in liability comes with the sale of the brownfield unless remediation takes place. Past owners of polluted sites retain a percentage of the liability based on factors such as contribution to the problem, length of ownership, and ability to pay. Riverberg has owned the property for the last seventeen years and is the only living owner of record (all other owners have passed away). However, over time, liability might shift to the next owners if they have "deep pockets" and continue ownership for an extended period of time. For these reasons, you are willing to sell the property for 40¢ on the dollar, or $4 million, even if no remediation takes place. No matter what the outcome, you also want to increase the room tax to at least 4 percent to help with other fiscal needs such as schools and energy production.

Confidential Information for Council of the Village of Tinyville

The Council of Tinyville wants to offset the expansion into the wetlands by flooding the property of Ruth Morgan, a very prominent citizen of the village. Developing the wetlands would create much needed tax revenue for Tinyville. The wetlands are being offered at a cheaper price than the value of the brownfield, with more area and a lower tax base. The $200,000 annual tax revenue from this land could allow the village to stay solvent. Without it, Tinyville may have to consider annexation to Riverberg. Nevertheless, you are not ready to hand everything to Aqualand on a silver platter; you are anxious to retain your bargaining position and must respect the wishes of Ruth Morgan. She is not at the table, but nothing can happen without her approval.

Morgan has publicly stated that she wants to protect her residential development and does not want her land to revert back to wetlands. She has built four luxury homes on the adjacent land and has plans to build eight more on the proposed mitigation land (the land to be flooded). Two of the completed houses are occupied; they are on the highest points of the land and would not be affected by any flooding. Morgan has no prospects for selling the two other completed houses and is willing to sell them and up to 400 acres of land. She wants to be discrete (to save her the embarrassment of stopping development and having two unmarketable houses); therefore, she is willing to drop the price of the land from $20,000 to $14,000 per acre if Aqualand agrees to buy all 400 acres (all of the land except the two occupied parcels). In addition, she wants to sell the two unoccupied houses at their $400,000 construction cost. Finally, she would like to make these gestures as a wealthy philanthropist, a supporter of humanity and the environment.

CONFIDENTIAL INFORMATION FOR HOTEL OWNERS ASSOCIATION

Your studies show that an expansion of Aqualand would generate a 2- to 5-percent increase in tourism, but only a 1- to 3-percent increase in the number of guests staying in hotels. Campers and day tourists generate 70 percent of the revenue of those staying overnight in a hotel. In addition, the last time Aqualand expanded, revenues at Clear Waters (the park owned by Pat Besley, president of the Hotel Owners Association) grew by 5 percent. For these reasons, you support the expansion of the park; however, you would like Aqualand to pay at least the market value of whatever land is acquired. Finally, you are willing to accept a smaller jump in the tax rate, even if the revenue generated is only be used to offset the cost of remediation.

CONFIDENTIAL INFORMATION FOR WHOLE WORLD FORCES (WWF)

Your number one priority is to avoid any net loss of wetlands. Your second priority is to leave the negotiation with good publicity and broader support for your national wetlands campaign. WWF is willing to vote for development of the wetlands only if both of the following conditions are met: 1) there is a 2 for 1 offset in the wetlands mitigation instead of the required 1 to 1 offset; and, 2) the water park agrees to offset the additional energy requirements with an alternative energy plan that includes the installation of at least ten wind turbines. Finally, field technicians from WWF found trace amounts of VOCs where the wetlands, Aqualand, and the brownfield sites meet. These may be naturally occurring substances or migrating toxins from the brownfield. Regardless, with an uninformed public and a city built on tourists who play in the water, neither situation helps Aqualand.

CONFIDENTIAL INFORMATION FOR THE MEDIATOR

You have been hired by the parties to mediate this dispute. Representatives of Aqualand, Riverberg, Tinyville, the Hotel Owners Association, and Whole World Forces are participating in the mediation. The parties have also agreed that if no consensus can be found, four out of five affirmative votes are necessary for the approval of any agreement.

REFERENCES

Amy, D. (1987). *The Politics of Environmental Mediation.* New York, NY: Columbia University Press.

Amy, D. (1990). Environmental dispute resolution: The promise and the pitfalls. In: N. J. Vig and M. E. Kraft (eds.), *Environmental Policy in the 1990s: Towards a New Agenda,* 211-234. Washington, D.C.: Congressional Quarterly Press.

Blackburn, J. W., and Bruce, W. M. (1995). *Mediating Environmental Conflicts: Theory and Practice.* Westport, CT: Quorum Books.

Bingham, G. (1986). *Resolving Environmental Disputes: A Decade of Experience.* Washington, D.C.: The Conservation Foundation.

Carpenter, S., and Kennedy, W. J. D. Managing environmental conflict by applying common sense. *Negotiation Journal, 1* (April, 1985): 149-161.

Emerson, K., Nabatchi, T., O'Leary, R., and Stephens, J. (2003). The challenges of environmental conflict resolution. In: R. O'Leary & L. B. Bingham (eds.), *The Promise and Performance of Environmental Conflict Resolution,* 3-26. Washington, D.C.: Resources for the Future.

Folberg, J., and Taylor, A. (1984). *Mediation: A Comprehensive Guide to Resolving Conflicts without Litigation.* San Francisco: Jossey-Bass.

Lake, L. M. (1980). Judicial review: From procedure to substance. In: L. M. Lake (ed.), *Environmental mediation,* 32-57. Boulder, CO: Westview Press.

Lind, E. A., and Tyler, T. R. (1988). *The Social Psychology of Procedural Justice.* New York: Plenum.

O'Leary, R. (1995). Environmental mediation: What do we know and how do we know it? In J. W. Blackburn and W. M. Bruce (eds.), *Mediating Environmental Conflicts: Theory and Practice, 17-36.* Westport, CT: Quorum Books.

O'Leary, R., and Bingham, L. B. (eds.) (2003). *The Promise and Performance of Environmental Conflict Resolution,* 3-26. Washington, D.C.: Resources for the Future.

O'Leary, R., Durant, R. F., Fiorino, D. J., and Weiland, P. S. (1999). *Managing for the Environment: Understanding the Legal, Organizational, and Policy Challenges.* San Francisco, CA: Jossey-Bass Publishers.

O'Leary, R., Nabatchi, T., and Bingham, L. B. (2004). Environmental conflict resolution. In: B. Durant, D. Fiorino, & R. O'Leary (eds.). *Building Common Purpose: Challenges, Choices, and Opportunities for Environmental Governance in the 21st Century,* 323-354. Cambridge, MA: MIT Press.

O'Leary, R., Yandle, T., and Moore, T. (1999). The state of the states in environmental dispute resolution. *Ohio State Journal of Dispute Resolution, 14*(2): 515-613.

Policy Consensus Initiative (1999). Balancing Environmental and Industrial Concerns in Delaware. In *States Mediating Solutions to Environmental Disputes,* 2-4. Santa Fe, NM: Policy Consensus Initiative. Available at: *http://www.policyconsensus.org/publications/reports/docs/MediatingEnvironmentalDisputes.pdf*

Riesel, D. (1985). Negotiation and mediation of environmental disputes. *Journal of Dispute Resolution, 1* (Fall): 99-111.

Stern, A. J., and Hicks, T. (2000). *The Process of Business/Environmental Collaborations: Partnering for Sustainability.* Westport, CT: Quorum Books.

Susskind, L (1978). It's time to shift our attention from impact assessment to strategies for resolving environmental disputes. *Environmental Impact Assessment Review, 2* (October): 4-8.

Chapter 8

Mediation in Crisis Situations

Tina Jaeckle

Crisis management, law enforcement, and mental health practitioners have long been familiar with intervention techniques to reduce and stabilize crises under the most difficult and dangerous of situations. Family mediators do not typically receive this type of specialized training and are often ill-equipped to manage crisis reactions, emotions, and behaviors during the mediation process and can therefore gain a substantial perspective from these arenas. Moreover, obtaining these basic skills is imperative as the very nature of these crises can serve to direct the mediation process away from one of collaborative and effective problem solving toward an increasing risk of impasse. It thus becomes critical to not only understand the foundation of crisis intervention but also the symptoms and behaviors involved.

Crisis intervention has been traditionally defined as a short-term helping process which serves to assist with the re-establishing of a person's normal and effective coping skills present during the pre-crisis phase (Hoff, 1989). This chapter will serve as a basic guideline to mediators who are seeking this knowledge and will offer insight and techniques through the presentation of various models of crisis intervention and negotiation.

Although the issues at the center of a dispute can vary significantly within the different types of mediation contexts, there subsists the potential for unique and challenging emotions that can ultimately lead to a crisis for one or more of the parties involved in the decision-making process. At the very heart of the mediation process is the need for the parties to effectively engage in the development of options to address the issues at hand. In addition, as mediators, one of the basic and most important ethical principles central in the mediation process is the parties' capacity in decision making and the right to self-determination. If a party in the mediation is experiencing an acute crisis, the lack of capacity may become a genuine issue for all involved. However, with appropriate intervention techniques, the mediator can assist a party in obtaining the emotional equilibrium required to move beyond the crisis, particularly in the arena of family and/or divorce mediation.

THE UNIQUENESS OF FAMILY AND DIVORCE MEDIATION

The role of mediation in family disputes is quite invaluable. According to Milne et. al. (2004), family and divorce mediation has emerged as distinct from commercial and civil claims due to the nature of family mediation striving to provide a model of interaction and communication for resolution of future disputes as well. In addition, while mediation is not considered therapy or involving diagnoses, potential insights and changes may occur in this process, although as a fringe benefit (Kelly, 1983; Milne, 1982). Understanding and mastering basic crisis intervention techniques can only serve to enhance the ultimate exchange of ideas, which serve the problem-solving practice inherent in alternative dispute resolution.

Divorce is considered one of the most dramatic and life-altering processes an individual and family unit can experience. The occurrence of difficult emotions in the context of family mediation is undoubtedly familiar to any mediator who regularly practices in this arena. The significant issues that parties must confront, such as custody and visitation of children, financial division of assets, and the often overwhelming sense of loss and grief associated with the dissolving of a marriage can indeed create crises situations. Additionally, these issues not only hold the possibility of creating a crisis in one's life, they can also serve to escalate the past and present conflicts between the parties.

Moore (2003) establishes that five problems commonly create negative psychological dynamics within negotiations: (1) Strong emotions; (2) Misperceptions or stereotypes held by one of more parties, about the parties or about issues in the dispute; (3) Legitimacy problems; (4) Lack of trust; and (5) Poor communication. The experience of crisis can exacerbate one or more of these frequent tribulations. Cohen and Smith (1972) have referred to these psychological stumbling blocks as "critical situations."

Divorce rates escalated rapidly in the United States beginning in the 1960s, a trend that foreshadowed similar increases in other English-speaking countries and throughout the industrialized world (Pryor and Rodgers, 2001; Emery, 1999). Currently, demographic estimates suggest that nearly half of first marriages end in divorce, affecting over one million children each year (Pedro-Carroll, 2005).

While numerous separations and divorces can be described as agreeable in many aspects, a significant number are characterized by high conflict and acrimonious emotions and behaviors. One thorough survey of divorces in two California counties found that 25 percent involved either substantial or intense conflict, and 24 percent required the involvement of a professional other than the parties' lawyers (a mediator, evaluator, or judge (Maccoby and Mnookin, 1992). Fortunately, the practice and utilization of family mediation has successfully evolved over the last twenty years and now includes numerous effective techniques to manage difficult conflicts and issues and ultimately reduces the adversarial nature of the process.

A significant part of the effectiveness in divorce mediation programs lies in the mediator's influence upon the parties who are frequently impacted psychologically, emotionally, and at times physically, by separation and/or divorce. Emery, Sbarra, and Grover (2005) conducted a longitudinal study within their own program of the importance of mediation on the overall psychological adjustment for the parents as well as the children. It was determined from this research that the most effective family mediations contained the following key "active ingredients": (1) the call for parental cooperation over the long run of co-parenting beyond the crisis of separation; (2) the opportunity to address underlying emotional issues (albeit briefly); (3) helping parents to establish a businesslike relationship, and (4) the avoidance of divisive negotiations at a critical time for family relationships (Emery, Sbarra, and Grover, 2005). The application of basic crisis intervention techniques allows not only for a transitory approach of these underlying emotional issues, but can also serve to reduce the overall level of conflict between the parties themselves.

Moore (2003) provides further exploration into the various dimensions of emotion, and highlighting these components is essential in order to more comprehensively understand the powerful influence on the crisis state. Lazrus (1994) explains that these components include behavioral or expressive, psychological, and cognitive. The behavioral component of emotion can be expressed in many ways, including verbal, nonverbal, and as direct actions (Moore, 2003). The psychological component can include, but is not limited to, the emotional and physical aspects of emotion. Adler et al. (1998) explain that experiencing strong emotions can in fact create physiological changes. Jones (2001) adds that when the body becomes physiologically overwhelmed by feelings, an emotional flooding can occur which ultimately affects the cognitive dimension, or the ability to make logical and rational decisions in the mediation process. The crisis experience can also create a level of irrationality through its interplay with the various emotions involved. Therefore, Taylor (2002) explains, it is the role of the family mediator to initially work as a crisis intervention specialist, particularly in cases in which the conflict is continuing to escalate in some form and when the party or parties present at mediation in a crisis state.

Defining Crisis

According to Greenstone and Leviton (2002), a crisis occurs when unusual stress (such as a divorce or family conflict), whether due to one or several events, temporarily renders a person unable to make decisions, and his or her normal coping mechanisms fail. Underlying any crisis are frequently significant feelings of loss of control, anger, revenge, hopelessness, fear, sadness, and grief. While all individuals experience crisis though the exhibition of various and unique behaviors, typically in all cases, the onset of crisis is sudden and unexpected. Before a crisis, the majority of individuals possess the ability to cope with stress, anxiety, and tension, and when these normal mechanisms fail, the individual can begin a downward spiral.

Perception also plays an integral role in the development of a crisis state. A crisis occurs when a person's individual interpretation of the events in his or her life, the overall ability to cope with these events, and the limitations of social resources ultimately lead to stress levels so severe that emotional relief cannot be found or obtained (Hoff, 1989). Moreover, the balance or sense of control in one's life is significantly compromised. To demonstrate, the following figures display the shift from a normal equilibrium (non-crisis state) to a crisis state:

Emotional/Non-Cognitive/Non-Rational   **Non-Emotional/Cognitive/Rational**

Figure 8.1
Normal Equilibrium/Balanced Non-Crisis State

Emotional/Non-Cognitive/
Non-Rational

Non-Emotional/Cognitive/
Rational

Figure 8.2
Non-Balanced Equilibrium/Crisis State

THE ROLE OF THE HELPER IN CRISIS

In the crisis intervention and management fields, it is generally understood that there are three goals for the helper or intervener in this process: 1) To help a person in crisis to at least return to their pre-crisis state; 2) To do all that is possible to help a person grow and become stronger as a result of the crisis and effective problem solving; and 3) To be alert to dangers signals in order to prevent destructive outcomes of a crisis experience (Hoff, 1989). It is crucial to explain that crisis intervention and management techniques are not considered a provision of therapy or counseling and therefore do not create a neutrality issue for a family mediator. Although mediators with professional mental health experience or training may be more adept at these various techniques, it is clearly not a requirement. The crisis intervention approach is designed to intercede into the present crisis of the party and to offer "emotional first aid" in order to assist with stabilization and the ability to problem solve. Psychotherapy and crisis intervention are two exceptionally different methods and approaches and should not be compared or measured at the same level.

IDENTIFYING CRISIS BEHAVIORS

It is imperative for any family mediator to first properly identify the behaviors which most commonly distinguish when a party is in a crisis state. While all individuals experience and exhibit crisis behaviors in a unique manner depending on their general coping mechanisms, Greenstone and Leviton (2002) provide the following basic guidelines to assist with assessment.

Indicators that Can Characterize a Crisis-Prone Person

- Alienation from lasting and meaningful personal relationships
- Inability to use life support systems such as family, friends, and social groups
- Difficulty in learning from experience; the individual continues to make the same mistakes
- A history of previously experienced crises that have not been effectively resolved
- A history of mental disorder or severe emotional imbalance
- Feelings of low self-esteem
- Provocative, impulsive behavior resulting from unresolved inner conflict
- A history of poor marital relationships
- Excessive use of drugs, including alcohol abuse
- Marginal income
- Lack of regular, fulfilling work
- Unusual or frequent physical injuries
- Frequent changes in residence
- Frequent encounters with the law

Common Signs and Symptoms of Psychological Reactions to Crisis

- Anticipatory anxiety
- Generalized anxiety
- Shock
- Denial
- Insecurity
- Fatigue
- Uncertainty
- Fear
- Helplessness
- Depression
- Panic
- Despair
- Guilt
- Feeling out of Control
- Grief
- Outrage
- Numbness
- Frustration
- Inadequacy
- Feeling Overwhelmed
- Anger
- Irritability

Common Signs and Symptoms of Cognitive Reactions to Crisis

* Confusion
* Poor Attention Span
* Poor Concentration
* Loss of Trust
* Difficulties in Decision Making
* Nightmares and/or Flashbacks

Common Signs and Symptoms of Physiological/Behavioral Reactions to Crisis

* Withdrawal
* Sleep Disturbances
* Angry Outbursts
* Change in Activity
* Change in Appetite
* Increased Fatigue
* Excessive Use of Sick Leave
* Alcohol or Drug Abuse
* Difficulty functioning at normal ability level
* Antisocial acts
* Frequent visits to physicians for non-specific complaints
* Anger at God
* Loss of desire to attend religious services
* Regression
* Crying
* Change in communications
* Pre-occupation with the crisis to the exclusion of other areas in life
* Diminished job performance
* Unresponsiveness
* Hysterical reactions
* Irritability

CRISIS INTERVENTION AND MANAGEMENT APPROACHES: THE POWER OF COMMUNICATION

Whether in the law enforcement, crisis/hostage negotiation, or mental health arenas, effective communication skills play an integral role in the reduction and resolution of the crisis state. As a family mediator, the integration of various techniques provided by the experts in these fields could prove beneficial for the overall process.

Dr. Lee Ann Hoff (1989), a mental health expert in the crisis intervention field, details seven stages or steps which can serve to assist in the de-escalation of crisis symptoms and behaviors. Moreover, crisis management and law enforcement negotiators have also built upon Hoff's early work to create a more well-rounded approach to the resolution of high-conflict and potentially deadly situations. These seven steps, as well as some of the various law enforcement techniques, are detailed as follows:

1. Listen actively and with concern: When a person is ashamed with his or her ability to cope with a problem, or feels that the problem is too minor to be so upset about, a good listener can dispel some of these feelings (Hoff, 1998). Lanceley (2003) describes the concept of active listening as essential in expressing to a person in crisis that you are truly empathetic to their concerns and problems. This approach is viewed as the first initial step in the movement toward positive behavioral changes which indicate the re-establishment of the pre-crisis state. Vecchi et al. (2005) also demonstrate the importance of active listening and empathy building through the Behavioral Change Stairway.

2. Encourage the open expression of feelings: The actual venting of feelings and emotions may serve to decrease the crisis state and simultaneously allow you, as the family mediator or helper, to exhibit empathy and build rapport. Hoff (1989) explains that people who are crisis-prone may habitually bottle up feelings such as anger, grief, frustration, helplessness, and hopelessness. Through allowing the overt expression of the feelings, the family mediator can begin to learn the reason(s) and/or content behind the crisis state, which is essential to move to the next step in this process. The following "donut" provides a visual of this process.

3. Help the person gain an understanding of the crisis: Hoff (1989) explains that the helper, or mediator for our purposes, can assist the party in examining the reasons for the crisis through exploration and encouragement. The goal for this step is to allow for thoughtful reflection on one's behavior in order to promote growth and ultimately a re-stabilization to the pre-crisis state. McMains and Mullins (2006), experts in the crisis/hostage negotiation field, suggest the use of embedded questions to assist with introspection. These can include, but are not limited to, "Take a moment. Can you think back to a time when you were not under so much stress?" This is an important technique to allow the person to emotionally and mentally concentrate on a more positive time period in his/her life so reframing can begin to occur (McMains & Mullins, 2006).

The techniques of active listening, while important in the initial first step, also remain central in the remaining stages as well. Bolton (1984) has described these various communication techniques as:

a. Paraphrasing: A response by the mediator which incorporates the essence of the message in the person's words.

b. Reflecting feelings (or mirroring): A response by the mediator which includes stating back to the person in crisis the emotion(s) being heard or communicated. Another reason for utilizing this technique is to allow the person in crisis to identify, and correct if needed, their own feelings and emotions. This, in turn, allows for the person in crisis to feel more in control and can begin to utilize their cognitive rather than affective skills.

c. Reflecting meaning (or emotional labeling with emotions): A response by the mediator which includes the understanding of the facts AND the feelings that are being communicated.

d. Summative Reflections: A response by the mediator which includes the main facts of the content of the story AND the feelings being communicated over a relatively long period.

Ware (2003; 2004) included other techniques such as:

e. Minimal Encouragers: Responses by the mediator, such as "Yes," "I see," or "Go on," to express active listening and empathy.

f. Open-Ended Questions: Questions offered by the mediator to encourage the person in crisis to open up and give a long, verbal answer.

g. I-messages: Utilized by the mediator to express his/her own emotions in response to what is being communicated by the person in crisis. This technique also assists in building rapport.

h. Effective Pauses and Extended Pauses: The mediator can utilize silence when the person in crisis is finished talking in order to encourage the filling of space with additional communications.

4. Help the individual gradually accept reality: Individuals in crisis tend to blame and scapegoat others for their current predicament, and this is particularly present in cases of marital or family conflicts (Hoff, 1989). This persona of "victim" can serve to maintain the crisis state: therefore, the role of the helper or mediator is to gradually assist the person to move away from this status. McMains and Mullins (2006) discuss the importance of being cautious at this stage because the person may still be in the affective or emotional aspect of crisis, rather than the cognitive, and may perceive this step as threatening. As a family mediator, be aware to first establish a solid foundation of trust and rapport before attempting this aspect of crisis intervention.

5. Help the person explore new ways of coping with problems: Sometimes people in crisis have given up on problem-solving devices that have actually worked for them in the past (Hoff, 1989). One of the essential steps offered by William Ury (1991) in his "Getting Past No" model is assisting the person in crisis to focus by asking the following specific questions: "What worked to help you solve this problem in the past?", "Why did it work?", "Why did it not work?", and "What if you tried it this way?" In the family mediation context, if a person in crisis can begin to respond to these questions from a cognitive perspective, this is an excellent sign that the pre-crisis state is beginning to become re-established.

6. Link the person to a social network: Hoff (1989) explains that the precursor to crisis is often the disruption of social ties, particularly during a separation or divorce; therefore, it is imperative to explore other options for social support with the person in crisis. Given that the family mediator must be cognizant of professional boundaries, including impartiality and neutrality, it may be beneficial to have a listing of the various social services in the community to offer to the individual. However, by allowing the person to directly select and initiate contact with these services, this returns more control regarding the decision-making process and will hopefully create some long-term coping mechanisms.

7. **Reinforce the newly learned coping devices:** Through the utilization of step six and seven, the person is given an opportunity to reinforce newly learned coping devices. This behavioral and emotional change may become apparent almost immediately through a focus on the problem-solving phase in family or divorce mediation and a willingness to participate openly in finding appropriate solutions.

EMOTIONAL AND BEHAVIORAL INDICATORS OF PROGRESS

There are several important characteristics and indicators of emotional and behavioral progress in crisis intervention. In family mediation, these may be exhibited as follows:

A Person's Behavior or Communication:

* Shifts from potentially threatening and/or potentially violent language to non-threatening language
* Person's disclosure of personal information becomes more open and honest
* Shifts from emotional (affective) to rational (cognitive) content
* Willingness to discuss topics unrelated to the ongoing crisis or central issue
* Lower voice level
* Less rapid speech pattern
* Conversations of increasing length
* Increased willingness or desire to speak with the mediator

CONCLUDING COMMENTS

This chapter has demonstrated that family mediators can undoubtedly benefit from learning and utilizing various skills and techniques from other experts and professionals in the crisis intervention and management arenas. The information presented in this context is solely considered a basic guideline for crisis intervention and should not be construed as advanced or applicable in all crisis situations. For family mediators who frequently work with high-conflict or crisis-prone individuals and families (particularly those involving domestic violence, suicidal or homicidal ideations, and/or mental health issues), it is strongly suggested that additional training in this area be obtained.

Case Study: The Divorce of Robert and Jenna

Robert and Jenna had been married for eleven years when Jenna shared that she was unhappy in the marriage and wanted a divorce. Jenna has a history of mild depression. They have been separated and living in different residences for six months. They have one child together, Matthew, age 7, who is presently living with Jenna. Jenna also has one child, Amanda, age 14, from a previous marriage. Two weeks prior to the court-ordered family mediation, Matthew told Jenna he wanted to live with his father and she allowed him to do so reluctantly. Once Matthew moved in with Robert, he began to refuse to visit or talk with his mother. Amanda also exhibited a significant amount of anger towards her mother and became withdrawn in the relationship. Jenna was emotionally overwhelmed but felt she was able to go forward with the legal proceedings. At mediation, she shared with the mediator that she was having trouble concentrating and felt like all that had happened was "not real."

QUESTIONS FOR DISCUSSION

1. Is Jenna in crisis at the present time? What symptoms/behaviors indicate this?
2. Is the mediation potentially at risk for impasse?
3. What crisis and/or communication techniques can the mediator utilize to assist Jenna?
4. Please examine your own thoughts/feelings on this case. Are they significant to how you would approach this situation?

Role Play: The Divorce of the Turners

INFORMATION FOR JAMES TURNER

James is a 45-year-old dentist who filed for divorce from his wife, Christine, approximately six months ago and is now ready to settle all financial and legal issues at this court-ordered family mediation. James and Christine have been married for twenty-two years. This was a very difficult decision for James: however, he is now moving forward with his life and feels confident in the outcome of his case and has arrived ready to mediate. James would like to sell the marital home, which has no mortgage balance, and then split the proceeds equally with Christine. They also have joint checking, savings, and retirement accounts totaling approximately $500,000. James feels he could split the checking and savings accounts, however, he wants to retain a larger percentage of the retirement since he was the primary contributor. He has no issues with Christine keeping the furniture in the marital home. They have three children, all adults at this time. His demeanor is calm and relaxed.

INFORMATION FOR CHRISTINE TURNER

Christine is a 44-year-old homemaker who has devoted her life to supporting James in his career as a dentist. Christine has been struggling financially since the separation, and two days before this scheduled court ordered mediation, a close friend revealed to her that James was in a relationship with a much younger woman and this was the "reason" he left the marriage. Christine is very hurt, angry, and in shock, and is not able to think clearly about any of the complicated financial and legal issues in this case. At the beginning of the mediation, Christine was very lethargic, complained of feeling "very tired," and could only focus on the information regarding James and his new relationship. The family mediator in this case must work with this couple and assess if a crisis is present and what approach would be most effective.

REFERENCES

Adler, R., Rosen, B., and Silverstein, E. (1998) Emotions in negotiation: How to manage fear and anger. *Negotiation Journal, 14*(2), 161-179.

Bolton, R. (1984). *People skills.* Englewood Cliffs, NJ: Prentice-Hall.

Cohen, A., and Smith, R. (1972). The critical-incident approach to leadership intervention in training groups. In W. Dyer (ed.), *Modern Theory and Method in Group Training.* New York: Van Nostrand Reinhold.

Crisis Negotiation Unit. (2002). *FBI National Crisis Negotiation Course.* Quantico, VA: FBI Academy.

Emery, R. E. (1999). *Marriage, Divorce, and Children's Adjustment (2nd ed.).* Thousand Oaks, CA: Sage.

Emery, R. E., Sbarra, D., and Grover, T. (2005). Divorce mediation: Research and reflections. *Family Court Review,* v. 43, no. 1, 22-37.

Greenstone, J. L., and Leviton, S. C. (2002). *Elements of Crisis Intervention: Crises and How to Respond to Them (2nd ed.)* Pacific Grove, CA: Brooks/Cole.

Hoff, L. A. (1989). *People in Crisis: Understanding and Helping* (3rd ed). Redwood City, CA: Addison-Wesley.

Jones, T. (2001). Mediating with heart in mind: Addressing emotion in mediation practices. *Negotiation Journal, 17*(3), 217-244.

Kelly, J. (1983). Mediation and psychotherapy: Distinguishing the difference. *Mediation Quarterly, 1*, 33-44.

Lanceley, F. J. (2003). *On-Scene Guide for Crisis Negotiators* (2nd ed). Boca Raton, FL: CRC Press.

Lazrus, R. Meaning and emotional development. In P. Ekman and R. J. Davidson (eds.), *The Nature of Emotion: Fundamental Questions.* New York: Oxford University Press, 1994.

McMains, M. J., and Mullins, W. C. (2006). *Crisis negotiations: Managing critical incidents and hostage situations in law enforcement and corrections,* (3rd ed). Albany, NY: Anderson Publishing.

Milne, A. L., Folberg, J., and Salem, P. (2004). The evolution of divorce and family mediation, an overview. In *Divorce and Family Mediation.* New York: Guilford Press.

Milne, A. (1982). Divorce mediation: An idea whose time has come, *Wisconsin Journal of Family Law, 2*(2), 1-10.

Moore, C. (2003). *The Mediation Process: Practical Strategies for Resolving Conflict* (3rd ed.). San Francisco, CA: Jossey-Bass.

Maccoby, E. E., and Mnookin, R. H. (1992). *Dividing the Child: Social and Legal Dilemmas of Custody.* Cambridge, Mass.: Harvard University Press.

Pedro-Carroll, J. L. (2005). Fostering resilience in the aftermath of divorce: The role of evidence based programs for children. *Family Court Review, 43* (1), 52-64.

Pryor, J., and Rodgers, B. (2001). *Children in Changing Families. Life after Parental Separation.* Oxford: Blackwell.

Taylor, A. (2002). *The Handbook of Family Dispute Resolution: Mediation Theory and Practice.* San Francisco: Jossey-Bass.

Ury, W. (1991). *Getting Past no: Negotiating with Difficult People.* New York, NY: Bantam Books.

Vecchi, G. M., Van Hasselt, V. B., and Romano, S. J. (2005). Crisis (hostage) negotiation: Current strategies and issues in high-risk conflict resolution. *Aggression and Violent Behavior, 10*, 533-551.

Ware, B. (2003). "Active listening." Presentation at the annual Crisis Negotiation Competition/Seminar. Texas State University, San Marcos, TX (January).

Ware, B. (2004). "Active listening for negotiators." Presentation at the annual meeting of the Kansas Association of Hostage Negotiators, Olathe, KS (April).

Chapter 9

Mediation in Juvenile Victim/Offender Conferencing

Andrea Bodtker

Victim/Offender Conferencing (VOC) is a special form of mediation which brings together parties who are related to one another through some criminal offense. In these cases, one party (or more) is identified as the offender, and the other (or others) as the victim. In this way, VOC differs from traditional mediation in that the nature of the conflict has already been determined by criminal law. Recall that in traditional mediation, part of the process involves learning what the conflict issues are for each party, and determining which (if not all) are key to focus during the conferencing session. In VOC, the legal system has already made this decision (due to the arrest of the offender), so the conflict, per se, has been defined prior to the disputants coming together.

While untraditional, given the pre-determined nature of the conflict, VOC cases are ideal for mediation because of the ability of the mediation process to humanize the criminal event and the subsequent justice process. It does so by creating a climate for engaged dialogue among the involved parties. Through this dialogue, the consequences of the offender's harmful actions on others can be realized; the opportunity for "victims" to have voice (power) in the justice proceedings is provided; and the community is called upon to support both victims and offenders in a process that can be truly restorative for all involved.

BRIEF OVERVIEW OF THE RESTORATIVE JUSTICE PHILOSOPHY

One might wonder how criminal cases could be appropriate for mediation since it is the judicial system which is responsible for determining justice in the United States. The answer lies in the definition of justice one uses. The current judicial system in the U.S. is based upon retributive justice. In this system, crimes are seen as offenses committed against the state (rather than against individuals) and the court system, with judges and attorneys, is called upon to assess the crime and apply appropriate penalties according to the law. Although reparations are sometimes made to individuals harmed in the offense, technically speaking, offenders pay their debt to the state (for instance, by serving jail time or paying fines).

Additionally, in these cases, offenders often never see or meet the people they have harmed, and the way they pay their "debt" doesn't allow them to see the true impact of their actions on others. The judicial system is therefore very impersonal and ineffective in resolving conflict because the parties are essentially seen as labels (offenders, victims) with no recourse for active participation in their recovery from the event. For instance, victims don't typically get to help determine how the offender should pay their debt; the harmful effects they have experienced as a result of the crime are usually not fully addressed (and therefore are difficult to gain closure on) and offenders are not held responsible for their actions on an interpersonal level.

On the other hand, VOC is based on a philosophical system of restorative justice which views crime as an offense committed by a person or persons, against another person or persons, as well as the community in which they live. In the restorative system, in order for justice to be served, the offender is called upon to "make things right" to the person or persons harmed as well as the surrounding community. In order to accomplish this, the people involved in the actual offense (victims, offenders, and community members) are given the responsibility to determine what harms have been suffered, and who suffered them, and then, what can be done to bring equilibrium back to all those involved (hence, the term "restorative") (Zehr, 2002). So, rather than letting attorneys and judges make those decisions, parties meet face to face (in most cases) with the assistance of a trained mediator to talk about the impact of the offense on all parties involved and how the offender can repair the damage. This process is much more personal than the legal system and is thought to bring about a more complete and productive resolution of the "conflict" for all of those involved, including the offender. The process helps the victim address emotional and informational needs central to their healing and to the development of empathy for the offender (Umbreit,

1998). Finally, the personal nature of the process is thought to reduce future criminal behavior in the offender.

THE IMPACT OF VICTIM-OFFENDER MEDIATION PROGRAMS

It is beyond the scope of this chapter to discuss at length the various risks and benefits of participating in victim-offender conferencing for victims and offenders. Offered below are two tables outlining the general pros and cons for each party (adapted from Umbreit, Bradshaw, & Greenwood, 1998).

Table 9.1: Understanding Benefits and Risks of VOC for Victims

Risks:
1. re-experiencing anxiety or trauma
2. learning painful new information related to crime
3. not seeing desired level of remorse in offender
4. unrealistic expectations of offender's rehabilitation

Benefits:
1. expressing anger and pain directly to offender
2. learning new information about crime
3. seeing remorse in offender
4. experiencing greater sense of closure
5. feeling more powerful and in control of one's life

Table 9.2: Understanding Benefits and Risks of VOC for Offenders

Risks:
1. re-experiencing anger, frustration, loss of control associated with crime
2. reinforcement of shame, despair through learning impact on victim
3. unrealistic expectations about the victim's response
4. feeling vulnerable as a result of expressing true feelings

Benefits:
1. learning the real impact of their behavior on others
2. moving beyond defense mechanisms to taking responsibility
3. building self-esteem through taking action to make things right with victim
4. having a chance to tell one's story, to represent oneself, to be heard
5. having a say in determining plan for restitution
6. feeling more powerful and in control of one's life

The Philadelphia Juvenile Court Victim-Offender Conferencing Program

The remainder of this chapter will focus specifically on the Good Shepherd Mediation Program (GSMP) in Philadelphia which mediates VOC cases for Philadelphia Juvenile Court. In this Court-involved program, first-time juvenile offenders arrested for misdemeanor or non-egregious felonies (e.g., physical altercation at school) are given the opportunity to divert their case from court (i.e., avoid getting a criminal record) by participating in the VOC program. In order for them to be eligible for the program, they must first accept culpability for the action that led to their arrest. In other words, they must admit their wrong-doing or guilt. At that point, the case is referred to GSMP for management.

The case manager then describes the VOC program to the offender and his/her family and ascertains whether the offender is willing to move forward. If the offender accepts the offer, the case manager then contacts the victim to briefly explain the program and to learn whether they are interested in participating. If the victim indicates willingness, an in-depth meeting is scheduled first with the victim to get a more comprehensive understanding of his/her perspective, including fears and concerns, and to urge him/her to begin thinking about what he/she might need in order to feel better about the event (to restore the harm).

It is during this meeting that the mediator makes an initial determination about whether or not the case is appropriate for mediation. Red flags cautioning the mediator against a joint session include a victim who exhibits or expresses tremendous fear in confronting the offender, or, conversely, is devoutly positioned on wanting the offender "to pay" for the crime through the criminal justice system (court). In each of these cases, the risk at further injuring one or both parties may be too great to warrant going further.

These issues are taken up in greater detail later when training and special skills emphases are discussed. If the victim expresses a genuine desire to move forward, he/she believes it will do themselves and/or the offender some good, then the case manager contacts the offender, and a similar in-depth meeting is held with the offender, the parent or guardian and the mediator.

During this meeting, the mediator assesses the extent to which the offender is willing to take responsibility for his or her actions and whether he/she possesses any regret or remorse (indicating the potential to empathize with the victim). Red flags that could prevent a joint session at this point include an offender who expresses regret for "getting caught" but not for the action itself, an offender who is apathetic (appears to be going through the motions JUST to avoid a criminal record), and/or one who clearly expresses contempt for the victim (e.g., "they deserved it" or "I'd do it again"). It is unlikely that a youth with this attitude will be able to engage in the meaningful dialogue which is at the heart of VOC process.

And, as is discussed further in the subsequent section, preventing re-victimization is the central ethical concern in these types of cases. That said, if the offender shows genuine willingness and desire to own up to the offense with the victim, a joint session between victim and a support person, and the offender and their guardian is scheduled. A co-mediation model is used and an effort to match gender and ethnicity is made in order to present a balanced mediator team. The joint session proceeds very much like other mediation sessions, although the mediators must be attentive to the special needs of the victim and offender and to the multi-party dynamics not always present in other types of cases.

SPECIAL SKILLS EMPHASIZED IN JUVENILE VICTIM-OFFENDER CONFERENCING

Arguably, the success of VOC as a restorative justice process is due to the fact that it reformulates an event categorized as a "crime" to one seen as a "conflict" (Strang, 2002). The word "conflict" differs widely depending on its nature and context; therefore requisite skills needed by the mediator vary. VOC mediators must not only acquire the generic communication and process skills necessary for other types of mediation, but strive to become proficient in understanding and attending to the: 1) special needs of victims, 2) special needs of offenders, and 3) dynamics of multi-party mediation.

ATTENDING TO THE SPECIAL NEEDS OF VICTIMS

In mediating criminal cases, mediators must be sensitive to the potential for crime victims to feel extremely vulnerable in confronting the offender and fearful about being re-victimized by him/her. The emotional pain felt by a victim is often far greater than any financial loss or even physical injury they experienced (Umbreit, 1995). For instance, in one case where a school-aged girl was pushed down and taunted by a male school-mate (a criminal offense in the Philadelphia school system), the mother expressed extreme concern for her daughter's future safety. Part of the concern centered around revealing to the male offender just how scared (hence, vulnerable) both she and her daughter were that there may be a "next time" and that the nature of that attack might be more serious. Although the victim's injuries were minor in the assault, she and her mother experienced continued anguish over the possibility that it could happen again.

A mediator must be able to empathize with this fear and treat it as an important issue during the mediation process. Because a mediator cannot guarantee that another harmful act will not occur, they must do their best to prevent re-victimization through the process by in-depth pre-screening of the offender where they ascertain the degree of guilt or remorse the offender feels, and by managing any interactions between the victim and offender in such a way the victim is empowered. Being able to ask questions and get answers from the offender is one form of empowerment. Receiving a genuine apology from the offender, along with a commitment to restore the harm is another. In the best case scenarios, victims develop empathy for the offender, and this can be the greatest form empowerment they experience.

Victims also often express confusion, particularly when there is no clear connection between themselves and the offender. Questions they may have are "Why was I targeted?" or "What did I do to cause the harmful action?" These questions speak to the need of the victim to make sense of what occurred and to place the event into a larger "normal" context. A mediator cannot answer those questions or normalize the event for the victim. There is usually no concrete cause-effect sequence that would provide a normalizing "reason" for what happened anyway.

What a mediator can do is listen sensitively and validate the victim's need to understand; they can normalize the feelings the victim is experiencing. In terms of process, the mediator may suggest to the victim that this is an issue they may want to address with the offender in the conferencing session.

Victims often learn that they were not singled out by the offender; that the act was truly random (e.g., as in the case of property damage or theft). While this information may not bring closure, it can provide some form of relief through the recognition that there is nothing they could have done to prevent the event; that they are not to blame. During joint session, dialogue around this issue helps the offender understand the personal nature of the crime; to see beyond themselves and therefore to better appreciate the impact of his/her actions.

Ultimately, then, victim needs center on security and understanding. In order to help mediators address these needs, VOC training spends a good deal of time helping mediators relate to victims' emotional experiences. This translates into practice that entails conducting individual meetings with victims where considerable time may be spent allowing the victim and his/her support person to vent their emotions surrounding the event. During this meeting, the mediator must be conscious of validating the feelings of the parties, even so-called "negative" emotions, such as the desire for retribution. Typical emotions a victim may be feeling include: anger or rage, fear or terror, frustration, confusion, guilt or self-blame, shame and humiliation, and grief or sorrow.

Part of the challenge in helping a victim share these emotions is in bearing witness to them. In other words, there may be some emotions that are very uncomfortable for a mediator to experience. A skilled mediator must identify emotions they are sensitive to, learn to monitor their reactions to the expression of these emotions, and develop a strategy for managing their reaction.

For instance, as a trained VOC mediator, I am easily triggered by hostile expressions of anger. I react with a desire to diffuse the anger; to make it go away. I have learned to be cautious of this tendency as it could cause me to cut short the victim's expression and exploration of the anger. In doing so, I may inadvertently disconfirm their emotional reality and loose an important opportunity to identify issues central to the victim's needs. Worse yet, I may re-victimize the party by not treating his/her anger as valid. Thus, an attentive mediator must monitor him/herself during the mediation process, making sure he/she is not "reacting" to the unpleasant nature of the venting.

ATTENDING TO THE SPECIAL NEEDS OF OFFENDERS

In working with juvenile offenders, the first thing that mediators need to keep in mind is that in nearly all cases in the Philadelphia area, youths are injured in some way. It is very likely that they come from a disadvantaged background, including an impoverished family life and/or lower socio-economic status as well as being a member of a marginalized community. Many juvenile offenders are victims of abuse as well. As such, these youth have not gotten their basic needs met in very many ways. The mindset of a young person who commits an act that gets criminalized, therefore, is poised to defend itself against the censure ("I am not merely a criminal; I am a human being!").

It is human nature to protect one's fundamental sense of identity against external threats. The skilled mediator must, therefore, appreciate the "place" an offender is coming from and learn how to identify the various ways they may be masking their own vulnerability. The psychological term for masking is a "defense mechanism." Principle defense mechanisms operating within a defender include denial ("What else could I do?"), minimization ("It wasn't a big deal"), projection ("My friend made me" or "I was provoked") and rationalization ("They're rich, they can afford it"). Each of these prevents an offender from taking responsibility and from participating wholly in dialogue during the joint mediation session. So, the adept mediator recognizes these mechanisms and attempts to intervene accordingly.

One strategy is to help the youth engage in perspective taking, to move them away from explaining their behavior toward recognizing the impact of their actions in a personal way. It is important to begin this work during the individual meeting with the offender. Not only does this help the mediator determine whether a joint session is warranted, but it prepares the offender for hearing the victim's point of view.

Another powerful strategy mediators use to move past defensiveness is to identify strengths of the youth and focus on them in discussing the past event for which they got arrested, as well as future events, and developing a plan for how the offender will avoid criminal behavior in the future. For instance, during discussion, let's say an offender shares a story of playing a pick-up game of basketball at the neighborhood courts where one kid tried to "get into it" with him during the entire game, and how "heated" it made him feel. A mediator might skillfully paraphrase (reframe) that account by pointing out that the offender successfully managed his emotions (didn't act on his impulses to want to fight the kid) and engaged in effective decision making. These are two competencies critical to success in life and helping the offender recognize them can really bolster self-esteem. It also helps the offender recognize his/her own ability to take responsibility for his/her actions which provide the groundwork for developing a restitution plan. Drawing out and emphasizing the various strengths a youth possesses treats him/her as a whole person and therefore helps to get beyond the stigmatizing label of "offender." Participating in a process that humanizes parties is one of the most powerful benefits of VOC.

Another possible impediment to the VOC process is the fact that an offending youth's participation is not necessarily voluntary. While youth do have the right to turn down the offer to engage in VOC, they don't really have another viable option (go to court and get a criminal record). So to say that a choice exists is a misnomer. What's more, because there are inherent power imbalances between court personnel who make the initial referral to VOC and the offender, the "opportunity" to engage in VOC may seem mandated or coerced. This is problematic because a fundamental assumption of any mediation process is that it is completely voluntary. When the voluntary nature is compromised, participation in the process can range from mere compliance to hostile or resentful acquiescence. A skilled mediator needs to bear this in mind, recognize that this initial condition may trigger a defensive and uncooperative stance and work to empower the youth through the process.

In subtle ways, youth can feel they have control when a mediator doesn't push them to reveal more than they are ready to reveal, and when they refrain from expressing judgment. Being "with" the offender, especially in early stages during the individual pre-mediation session, can help to develop trust and lead to acceptance that the process is a fair one. When people feel they have a choice, they're better able to abandon their defensiveness and participate genuinely.

Pressure to participate comes not only from "the system," but may come from the parent or guardian as well. In ideal situations, parents or guardians play a supportive role in helping their child take full responsibility for their actions, which often includes offering a sincere apology and committing to follow through on a restitution plan. Supportive parents refrain from criticizing and blaming, and instead try to provide a sense of unconditional love and regard so that a youth feels protected as he/she admits wrong-doing.

Unfortunately, what happens all too often is just the opposite. A parent or guardian, understandably angry and concerned about the arrest, berates the child for being "foolish" and "not using the good sense they were born with." Parents may also impel their child to apologize and give the victim whatever he/she wants to "pay for" the offense. Clearly, that kind of pressure does little to foster a youth's self-esteem and true ownership of the offense. Indeed, such a stance robs the youth of dignity and undermines the restorative nature of the process. Of all the challenges in VOC, this is among the most difficult for a mediator to deal with. In the most effective VOC cases, this information is revealed during the individual offender meeting where a mediator has the opportunity to trouble-shoot the behavior.

One approach is to caucus separately with the parent or guardian. During the caucus, the mediator needs to validate the guardian's concerns for the child. The mediator can also try to empathize with the guardian with respect to the myriad difficulties he/she may be experiencing as a parent. And they can try to instill a sense of common ground between the parent and the VOC process in that both want to help the offending youth to become a more responsible person. Once a level of trust is developed, the mediator can suggest more productive communicative options they can both use to accomplish that goal. This is a very sensitive dialogue to engage in, and a mediator must be cautious not to trigger defensiveness in the parent.

In dire cases, a situation like this may pose an ethical dilemma for a mediator if he or she suspects some form of abuse. Most mediation programs have exceptions to confidentiality, and this is clearly one of those cases. On the other hand, a successful caucus will leave the parent feeling supported and better able to engage productively with his/her child in the individual meeting. The ability of a mediator to accomplish such work before the joint session vastly enhances the productive and restorative potential of the process.

VOC Training

Mediators who work on VOC cases are usually experienced mediators who have had basic mediation training (40 hours) and undergo an additional 32-hour advanced training which includes: 1) education on the values of restorative justice, 2) the potential benefits and costs of conferencing for both victims and offenders, 3) the special needs of the victim, 4) the special needs of the offender, and 5) a focus on a four-phase process which emphasizes in-depth initial meetings with victims and offenders (and their support members) individually as well as more involved follow-up. Most of this information has been provided throughout this chapter, so the remainder of this section will briefly recap key points in each of the four phases of the VOC process that are addressed in training.

Phase 1: Intake: Entails the referral of the case from court to the mediation agency. Case manager contacts offender to briefly describe program and to ascertain interest in proceeding. If offender fails to accept responsibility for the crime behavior or indicates a lack of willingness to engage in the process, then the case is sent back to court. This is the first screen to prevent re-victimization. The case will go on to the next phase if the offender wants to proceed.

Phase 2: Preparation (pre-mediation): Initial contact with the victim is made, and the program is described to them. If the victim indicates willingness, a face-to-face meeting is scheduled to hear the victim's story of the event, to more fully explain the process, to gain consent and to prepare him or her for face-to-face participation with the offender. A similar meeting is held with the offender and his/her guardian. Preparation for both victim and offender also includes identifying possible options for restitution such as financial payment, personal or community service, and/or social services for offender.

Phase 3: Joint Mediation Session: Parties are brought together to discuss the crime event and its impact on each party, and to develop a restitution plan. This phase proceeds much like "standard" mediation. If successful, the phase concludes with a signed agreement and a sense of emotional healing for all of the parties.

Phase 4: Follow-up: The case manager follows up with both parties to monitor progress on restitution agreement, and whether it is accomplishing the restorative goals it was designed to meet.

CONCLUDING COMMENTS

The traditional criminal justice system has been ineffective in rehabilitating youth and reducing recidivism of offenders. Nor has it addressed the needs of victims. Victim offender mediation/conferencing is a restorative justice process based in the humanistic tradition which seeks to address those shortcomings. It does so by providing a unique opportunity for victims of crime to confront their aggressors and take an active part in deciding what should be done to restore the harm. In this way, victims are empowered.

The VOC process also transforms the impersonal criminal justice process into an interpersonal encounter for offenders where they are better able to understand the personal nature and impact of their criminal behavior on others, take ownership for the harms they have inflicted, and then be given the chance to redress these harms. Such a process allows offenders to transcend the stigmatization of being labeled a criminal and move beyond the incidence with improved self-esteem and regard for others. Mediators skilled in facilitating this process contribute to a society that endeavors to take responsibility for and foster constructive development of all its members.

Case Study

The following case study is an example of a joint conference that went awry. It is offered here to illustrate the particular challenges inherent in complex family dynamics and the need to be sensitive to subtle cues parties may be expressing. In this particular case, the offender was a 14-year-old African-American male who was arrested for harassing a 13-year-old Caucasian female student on the bus. According to the arrest warrant, the harassment involved a physical shove as well as intimidating threats of future abuse. The bus driver reported the case and the next day the offender was arrested at school, taken to the Youth Study Center (the juvenile detention center) and placed in a holding cell until his mother came to pick him up. When she arrived later that afternoon, the detention officer discussed the arrest with them and gave them the option of avoiding a criminal record by participating in the VOC program. The officer informed them that a case manager from Good Shepherd Mediation Program would be contacting them to describe the program further and to set up meetings. They agreed to give the program a try.

Within a week, the case manager called, described the program, and explained that before they could move forward, the victim and her family needed to give their consent. At that time, individual meetings with each of the parties and their families would be scheduled, followed by the joint conference if both parties still wanted to meet. The individual meetings took place and the mediators gathered enough information to feel confident that a joint session was appropriate. There was one interesting difference in this case as it went to joint conference, and that is that the mother was extremely concerned about her daughter being further intimidated by confronting the male offender. Yet she wanted to meet with him face to face to convey to him how angry she was about the attack and to ask him for a commitment that he would refrain from any further harassment. So the joint conference took place without the actual victim, but with her advocate (her mother). Additionally, the offender showed up for the joint session not only with his mother (who had participated in the individual meeting) but with his stepfather (who had not participated in the individual meeting).

It is acceptable in VOC cases for a victim or offender to have more than one support person with them, so the presence of the stepfather was not an initial concern. The mediators were both male; one was African American and the other Caucasian, to mirror the ethnicity of the parties. The parties were invited into the conference room and took their seats. The mediators gave their opening statements, which included explaining that they had met privately with both parties and that all parties present were willing to participate to work things out. They also explained how the process would unfold. In this case, the victim's mother wanted to speak first, so she was given the floor to tell her story. As she described the aftermath of the event and how frightened her daughter had been (and still was), you could see how visibly uncomfortable the offender was. His hands were folded in his lap and his head was hung low; he had difficulty trying to hold any eye contact with the victim's mother as she related her story. He clearly looked ashamed and remorseful.

After the victim's mother had finished, the mediators asked the offender to summarize what she had said. The offender was soft-spoken and related back with few words what he'd heard, emphasizing that the victim had been and still was really afraid of him. The mediator then asked if he was surprised to learn that information. The offender answered "yeah" and kind of grinned. The mediator, catching the flash of a grin, asked what the offender was thinking and feeling at that moment. The offender, with his mother and stepfather sitting beside him, said "I dunno . . . I guess I'm surprised cuz I was just messin around with her. I didn't mean it to be serious."

The mother seemed to find this statement both reassuring and incredulous. In fact, when the mediator asked her how she felt now, she responded that she was relieved to hear him say that he intended no harm, but was dumbfounded that the youth thought he could push a girl and threaten her and think that she wouldn't feel intimidated. The mediator then asked the youth to tell his version of what happened. He explained that rather than shoving the girl, he actually intentionally bumped into her with the side of his arm and while smiling said, "ya betta watch out girl or I'm gonna mess with ya." He explained that he thought the girl was "down" (cute) and that he was just trying to show off in front of his friends. He further explained that he was surprised when she ran off the bus, and was even more surprised when he got arrested the next day at school.

He finished his story by looking down and shyly saying, still in a very quiet voice, "Ma'am, I'm really sorry I scared your daughter." The mother seemed clearly relieved at this point as she smiled at the offender and nodded her head. All seemed to be going really well with the session up until now, as there appeared to be a palpable understanding of the nature of the event and the mediators were poised to bring the discussion of what could be done to "make things right"; to restore the harm.

However, at this point the offender's stepfather jumped in, slapped the offender on the upper arm and said, "Come on son, be a man, give the lady a real apology." Up until now, the offender's mother had been very quiet and maintained a demur posture. The stepfather had been listening intently, occasionally trying to butt in, but had not interrupted the process. After issuing this command, however, the rhythm of the process was broken. The offender looked up at one of the mediators, with a pleading sense in his eyes, but remained silent. The mother attempted to say something to support her son, but the stepfather put his hand on her forearm as if to say, "don't say a thing." The stepfather continued to berate the offender to "give the woman the apology she deserves; don't be a sissy."

All parties were alarmed and taken off guard by this abrupt interruption. Clearly trying to gain composure, one of the mediators remarked that the stepfather seemed very agitated and "would he mind taking a seat in the lobby for a few minutes." He angrily acquiesced to the request.

As the parties attempted to regroup, sounds of the stepfather grumbling just outside the door were apparent. The offender looked intently at the mediator with eyes imploring him to do something, but would not say a word. As the mediators awkwardly attempted to get back on track, the stepfather burst into the room, grabbed the offender's mother arm and yelled at the offender, "We're leaving . . .

this is bullsh*t." The room in a panic, the three exited before anyone could stop them and the mediators and the victim's mother were left at the table looking at each other with shock. The mediators attempted to reach closure with the victim's mother, explaining how the process would proceed from here. After she left, they debriefed for an hour.

QUESTIONS FOR DISCUSSION

1. What went wrong in this mediation?
2. Could anything have been done to prevent the outburst from the father?
3. What could the mediators have done to prevent this?"
4. What are the mediator's ethical responsibilities to the families?
5. What are the ethical responsibilities of the mediators with respect to the family, particularly the offender, now?
6. Should law enforcement notified be about this situation?
7. Do we suspect abuse by the stepfather that would warrant us revealing the details of the case?

Role Play: The Fight Between Friends

The following role-play is fairly typical of the types of cases that get referred to the Philadelphia VOC program. In this case, both victim and offender are 15 year old females who attend the same school and have known each other for several years. They both come from single parent families and each has a younger sibling. Mediators should consider the family dynamics of each party and discuss how they may be impacting the girls' behavior.

INFORMATION FOR ERIN ANDREWS

You were arrested for assaulting another classmate on the bus while going home from high school. You hit Irene Dunn in the face, giving her a black eye and a broken front tooth. Because school officials could not reach your mother, you had to spend the night in a holding cell with other juvenile offenders. You are mad at Irene for a number of reasons, but what upsets you the most is that she is dating someone you were interested in and she knew this. You also are upset with her because she has been spreading rumors that you have been sexually active with a number of boys in school.

You have been told that if you participate in a victim/offender conference, you will not have to go to court, and possibly jail. You feel that you have nothing to lose, so you and your mother have agreed to the conference.

INFORMATION FOR IRENE DUNN

On your way home from high school last week, you were assaulted by Erin Andrews. She punched you in the face, giving you a black eye and a broken front tooth. When Erin attacked you, she said that you were a "disloyal, back-stabbing bitch who needed to be taught a lesson." You were shocked by Erin's behavior, and covered yourself until other students could pull Erin off of you.

You were surprised by her behavior, because you had no idea what Erin was talking about. You used to be good friends until about a month ago when you started dating a guy named Tony. You knew that Erin liked him, but you also knew he was not interested in dating Erin. Once you and Tony began dating, Erin stopped talking to you. When you asked her what was wrong, she would just roll her eyes and walk away with no explanation. You think that she might be upset with you because you jokingly told some people that she was sleeping around.

REFERENCES

Strang, H. (2001). The crime victim movement as a force in civil society. In H. Strang and J. Braithwaite (eds.), *Restorative Justice and Civil Society,* 69-82. Cambridge, UK: Cambridge University Press.

Umbreit, M. S., Bradshaw, W., and Greenwood, J. (1998). Victim offender mediation training manual. Center for Restorative Justice & Peacemaking. School of Social Work, University of Minnesota.

Umbreit, M. S. (1998). Restorative justice through victim-offender mediation: A multi-site assessment, *Western Criminology Review,* available at http:/wcr.sonoma.edu/v1n1/umbreit.html.

Zehr, H. (2002). *The Little Book of Restorative Justice.* Good Books: Intercourse, PA.

Chapter 10

Mediating Disputes Involving Youth Gangs

Bruce C. McKinney

One of the more important points for advocating mediation to resolve disputes is that it's most effective when the disputing parties have a *continuing pattern of interaction.* People are usually not too concerned about digging into issues with other disputants when they know they will never see the other disputant again. However, when disputing parties know they will have to continue to interact with the other disputant, mediation becomes a more viable option.

The fact that mediation does not identify a "winner" or "loser" in the conflict makes it especially useful for mediating disputes involving youth gangs. Gangs that will continue to interact for issues such as turf and self respect only prolong the agony when there is a clearly identified winner or loser. The fact that mediation empowers disputants is especially important for gangs. Gangs who feel disrespected and powerless are more prone to lash out with violence. Once a gang loses face, many see violence as the only proper response. The use of mediation which addresses all of these issues makes it a much better option for reducing gang violence than other forms of dispute resolution.

THE YOUTH GANG PROBLEM

Youth gangs are not just problems of big cities. Older Americans might recall the 1961 film *West Side Story*. It might surprise them that many that gangs now inhabit locations more consistent with *The Music Man* than *The Naked City;* there is trouble in River City. In its most recent survey on gang activity in the United States, the U. S. Department of Justice reported that almost 30 percent of locations classified as "rural" had at least four to six gangs and at least 51-200 gang members. The situation is far worse in cities with populations greater than 250,000. Sixty-one percent of the cities studied reported having more than 30 gangs and more than 1000 gang members (Egley, 2005). According to a study by Egley and Arjunan (2002), there are more than 24,500 different youth gangs in the U.S., and more than 750,000 teens and young adults involved in gang activity. Another problem identified by the U.S. Department of Justice is gang migration, where members of big city gangs spread out across the country in their search for new markets for drug distribution. However, the Department of Justice concludes that local, indigenous gangs are the major cause of gang problems (Maxxon, 1998). Though the type and nature of youth gangs can vary as much as the geography from where they exist, the National Youth Gang Center defines a youth gang as:

> a self-formed association of peers having the following characteristics: three or more members, generally ages 12 to 24; a name and some sense of identity, generally indicated by such symbols as style of clothing, graffiti, and hand signs: some degree of permanence and organization; and an elevated level of involvement in delinquent or criminal activity. (National Youth Gang Center, 2006).

While a gang from New York City may have many differences from a gang in rural Kansas, Moore (1998) identifies conditions within a community that must exist before a gathering of individual youths becomes an organized gang: 1) ineffective and alienating family and school systems, 2) too much free time that is not consumed with prosocial roles, 3) lack of employment, and 4) a place to congregate. The major reasons youths join gangs are ones any adolescent can identify with: socialization and protection (Decker & Van Winkle, 1996; Pererson, Taylor, & Esbensen, 2004). If these reasons are combined with an environment with few or no extracurricular activities, obviously there would be a greater tendency for an individual to join a gang. However, as Peterson et al. (2004) conclude, youths are far more likely to be a victim of a violent crime while in a gang.

In an attempt to answer the question "What are the characteristics of individuals who join gangs?" the U.S. Department of Justice's research concluded that gang members are socially inept, have lower self-esteem, sociopathic tendencies, a high level of interaction with antisocial peers, and a low level of interaction with prosocial peers. (Esbensen, 2000). The wide variety of offenses committed by youth gangs are enough to cause any community concern, especially those in large cities. The most common offenses committed by large city gangs are drug use, drug trafficking, and violent crime (Howell & Decker, 1999). The use of a firearm is a major practice in gang violence; 84 percent of the gang-problem jurisdictions, reported at least one use of a firearm by one or more gang members in a crime of assault (Egley & Arjunan, 2002).

However, the problems associated with gangs in school settings, though less frequent than on the city streets, are still a cause for concern. Gottfredson and Gottfredson (2001) found a -.49 correlation between school safety and presence of school gangs, and there was an increased amount of victimization in schools with gang members present. Chandler, Chapman, Rand, and Taylor (1998) reported that between 1989 and 1995 the percentage of students reporting the presence of gangs at their schools nearly doubled. Additionally, Chandler et al., found a strong correlation between the presence of gangs in schools and the presence of drugs and firearms at these schools. Their study listed the reasons why students concluded that there were gangs in their schools: 1) the gang had a name, 2) had a recognized leader, 3) had their own identifiable territory, 4) turf was tagged or marked with graffiti, 5) there were identifiable violent acts committed by the gang, 6) clothing was identifiable with gang membership, and 7) they were aware of gang member tattoos (Chandler et al., 1998).

REACTIVE APPROACHES TO GANG PROBLEMS

While it is only speculative that the existence of gangs in schools may increase, it seems a logical conclusion with schools cutting extracurricular activities as states try to balance budgets. What is most alarming about gang activity in schools is that measures to curb gang violence and activities are largely reactive and not proactive. Howell and Lynch (2000) identified typical security steps schools used as measures against gangs: 1) security guards, 2) school staff supervising hallways, 3) metal detectors, 4) locked doors during the day, 5) requiring visitors to sign-in, and 6) locker checks. The National Institute of Justice (Kenney & Watson, 1999) call this process called "target hardening" and offer common criticisms of this approach: 1) an oppressive security environment might worsen relations between educators and the police, and 2) such an environment might harm the function of the educational process in schools. While such measures may protect students during the school hours, they do nothing to prevent gang violence after school is dismissed.

GANG DISPUTES AND MEDIATION

With the plethora of studies reporting the success of peer mediation programs in schools, it is interesting that the two agencies that are responsible for much of the published literature on gangs in the United States—the U.S. Department of Justice's Office of Juvenile Justice and Delinquency Prevention and the National Youth Violence Prevention Resource Center—do not report on any studies on the result of school mediation programs for the reduction of gang-related problems. In fact, there are few if any studies on the use of mediation to curb gang violence. The prevailing thought seems to be one of gang prevention with programs such as G.R.E.A.T. (Gang Resistance and Education Training) modeled after the drug resistance program D.A.R.E.[1] There are many publications available that discuss programs to solve problems in schools, but once again these do not involve any material on mediating gang disputes.[2]

One of the few published studies on the use of mediation as a gang prevention strategy was published fifteen years ago (Mendelsohn, 1991). Mediation was used to solve problems between two gangs in which violence had escalated to the point that several people were stabbed and beaten. One gang was predominantly female, the other male. The two groups discussed the two issues that were causing problems between the gang—gender and cultural problems—and were able to reach a mediated agreement that lasted over a year.

Tabish and Orell (1996) reported on the use of mediation between gangs at a middle school in Albuquerque, New Mexico. The results were promising. They concluded that the formal mediation process, when used between two rival gangs, markedly curbed inter-gang violence and made the campus a safer place for the student body and adult population. This school did not use student mediators, but mediators from the New Mexico Center for Dispute Resolution.

CONSIDERATIONS FOR GANG MEDIATIONS

While metal detectors might reduce violence in the halls of schools, they do not prevent future violence by gang members who leave school property. It is hoped that administrators realize that gang mediation should be seen as a proactive process to reduce gang problems, and are not an attempt to throw water on a fire after it has already begun.

An important initial question to consider when planning mediations involving gangs in schools is whether to use student mediators or professional adult mediators? As reported in the New Mexico study, when there were mediations between individual gang members, student peer mediators were used which were drawn from a long standing and successful peer mediation program. However, when mediations were needed for disputes between two groups of gang members, professional adult mediators were employed.

Because of the potential for violence while mediating gang disputes, adult mediators with extensive mediation experience *and knowledge of local gangs should be employed.* Mediators who have training in social services and experience dealing with delinquent youths would also be good candidates for gang mediations. Mediators should not be local school administrators—some may question their neutrality or motives—but qualified mediators from community mediation centers, or professional mediators who are viewed as neutral by the gang members. While mediation might not be a panacea for all gang problems, it certainly could be an extremely effective preventative and proactive measure for gang related problems. Some basic tenets of mediating disputes that involve gang members will be discussed, but first there are several important decisions that must be made before gang mediation can be implemented.

While a plethora of books have been devoted to community mediation, family mediation, etc., there is a void of information when it comes to the mediation of gang-related conflicts. The most comprehensive guide for mediating gang disputes is presented in *The School Mediator's Field Guide* (Cohen, 1999).

GANG MEDIATION PROCEDURES

First and foremost, if gang mediation is to be successful, mediators must work with community-based agencies that have experience in dealing with gangs. These agencies can serve vital functions for mediators by helping them learn about the gangs they will work with, arrange preliminary meetings between gang members and mediators, and help with the follow-up and support of mediated agreements (Cohen, 1999). Perhaps the most important variable in gang mediation is trust between gang members and mediators. Simply put, trust must be based on mutual respect. If the mediators do not show respect for the gang members, they should not expect trust to be reciprocated, defeating the mediation before it begins.

Intake procedures are probably even more important when mediating gang disputes. Since each side will usually be represented by more than one individual, the mediators should learn of the specifics of the dispute before the disputants meet face-to-face. If the dispute between the gangs is hostile, it is best to give parties a chance to vent in a preliminary intake than in the open mediation session (Cohen, 1999).

During this intake, the mediators can judge the severity of potential for violence between the two parties, and assign security personnel as needed. As Cohen (1999) points out, when conflicts are between two groups, it is too risky to begin the mediation without any knowledge of the dispute. This is especially true for gang mediations. Additionally, mediators can use preliminary sessions to demonstrate their neutrality. The following should be covered during the preliminary meeting between the mediators and the disputants:

> (1) A discussion of the mediation process and determination as to whether mediation is appropriate for the current dispute. (2) An analysis of the urgency of the conflict—what will happen if the dispute is not resolved? (3) If appropriate, encouragement to use mediation to resolve the dispute (Cohen, 1999).

It is also easier for the mediators to get parties to agree to the ground rules before the mediation, so hostile remarks will less likely to be aired during the mediation. It is essential that the ground rules of mediation be clearly stated and enforced when the mediators introduce the process. As one gang mediator says, "Some of these kids in gangs have never followed rules. They do not know what rules are for. Even when you state them, they will break them to challenge you."[3] If the mediators allow gang members to break rules that are not enforced, chaos and physical violence could follow.

SPECIAL CONSIDERATIONS FOR GANG MEDIATIONS

In general, community mediations are usually held at mediation centers across the country where a safe environment is taken for granted. However, issues of security are the most pressing concerns for the location of mediations involving gang disputes. This is essential for the protection of both the mediators and the disputants. If either feels threatened, the success of the mediation is questionable. To achieve a safe environment, Cohen (1999) recommends the following: 1) the implementation of a "no weapons" policy, and informing all disputants that they will be frisked before the mediation begins; 2) the prohibition of wearing gang-related clothing; 3) encouraging spokespersons from the gangs to appear, not all gang members; 4) security personnel located outside or inside the mediation room, and 5) the escorting of gang members to "safe zones" after the mediation has concluded.

This information must be communicated to and agreed upon by all participants in the mediation before the process begins.

Gang disputes that cause problems in both rural and urban areas are usually caused by gang members of high-school age. An important question to be considered is whether or not gang mediations should take part on a school campus or at another site perceived as neutral to gang members. One problem with allowing gang mediations on school grounds is the reluctance of school administrators to allow this type of intervention. By allowing gang mediation on school grounds, administrators are admitting that there are gangs in their schools—something administrators might not like to admit. Simply being identified as a gang member (e.g., wearing gang colors or tattoos) may warrant suspension. If the dispute is between gang members who attend the same school, the local school may be perceived as a neutral site. If the dispute is between gang members who attend different schools, a neutral site independent of the schools is preferable.

As with other types of mediation, confidentiality is an issue that mediators must deal with effectively. If a mediator learns of crimes committed or other laws broken, what are their moral and/or legal responsibilities? Does their state allow mediators with the same privilege as given to attorneys and their clients? These questions are crucial if the gangs have previously engaged in violent or illegal behavior. Therefore, the expediency of the mediation must be carefully assessed by the mediators, as well as the consequences of not holding mediations when the consequences are clearly identified. While models of mediation may vary, the traditional mediation model (introduction, explanation of mediation, defining the conflict, seeking solutions, reaching agreement) may be employed in gang mediation.

It is not recommended that the traditional seating arrangements be employed in gang mediation. There should be as much physical space as possible allowed between the opposing gangs. Additionally, any instruments that could be used as weapons should not be allowed in the mediation room—this includes pencils and pens.

When agreements are reached in gang mediation, they must involve all gang members. This may take time to allow gang representatives to discuss the agreement with their respective gang members. If this is not done, the empowering aspect of mediation will not be recognized by all gang members, and agreements might fall apart. However as with any mediation, mediators must not pressure gang members into agreement that they feel they do not own. Another important aspect in the agreement is to determine if the agreement reached is realistic based on past behaviors. If two disputing gangs reach an agreement that does not seem tenable based on past events, the mediators should test this with the disputants.

THE AQUARIUS PROJECT

The Aquarius Project, a highly successful gang mediation program in the San Francisco Bay Area, deals with gang disputes that have life or death consequences.[3] This program was initially conceived to stop gun violence in Boston through the "Streetworker Program." Staff members in this program are trained in conflict resolution and mediation, and are available to gang members and their families to mediate gang dispute and truces, and act as a go-between for gang members and existing governmental and community programs. Because of the volatile nature of the gangs they deal with, the Aquarius Project utilizes some practices that are different from what might be considered a typical mediation. Hewitt R. Joyner, III, the vice president of the Aquarius Project in the San Francisco Bay Area, says that the most important thing in mediating gang disputes is the preparation before the actual mediation, to find out as much as possible about the nature of the gang, its members, and the type of dispute. This involves getting information from a variety of sources that have had contact with the gangs before (e.g., police gang task forces, probation agencies, youth-service agencies, etc.).

When gang members arrive for the mediation, they are searched and are seated at the same table but at different ends from the other gang. The number of mediators and law enforcement officers at the mediation always outnumber the number of the disputants. As Joyner says, "The gang members need to respect who we are and the fact that we can always be more aggressive than they are."[4] An important aspect of this type of mediation is reality testing because the "what-ifs" have deadly consequences: lives may be lost if the mediation does not take place. This project does not allow any more than three disputants from each side during the mediation. Disputants are told to only discuss the current dispute and not bring up other complaints from past grievances with the other gang. This is a proactive program with the purpose of stopping gang violence before it begins, and is used with more violent gangs that contribute to the large number of homicides and criminal offenses committed by gangs.

CONCLUDING COMMENTS

Gang mediation is probably the least studied and least understood of all the forms of mediation; Y the consequences of not resolving gang disputes can have deadly consequences. While reactive measures (e.g., metal detectors) may give those in school a feeling of protection from gang violence, they do little to prevent gang violence outside of the school. The gang problem in the United States is rising, not declining. Until more effective measures of *preventing* gang violence are implemented, the crisis of gang-related criminal offenses will continue, not only in the inner city, but in more suburban areas as well. Even more important, mediations between gangs are seen as proactive measures—an attempt to stop violence *before* it takes place. With the success of such programs like the Aquarius Project, it seems that mediation can be a more viable method of dealing with conflicts associated with gangs. The alternative will only be a rise in gang-related problems. The success of mediation in resolving a wide variety of disputes is widely published and understood; why more attempts like the Aquarius Project are not implemented to reduce gang problems is a troubling question. Our children deserve better.

Case Study: The Street Wizards and the Castle Boys

The Castle Boys' turf is located in an eight-block square area bordered by Franklin Street, Market Street, South Quincy Street, and Oak Street. This area is "tagged" with their blue and gold colors, with "CB" painted on many buildings, fences, and billboards. This is a Hispanic gang, and they have controlled this area for over ten years. Two people have been murdered since the Castle Boys took control of this area: one was an unfortunate tourist who got lost and wandered onto their turf looking for directions; the other was a member of their rival gang the Street Wizards who was caught tagging while on their turf.

The Street Wizards turf begins on the other side of Main Street. The Wizards, an African American gang, once occupied some of what is now the Castle Boys turf. However, with the rapid influx of Hispanics into the city—many who have joined the Castle Boys—the Wizards decided to give up a two-block area of their former turf and move four blocks south of Main Street. This created a two-block buffer between the two gangs, which is now referred to as the Demilitarized Zone (or DMZ). However, each gang sees the DMZ as an extension of their territory. Though they do not occupy it, violent incidents have occurred when a rival gang member was seen in the DMZ. However, if no one from either gang encroaches on this territory, the gangs are willing to accept this as a buffer between their two gangs.

Though the Castle Boys and the Street Wizards are violent enemies, they respect each other's turf, and are well aware of the consequences of trespassing onto enemy turf. However, a new and more volatile set of circumstances occurred when a playground was built in the DMZ. There are many younger children—brothers, sisters, offspring—of both gangs who want to use the new playground.

Two weeks ago, a fight broke out between opposite gang members who accompanied the children to the playground. Additionally, members of the Street Wizards tagged the playground with their black and orange colors, angering the Castle Boys, who then tagged the playground as well. Because of these problems, the playground in the DMZ is now used very little because people in the neighborhood see it as an extremely dangerous environment and they are afraid to let their children play there. The children and younger siblings of gang members are upset because they all liked the playground and want to continue to use it. However, it is now a matter of pride between the two gangs as to who can claim the playground as the its turf. Saving face is very important to each gang, and both gangs feel that it would be destructive to gang morale and pride if they conceded the playground to the other gang. Additionally, members of both gangs indicated that they would lose respect for their gang leaders if they did not try to claim the playground as their own.

QUESTIONS FOR DISCUSSION

1. Do you think this conflict can be resolved through mediation? Why or why not?
2. If this dispute is mediated, what information should the mediators try to discover during preliminary sessions with each gang?
3. What are the underlying issues in this conflict?
4. Which gang members should appear in the mediation?
5. What topics of discussion should the mediators try to avoid?

Role Play: The Turf Dispute

INFORMATION FOR CARLOS BELTRAN

You have been the leader of the Castle Boys for the last three years. In that time, you have seen your gang continue to grow and feel that you have a very strong membership. Your main problems have been with the Street Wizards. Though they no longer claim some turf your gang now controls, every now and then there is an incident in which a gang member from the Street Wizards tries to tag buildings on your home turf. This has led to several violent incidents, and there is a great deal of tension between the two gangs.

Recently, some residents in the neighborhood between your gang and the Street Wizards built a playground for local children. It is not a problem when these children play there, but every time a child who is related to a member of the Castle Boys wants to play there, he or she must be escorted to the playground by a gang member. Unfortunately the Street Wizards have been doing the same thing, and this has led to violent confrontations between the members of the rival gangs who have brought their children to the playground. One member of your gang was stabbed by a member of the Street Wizards right in front of his little brother.

You realize that this area between your gang and the Street Wizards (known as the Demilitarized Zone or DMZ) will never be controlled by either gang. You need to resolve this problem before a child is hurt by violent interactions between your gang and the Street Wizards. The local police have told you that if you do not want them harassing your gang, that you have to meet with the leader of the Street Wizards in a mediation.

INFORMATION FOR TERRELL DAVIS

You are the leader of the gang known as the Street Wizards. You used to control ten city blocks, but your area of control has declined because of a newer and more powerful Latino gang, the Castle Boys. You have had several encounters with this gang, and usually the result is a shooting or a stabbing. There is a two-block wide buffer between you and the Castle Boys which the local residents call the "Demilitarized Zone." Neither gang claims this territory as their own turf even though your gang used to control it several years ago. A serious problem has now arisen between you and the Castle Boys. Two months ago a civic leader approached you and asked you if your gang could help built a playground on the DMZ, and all of your members were happy to help with this project since many of your gang members have younger sisters and brothers, and some even have children. Though you know that helping with this project did not give your gang exclusive rights to this project, you still you have more of a claim to this territory than the Castle Boys. Problems have arisen because when the children and siblings of the Castle Boys come to play on this playground, they usually bring their older brothers who are active gang members. This has resulted in a number of violent conflicts between you and the Castle Boys. You think it is okay for the children of the Street Wizards to play in the playground of the DMZ, you just do not want their older brothers accompanying them.

NOTES

[1] For an explanation on a G.R.E.A.T middle school component, see http://www.great-online.org/corecurriculum.htm.

[2] See for example, Crawford D., and Bodine, R. (1996). *Conflict Resolution Education: A Guide to Implementing Programs in Schools, Youth-Serving Organizations, and Community Juvenile Justice Settings:* Program Report. Office of Juvenile Justice and Delinquency Programs, U.S. Department of Justice, and Safe and Drug-Free Schools Program, U.S. Department of Education.

[3] For further information see http://aquariusproject.org/.
[4] Hewitt Joyner, III, June 30, 2006, personal interview.

REFERENCES

Chandler, K. A., Chapman, C. D., Rand, M., and Taylor, B. M. (1998). *Student reports of school crime: 1989 and 1995.* Washington, D.C.: United States Departments of Education

Cohen, R. (1999). *The School Mediator's Field Guide.* Watertown, MA: School Mediation Associates.

Decker, S. H., and Van Winkle, B. (1996). *Life in the Gang: Family, Friends, and Violence.* New York: Cambridge University Press.

Egley, A., Jr. (2005). Highlights of the 2002-2003 national youth gang survey. *Juvenile Justice Bulletin.* Washington, D.C.: U.S. Department of Justice, Office of Juvenile Justice and Delinquency Programs.

Egley, A., Jr., and Arjunan, M. (2002). Highlights of the 2000 national youth gang survey. *Juvenile Justice Bulletin* Washington, D.C.: U.S. Department of Justice, Office of Juvenile Justice and Delinquency Programs.

Ebensen, F. (2000). Preventing adolescent gang violence. *Juvenile Justice Bulletin.* Washington, D.C.: U.S. Department of Justice, Office of Juvenile Justice and Delinquency Programs.

Gottfredson, G. D., and Gottfredson, D. C. (2001). *Gang problems and gang programs in a national sample of schools.* Ellicott City, MD: Gottfredson Associates, Inc.

Howell, J. C., and Decker, S. H. (1999). The youth gangs, drugs, and violence connection." *Juvenile Justice Bulletin.* Washington, D.C.: U.S. Department of Justice, Office of Juvenile Justice and Delinquency Programs.

Howell, J. C., and Lynch, J. P. (2000). Youth gangs in school. *Juvenile Justice Bulletin.* Washington, D.C.: U.S. Department of Justice, Office of Juvenile Justice and Delinquency Programs.

Kenney, D. J., and Watson, S. (1999). Crime in schools: Reducing conflict with student problem solving. *Research in Brief.* Washington, D.C. National Institute of Justice.

Maxson, C. L. (1998). Gang Members on the move. *Juvenile Justice Bulletin.* Washington, D.C.: U.S. Department of Justice, Office of Juvenile Justice and Delinquency Programs.

Mendelsohn, D. O. (1991). Mediation: A gang prevention strategy. *MCS Conciliation Quarterly, 10,* 5-6.

Moore, J. W. (1998). Understanding Youth Street Gangs: Economic Restructuring and the Urban Underclass. In M. W. Watts (Ed.), *Cross-Cultural Perspectives on Youth Gangs and Violence* (pp. 65-78), Stamford, CT: JAI.

National Youth Gang Center, (2006). *Frequently Asked Questions Regarding Gangs.* Available from http//www.iir.com/nygc/fac.htm.

Peterson D., Taylor, T. J., and Esbensen, F. (2004). Gang Membership and Violent Victimization. *Justice Quarterly, 21,* 794-815.

Tabish, K. R., and Orell, L. H. (1996). "Respect: Gang Mediation at Albuquerque, New Mexico's Washington middle school." *School Counselor, 44,* 65-70.

Chapter 11

Faith-Based Disputes and Mediation Intervention

William D. Kimsey
Sallye S. Trobaugh

Faith-based organizations, like synagogues, temples, churches, and others, create a reality for their membership, which defines a member's worldview and how the organization governs through interlinked systems of symbols, schemas, and standards. Talk, dialogue, and negotiation at all levels, including interpersonal, group, and organizational shape believers' identity and experience. This shared reference sustains the substance of group and individual identity. Social and religious contexts provide for experiences where believers reify virtues, priorities, and ideals of their faith culture (Said & Funk, 2001; Said, Funk & Kunkle, 2003); normative practices make social interaction meaningful.

Deep-seated standards provide boundaries for achieving individual growth and transformation promised by faith-based organizations. Individual behavior must derive from and reflect organizational beliefs and higher-level cognitive schemas such as ideologies, orthodoxies, orientations, and more. Compliance with organizational values is implicit in all activities of the group. Yet, the premise of choice coupled with conviction often creates defensive communication patterns when faith-based members debate and dialogue amongst themselves. Members with minority opinions risk persecution within the organization if they do not represent the "official" position.

Faith-based organizations typically operate in religious paradigms, which impact all aspects of group and organizational life, including setting values, solving problems, resolving conflict, and more. Conflict in faith-based organizations often is tempered with unspoken tenets threatening rupture among member believers and severance of relationship with deity, both critical for definition of self, others, and worldview. Uncertainty, which surrounds faith-based disputes, coupled with difficulty of not knowing precisely the best way to respond, often starts a conflict-avoidance cycle that may create an appearance of submission to organizational values when just the opposite is true.

The purpose of this chapter is to present a framework for understanding faith-based conflict and resolving believer disputes through mediation. A seven-phase model of believer conflict is described with a comparative discussion of facilitative and transformative mediation practices. Examples of ways the authors have used the conflict schema and different experiences serving as mediators in faith-based organizations are presented.

A Schema for Faith-Based Mediators

The seven-phase model of conflict identifies patterns of conflict behavior individuals may choose when their commitment to the organization and its members is disturbed, distressed, or deteriorating. The model hypothesizes that there are points within the seven phases in which organizational leaders can resolve developing problems in the organization.

Critical moments in the conflict process present opportunities for intervention. Organizational leaders and mediators will intervene when conflict resolution is most likely to be successful. Use of mediation in key conflict phases can reduce or prevent destructive outcomes.

The attributes of the seven-phase model as presented by Kimsey, Trobaugh, McKinney, Hoole, Thelk, and Davis (2006) include worldview, frame of irony, relational dialectics, and conflict phases. Figure 11.1 presents a schema of the model.

Worldview constitutes values, attitudes, and behavior which provide meaning for an individual (Kimsey & Fuller, 1998).

The War on Terror demonstrates the power of religious paradigms for spawning different groups with similar visions about what people should believe and how they should live, such as the Hezbollah or the al-Qaeda both declaring jihad against the Capitalist and Judeo-Christian worldviews.

Worldviews are reinforced by systems that justify individual beliefs. Frame of Irony deconstructs challenges to worldview by dissembling thoughts, making as-

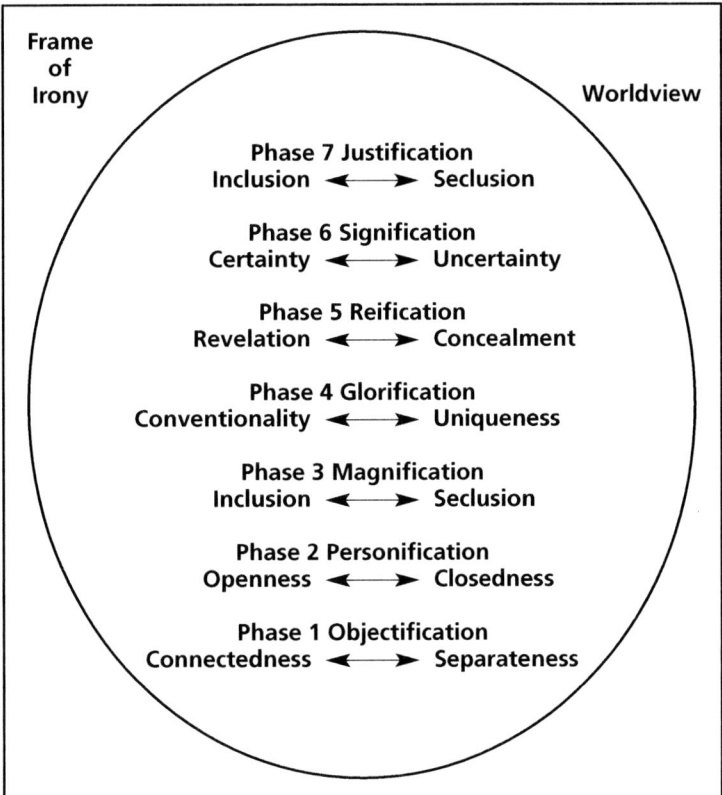

Figure 11.1
The Seven-Phase Model of Conflict

sertions or performing actions that negatively project the motivation behind a challenge. For instance, if inquiry is made into why the religious leader lives a higher standard of living than the believer members, the inquiry is met with rebuke, suggesting the intent behind the question reflects a critical spirit that harbors jealousy. The frame of irony serves the purpose of deflecting reasonable inquiry for finding the truth, thus ensuring the existing worldview.

Relational dialectics create push-pull contradictions inherent in engaging frames of irony and making challenges to existing worldviews. Unified by interdependence, the dichotomous predispositions coexist in a nexus of tensions which achieve resolution by negating each other. The interplay between relational dialects, including *Connectedness-Separateness, Predictability-Novelty, Openness-Closedness, Inclusion-Seclusion, Conventionality-Uniqueness, Revelation-Concealment,* and the frame of irony creates a link where the interdependence with the opposite impulse and independence from the opposite impulse occurs. The following describes the seven phases of conflict in faith-based organizations.

SEVEN PHASES OF CONFLICT

Phase 1: Objectification. The first step involves the believer objectifying self and others. Objectification is the base step for ultimately proving that one is right. When the believer objectifies, he or she projects an independent reality, making another individual impersonal. In other words, people are put in categories or boxes. For example, a woman, whose name is Elizabeth teaches Sunday school at a church and has been doing so for over twenty-five years; she is now 83. The church elders hired a young, new minister, Bob, who, through his inexperience, promptly dismissed Elizabeth because, in his interpretation of the Bible, women should not be teaching. The minister used his interpretation of the Bible to justify his actions—dismissing the Sunday school teacher, whom Bob framed as an object and did not acknowledge as a person. A dialectical tension occurs in Phase 1: Objectification, when the individual believer attempts to achieve connectedness by agreeing with the organization's worldview while at the same time attempts to speak out, knowing such boldness may pose a threat of separation.

Phase 2: Personification. The second step, personification, starts with the believer's casual conversation with other members of the group without disclosing his or her position. Interpersonal discussion focuses now on personal deficits of others who are not like-minded, particularly those in leadership. Elizabeth, in the above example, could have challenged the minister's actions, but instead starts talking to friends and parents of children whom she has taught, asking for their opinions about her dismissal. Likewise, Bob responds to friends' and members' inquiries about the dismissal citing the Bible as his authority for the action, all the while marking who agrees or disagrees with him. The relational dialectic in this phase exemplifies openness-closedness: "Do I personify by openly disclosing my position, or do I remain silent and closed, not voicing my dissatisfaction?"

Phase 3: Magnification. The third step, magnification, involves the act of enlarging the rightness of one's position by complimenting others who express support. Using the same example above, having focused on personal deficits in personification, a choice for creating facts out of unwarranted perceptions is the focus. Both the minister, Bob, and the member, Elizabeth, can spiral into detracting obvious shortcomings of one another, e.g. making comments like "He seems very legalistic about administration," or "It's really great to have more men involved in church work." The goal here is to convince oneself and other like-minded believers that what has been attributed in personification not only exists but is supported by fact–fact often taken out of context, overstated, or used as puffery. The relational dialectic of *Inclusion-Seclusion* surfaces at this point where the supportive communication achieves inclusion, and defensive communication creates seclusion.

Phase 4: Glorification. Step 4, glorification, is the act of exalting, glorifying, and venerating, often characterized by self-elevation. For instance, the glorifier talks about other spiritual experiences and notes how wonderful, powerful, and anointed the other leaders were that led that organization to fame and blessing. Likewise, alliances emerge for the purpose of recognizing those who have been suffering under the same injustice caused by the worldview and frame of irony set in place by the other side. In the case of Bob and Elizabeth, Bob has a few men in the Church whom he trusts, who will pray through the difficulty created by his position on women in leadership. Elizabeth, who has seen the minister's type of disingenuous acceptance of women in other churches, knows that women, in general, may harbor ill feelings over being treated as "second-class" citizens in the Kingdom of God. Also, she can prove Bob's scriptural position is too narrow. The relational dialectic for the glorification phase is *Conventionality-Uniqueness.*

Phase 5: Reification. Reification is creating a reality which is believed to be true by producing the behavior and actions to support that truth. In reification, the believer creates situations that provide evidence for his or her worldview whether in error or not. It is in this phase of reification that the believer may become more entrenched in imagination and no longer examines the accuracy of his or her actions. At this stage of the conflict progression, the believer is convinced of the rightness of his or her understanding of what is happening. It is not uncommon to see self-fulfilling prophecy expanding and being assigned greater importance than necessary. This is often the place where the believer forms his or her own frame of irony for the purpose of defending positions. For instance, Bob, who "knows" he is called of God to be positional about the place of women in the Church, and Elizabeth, who knows God has used her to touch a lot of people's lives through teaching Sunday school, may use every example and expression of their individual work as a "see, God is in what I am doing" attitude. The dialectical tension in reification is *Revelation-Concealment;* the believer can go along with the revelation and demonstrate the appropriate behaviors or secretly conceal disbelief. Bob and Elizabeth want the rightness of what they are doing individually to be revealed to others, while at the same time discrediting the claims of their opponent.

Phase 6: Signification. Assigning meaning for the purpose of drawing conclusions that support judgments and evaluations that have been made in phases 1-5, is the role of phase 6, signification. Examples of signification could be that the organization is beginning to suffer because of the growing disagreement between two factions that are now taking sides in the biblical interpretation Bob has placed on his action. Everything that does or does not happen in the lives of leadership or membership is used to provide proof that the individual believer, the one who assigns meaning, is right. Power derived from earlier phases makes it punishing for the believer to change his or her course, and the fundamental judgments made early in objectification and reinforced in phases 2-5 cannot be deserted.

Justification must now be achieved; too much has been committed, too much has been ventured, and too much is public. Elizabeth and Bob point to the illnesses, problems, and crises that occur in the other's life as proof that the other is out of God's will and therefore out of God's blessing. The dialectical tension of signification is *Certainty-Uncertainty;* everything must happen in a manner that is in line with the "truths" of the believers, and if that does not happen, the seeds of uncertainty are sown.

Phase 7: Justification. The final phase of the believer conflict, justification, involves exoneration for the purpose of normalizing assertions made earlier when no real information was present to sanction the positions taken. Phases 1-6 sequentially build to a critical mass for achieving assent to the position of the believer. A mindset of "I told you so" prevails. The goal that the believer is exact, fair, and has the heart of deity on the matters in dispute is now revealed to those objectified. Examples of this could involve being part of a plan to challenge the organization's leadership; to initiate prayer with other members for the purpose of resisting the other side's agenda; or even going to court to repossess the assets of the organization.

In this stage, the believer is ready to take action and fight for what he or she believes. Everything at this point is made right by winning battles; a win-lose approach concerning who is right and who is wrong is the mindset (Fisher and Brown, 1988). When the believer reaches justification, it is often difficult to reason and turn him or her from a course that could easily take on a life of its own. In short, a movement bringing forth a new worldview for the organization could result if enough believers of a similar mentality come together as a power. In our example, both Elizabeth and Bob have now talked to enough members at all levels of the organization during the previous six phases. The results culminate in a conflict episode where there is a "showdown" to prove who is right, even to the point of splitting the church.

Bob is convinced he is right because Elizabeth's actions now prove she is a power-seeking troublemaker. Elizabeth is sure she is right because Bob has proven that he is a legalistic, insensitive leader with chauvinistic values. The dialectical tension associated with justification is *Inclusion-Exclusion:* You are either with us or against us; since we have the truth, we will watch you lose. Moving to the *Win-Lose* framework allows the conflict to be brought into the open and for the first time more clearly defined.

The seven-phase model of conflict presented in this chapter identifies a conflict continuum that mediators and organizational leaders can use to conceptualize conflict (Kimsey, et al., 2006, p. 497) (see Figure 11.2. Hypothesized Conflict Model Continuum).

When objectification is high, the believer may be intense in judgment, but he or she is still likely to be alone still in his or her thinking. If leadership in the faith-based organization can resolve the issue, the conflict can be contained before growing and spreading. Within the phase of personification, leadership also has the opportunity and ability to resolve the believer's issues, prior to critical mass growing. When members are in the process of magnifying, glorifying, or reifying, it is likely that outside mediation may be necessary. A group of like-minded believers is forming and may be resistant to the other side's attempts to solve the issue, especially if glorification is high or the conflict is with the leadership.

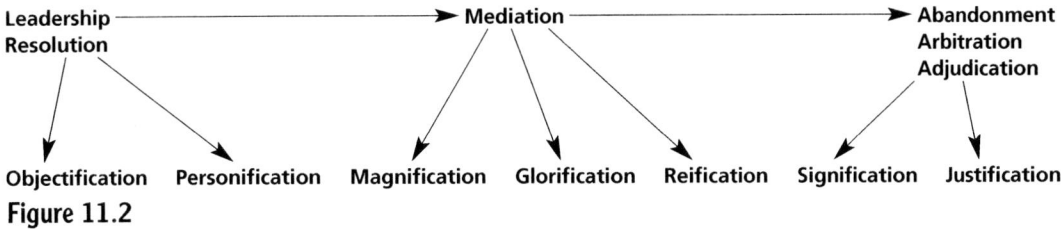

Figure 11.2
Hypothesized Conflict Model Continuum

Problem-solving and transformative mediation practices are choices available to organizational leadership. Problem solving is recommended for non-faith-related issues while transformative is best for faith-related issues. When a cadre of believers has reached the point of signification or justification, the likelihood of successful mediation quickly diminishes. All egos are involved and too much face would be lost even in a win-win situation.

FAITH-BASED MEDIATION PRACTICES

A facilitative process, using a mediation procedure, in most instances, is perhaps the only real means of achieving reconciliation among believers. Guilt accumulated as the believer passes through each of the seven phases of believer conflict creates a critical moment during which it is imperative that intervention helps believers reframe their positional, win-lose ploys to principled, win-win approaches (Sandford, 1989; Fisher & Ury, 1991). If this does not occur, the guilt resulting from fragmenting the group will not only hurt the believer but could eventually harm the organization (Cloud & Townsend, 1999).

It is essential for the individual believer to recognize that conflict is omnipresent. The believer's testimony, regardless of the person, is all about resolving conflict as the individual progresses through life cycles, starting with conception and birth, and ending with death and release.

The requirement for interdependence compels believers to be in fellowship, and the expressed struggles now focus on commitment to relationships and commitment to positions, e.g. doctrine (Lulofs & Cahn, 2000). Empowering the individual believer to have high concern for both relationships and individual goals is a natural consequence of engaging doctrine and the body of faith members. It is here where the believer must make a choice to work through conflict resulting from competing worldviews, frames of irony, and difficult people while not separating themselves from the faith-based organization (Kimsey & Fuller, 1998).

Key elements in achieving principled win-win resolutions should include a) separating other believers from the problem, b) focusing on interests, not positions in believer conflict, c) proceeding independent of trust and dependent on faith, d) achieving transparent communication with other believers for the purpose of finding options which achieve mutual gain, and e) insisting on outcomes separate from individual will—yielding to principle not pressure (Fisher & Ury, 1991).

Mediation is facilitated, principled discussion with an emphasis on achieving win-win outcomes by using a neutral intervener for the purpose of equally empowering the believers to solve problems resulting from competing worldviews, frames of irony, and difficult conflict styles. The mediation procedure provides a framework for achieving the above-identified key elements in win-win resolutions. The following are discussions of problem-solving and transformative mediation practices used to help believers be true to themselves and allowing for what their doctrine requires while navigating organizational pressure to conform. *The Promise of Mediation: Responding to Conflict Through Empowerment and Recognition* (Bush & Folger, 1994/2005), *Mediator Communication Competencies: Problem Solving and Transformative Practices 5/e* (Kimsey, McKinney, Della Noce, & Trobaugh, 2005) and other mediation texts provide elaboration of the concepts presented.

PROBLEM-SOLVING MEDIATION IN FAITH-BASED SETTINGS

The first step, *introducing the process,* involves establishing a positive communication environment. Believers in conflict and mediators meet and reach agreement through discussion about schedule, procedure, rules, and other matters necessary for satisfactory interaction. The purpose in the first step of mediation is to create a setting in which believers can pursue a clear and open discussion of the issues in dispute. Before meeting with believers, mediators should a) review available information about the dispute, b) discuss potential problems or difficulties, c) discuss roles, duties, and responsibilities, and d) become familiar with the physical setting selected for the mediation.

When appropriate, mediators should a) welcome the believers and affirm his or her choice to use win-win approaches in problem-solving mediation, b) clarify the purpose of mediation, c) explain the procedure and the mediator's role and function, d) describe the potential for private caucus sessions with the parties, e) discuss confidentiality and note-taking, and f) establish rules for interaction and secure agreement from the parties.

At the conclusion of the opening phase of a mediation session, the members and the mediators should be acquainted and comfortable with each other, understand and agree to the process for discussing the conflict, feel confident that they will be treated fairly and ethically, and know that the conflict and the process are owned by the believers.

The second step, *defining the conflict,* provides an opportunity for each believer to disclose, as fully and as completely as possible, his or her perception and understanding of the conflict. Each member will describe the conflict from his or her perspective. The parties' description will be unrestrained and uninterrupted. The mediator will summarize each believer's descriptions and ask for elaboration, clarification, or explanation necessary for developing a complete and accurate understanding of the conflict.

The procedure in this step includes: a) each member describes the conflict from their perspective, b) believers are encouraged to identify facts, share their feelings, and describe their desired outcome, and c) the mediator summarizes each parties' description. At the conclusion of the defining the conflict step, the parties and the mediators should have a complete understanding of the conflict—the facts, and the feelings—and have identified a tentative agenda of issues to resolve.

Step 3, *solving the problem,* focuses on gaining consensus regarding relevant issues and develop strategies, procedures, and solutions, acceptable to all members, which will allow the believers to reach successful agreement. The purpose of step 3 is to generate positive communication interaction while creating a supportive environment.

Procedures for the solving the problem step require the mediator to a) facilitate identification of issues in conflict, b) prioritize issues for discussion, c) pursue discussion of interests and positions concerning each issue, d) encourage members to use dialogue relevant to issues under discussion, e) provide periodic summary of progress and positive reinforcement, and f) caucus when necessary to overcome impasse or explore ideas privately.

At the conclusion of the solving the problem step, the members and mediators should have reached an oral agreement concerning each issue, be satisfied that all dimensions of each issue have been considered; be satisfied that the believers have been given full opportunity to participate in the discussion; and be confident that the strategies, procedures, and solutions are fair, ethical, and practical.

The last step, *implementing the agreement,* provides a device to insure, to the degree appropriate and possible, that the believers accept responsibility for implementing their agreement and provide documentation, if necessary, of that commitment. The purpose of step 4 is to bring the mediation session to a close and provide for some documentation of what has been agreed and what has been resolved.

Procedures for facilitating the Implementing the Agreement Step are for the mediator to a) write a statement of agreement, if needed, in clear and precise language and b) specify who is agreeing to what, when, and how. At the conclusion of this step, the members and mediator should achieve some closure with specific understanding of what is resolving the conflict and be satisfied with the steps taken for resolution.

It is in facilitated discussion where the individual believer now has a greater appreciation for his or her conflict over worldview, frame of irony, and difficult believers. Engaging the conflict using a principled win-win procedure like mediation allows all involved to find individual growth in their faith experience while engaging the relational dialectics inherent in organizational pressures for conformity.

The promise of mediation achieved through empowerment and recognition provides the believer the opportunity for solving problems in several of the seven phases of believer conflict while transforming the individual believer according to his or her faith structure. For believers, transformation of the inner person is a lifelong pursuit and challenge, and most faith-based organizations provide some approaches for achieving those goals. The following section describes how transformative mediation works.

Transformative Mediation and Faith-Based Organizations

Transformative mediation is defined as "a process in which a third party works with parties in conflict to help them change the quality of their interaction from negative and destructive to positive and constructive as they explore and discuss issues and possibilities for resolution" (Bush & Pope, 2002, p. 83). The goal of a transformative mediator in faith-based organizations is to help believing members identify the opportunities for empowerment and recognition shifts that arise in their own conversation, and to choose whether and how to respond to these opportunities (Della Noce, Bush, & Folger, 2002, p. 51). Thus, competent mediator practice focuses on 1) fostering empowerment shifts by supporting each believer's efforts at deliberation and decision making at every point in the session where choices arise, and 2) fostering recognition shifts by supporting, but not forcing, each member's freely chosen efforts to achieve new understandings of the other believer's perspective (Bush & Pope, 2002, p. 84). This means that the transformative mediator maintains a dual goal focus throughout the mediation process.

The transformative model presumes that transformation of the interaction is what matters most to members–even more than a tangible settlement agreement (Della Noce, Bush, & Folger, 2002, p. 51). Success is measured not by a settlement agreement, but by member shifts toward empowerment and recognition. The mediator observes these shifts in the believers' interaction.

The mediator in a faith-based organization begins the mediation session by having an opening conversation with the believers. A transformative mediator relies on the metaphor of conversation to convey to the members the nature of the process in which they are taking part. The opening conversation between the mediator and the believers emphasizes empowerment and recognition. Transformative mediators focus attention on the conversational quality of the members' interaction; emphasize believer autonomy, choice, believer-to-believer communication and understanding; and frame settlement as one of a number of possible valuable outcomes.

The transformative mediator listens to the members' conversation with an ear to opportunities for empowerment and recognition. The mediator "punctuates" the conversations occurring in the mediation. The mediator does not lead the discussion; the believers lead the discussion. The transformative mediator does not intervene each time he or she hears an opportunity in the conversation; the mediator remains quiet and allows for silence and space so the members hear and respond to each other.

When appropriate, transformative mediators use three kinds of responses: reflecting, summarizing, and questioning. Reflection is powerful in supporting both empowerment and recognition. Mediator reflection amplifies the conversation for each believer; the members hear and understand what is being said. Mediator reflection confirms and elicits an immediate affirmation.

Mediator summary amplifies and clarifies the developing conversation between the believers. The summary makes the believers' conversation an entity unto itself; it includes the differences revealed and the choices offered in a more visible manner so the members can make clearer choices about what to do. The parties respond to the mediator's summary by moving the conversation forward and often in new directions.

Mediator questioning and checking-in are used when members request help. While transformative mediators favor open-ended questions, "checking-in" is a particular use of a closed-ended question. A check-in focuses on a decision about the mediation conversation itself, e.g., "You just said . . . is that what you want to do now?" or "Did I miss anything, what are you really wanting done?"

Mediator questions provide opportunities for a believer to elaborate on and get clearer about what he or she has said. Questions stimulate recognition shifts by letting the non-speaking member hear different elaborations of what the believer is saying, which may lead to new understandings.

Check-in allows a member to correct a mediator reflection or summary and maintain some control. Mediator check-ins emphasize decision points and support recognition shifts by allowing each believer to become aware of the choices and priorities of the other, as decisions are faced and made in different ways.

Separate meetings are used often between the transformative mediator(s) and one member. Separate meetings help believers think through goals, resources, options, alternatives, and consequences. The mediator helps a believer to explore new information, consider what new understandings he or she could extend to the other, and explore whether there is something else that may need to be disclosed. The transformative mediator suggests separate meetings by checking in with the members.

In recessing and resuming after separate meetings, the mediator discusses what is happening and why. The mediator instructs how information shared in separate session is handled, e.g., if there are confidentiality issues. The mediator facilitates the conversation, during separate session, about what a member wants to share, and how he or she might do so. Finally, the mediator summarizes what has happened in the joint session before adjourning and after starting in a subsequent session.

At the conclusion of a transformative mediation, believers have a better understanding of each other's position, what is wanted, and where they would like to go.

Because of the emphasis on conversation, the members have openly clarified their perceptions and with new understanding can proceed to a more harmonious relationship. Out of the *Nova Harmony* they are better equipped to continue.

SELECTING BEST MEDIATION PRACTICE

Criteria for selecting the appropriate mediation practice, problem-solving or transformative, are suggested as follows:

Criteria	Practice
✱ Faith-related problems	Transformative Mediation
✱ Non-faith-related problems	Problem-Solving Mediation
✱ Compounded issues	Either Mediation Approach

A compounded issue may combine these mediation practices. Analyze the parts; the faith portion and non-faith portion may each be isolated, proceed then to mediate separately.

In order to assist understanding for making a selection of mediation practice, which is best suited to the issues, the following examples are offered.

Dispute Category	Mediation Practice
1. Philosophies	Transformative
2. Redemption/Sin	Transformative
3. Abortion/Right to Live	Transformative
4. Same-Sex Marriage	Transformative
5. War/Peace	Transformative
6. Administrative	Problem-Solving
7. Communication	Problem-Solving
8. Education	Problem-Solving
9. Divorce	Problem-Solving
10. Marriage & Family	Problem-Solving
11. Worship/Traditions	Either
12. Political Responses	Either
13. Community	Either
14. Medical vs. Faith Healing	Either
15. Sacraments	Either

Faith-based members in low-context societies typical of Western countries often associate with people in short time increments across a variety of contexts. Language, knowledge, and rules define how members in faith-based organizations problem solve and build community. Relationship development for faith-based members is often driven by deterministic thinking emphasizing personal achievement. Judeo-Christian worldviews not uncommon in Western psyches are, generally speaking, empirical, cause-effect, linear, solution-oriented, individualistic, and motivated toward managing the individual rather than the group. The drive toward solution inherent in the facilitative, problem-solving mediation practice often assumes a low-context individualistic approach to conflict resolution.

High-context societies found in Eastern countries typical of Asia or the Middle East are often characterized as placing emphasis on process and ceremony over content and structure. They are less direct and give less information in written form. Emphasis on group identity, setting strong boundaries over who is or is not accepted and the importance of "face" creates complex frameworks, making problem-solving techniques difficult (Ting-Toomey, 2005). The transformative method, being nondirective, or member driven, allows for more conversation which is consistent with high-context signification of situations and relationships. Faith-based organizations rely on high-context events and rituals which serve to justify choices made for the group and the believer member.

Problem-solving mediation may achieve outcomes typical of transformative practices, e.g. empowerment, recognition, etc.; yet the transformative process often is longer in duration, mediator authority is less noticeable, and outcomes may appear less clear and, perhaps, even less controllable than problem solving. This is evident, particularly, with a first-time introduction to transformative. Faith-based leaders favor transformative practices over problem-solving mediation when the issues of the conflict are over values, beliefs, or doctrines and not about disputes over administration.

CONCLUDING COMMENTS

With practice, discerning which mediation method to use will become clearer. The believer's choice for faith-based mediation is usually difficult to initiate for the members who are more comfortable thinking that working on their issues separately without confrontation will make the problems go away. Therefore, many times there will be approach/avoidance with the idea of mediation for fear of escalation of the conflict. The parties' concern may be that open discussion through mediation may expose their true position and somehow make them appear to be less worthy in the eyes of deity, when in reality the very opposite holds true. Mediation offers an organized direct approach to solving issues without either party losing.

Case Study: Charismatic versus Seeker-Sensitive Focus

A non-denominational church with a charismatic focus, approaching the celebration of their 15th year anniversary has been considering for some months how best to move forward and meet the evangelistic goals in their strategic plan.

The charismatic focus has been on praise and worship, experiencing the gifts and visitation of the Holy Spirit and allowing prophecies to be spoken on Sundays. Many meetings become very emotional and uplifting for the congregation and validate that God is present and blessing this group. Emphasis is on the biblical mandate to win the lost at any cost; weekend morning services are directed toward reaching the un-churched.

However, the administration and many members of the governing body have concluded that the evangelistic goals can be best met by changing the focus from charismatic to a seeker-sensitive orientation with a more traditional church atmosphere. Citing that the highly emotionally charged atmosphere has been proven in sister churches to scare away new members, the decision is announced for consideration.

This positioning had been discussed in private throughout the membership for months. The final announcement came forth with the following rationale. God is tired of us proclaiming the truth on street corners, like the man with a loudspeaker. In fact he will go as far as to say that Christians who try to witness to their friends and preach the gospel to them are down right annoying.

Our church needs to be purpose driven and we need to make our church so appealing that the whole world will want to be part of it. We don't need to drive Jesus down the visitors' throats; we'll let people decide for themselves as our church meets their needs. But we need to get them through the church's doors first.

Shortly after the announcement of the church's new direction, conflict erupted among different groups: the praise and worship team over songs and style of presentation, Sunday school teachers over programs and materials, youth group leaders seeking appropriate direction, the finance committee on budget allocations, and other staff. Reports began streaming into the administrative staff regarding increased disagreements and divisions. The congregation was splitting right before their eyes. The administrative board is split on administrative issues. The board of elders is split on spiritual issues and doctrine.

Seeking the outside counsel of the community mediation service, their problem was broken down into two types of conflict. The first was administrative issues, the second category was spiritual. The mediation service recommended the administrative board meet first to mediate conflicts over finance, programs, and staff issues. Secondly, the administrative board would agree to allow the elders to mediate on behalf of the spiritual issues related to worship service, sermons, youth group issues, doctrine, and the prophetic direction of the church.

QUESTIONS FOR DISCUSSION

1. Where in the Seven-Phase Model of Conflict would you say the Church presently finds itself? Why?
2. What style of mediation practice, problem-solving or transformative, best fits the conflicts? Why?

3. If mediation is not successful, what methods of negotiation could be used to reach a satisfactory solution?

Role Play: Administration Group versus Spiritual Group

Mediate the above conflict using the combined approach to mediation. Separate the conflict issues into the two categories of 1) faith related and 2) non-faith related. Use transformative mediation practice for 1) above and use problem-solving practice for 2) above. Decide who will represent the following beliefs/positions in the mediation session(s) and who will serve as the mediator(s).

INFORMATION FOR GROUP 1 ADMINISTRATION BELIEFS/POSITIONS

The administrative board is split on how to change the budget to accommodate the additional expenses for the seeker-sensitive approach versus dropping some programs in the original charismatic strategic plan. The budget is fixed and cannot be increased. Additional expenses are for continental breakfast every Sunday morning, a new advertising program, a new lighting system for stage productions, and materials for seeker-sensitive drama skits and props. Budget items which may be dropped include the scouting program, hospital visitation, Golden Glow dinners for the elderly, and the Christian marriage workshops.

INFORMATION FOR GROUP 2 SPIRITUAL BELIEFS/POSITIONS

Predominantly the worship team is being told that the order of worship is going to change. There will only be two praise songs during the fifteen minutes of time allotted out of the two-hour service. The remaining forty-five minutes prior to the sermon will be divided up between skits and stage performances for storytelling and the welcoming breakfast. The praise and worship team is heavily invested in praising God and bringing the congregation into the "Throne Room of God" for an emotional/spiritual experience. They have invested in the best instruments and music. They are accustomed to having a full hour to use their creativity to honor God. Musicians and worship leaders are essential on any church staff. With these impending changes, the church is risking loosing this portion of their staff.

REFERENCES

Bush, R. A. B., and Folger, J. P. (1994/2005). *The Promise of Mediation: Responding to Conflict through Empowerment and Recognition.* San Francisco: Jossey-Bass.

Bush, R. A. B., and Pope, S. G. (2002). Changing the quality of conflict interaction: The principles and practice of transformative mediation. *Pepperdine Dispute Resolution Law Journal, 3*(1), 67-96.

Cloud, H., and Townsend, J. (1999). *Boundaries: When to Say Yes, When to Say No, to Take Control of Your Life.* Grand Rapids, MI: Zondervan Publishing House.

Della Noce, D. J., Bush, R. A. B., and Folger, J. P. (2002). Clarifying the theoretical underpinnings of mediation: Implications for practice and policy. *Perppperdine Dispute Resolution Law Journal, 3*(1), 39-65.

Fisher, R., and Brown, S. (1988). *Getting Together: Building a Relationship that Gets to Yes.* Boston: Houghton Mifflin Company.

Fisher, R., and Ury, W. (1991). *Getting to Yes: Negotiating Agreement without Giving In* (2nd ed.). New York: Penguin Books.

Kimsey, W. D., and Fuller, R. M. (1998). A path model of world view, intolerance and violence. *Peace Research: The Canadian Journal of Peace Studies, 30*(4), 56-69.

Kimsey, W. D., McKinney, B. C., Della Noce, D. J., and Trobaugh, S. S. (2005). *Mediator Communication Competencies: Problem Solving and Transformative Practices* (5th ed.). Boston: Pearson Custom Publishing.

Kimsey, W. D., Trobaugh, S. S., McKinney, B. C., Hoole, E. R., Thelk, A. D., and Davis, S. L. (2006). Seven phase model of conflict: Practical applications for conflict mediators and leaders. *Conflict Resolution Quarterly, 23*(4), 487-499.

Lulofs, R. S., and Cahn, D. D. (2000). *Conflict: From Theory to Action* (2nd ed.). Boston: Allyn and Bacon.

Said, A. A., and Funk, N. C. (2001). The role of faith in cross-cultural conflict resolution. A paper presented at the European Parliament for the European Centere for Common Ground, September, 2001.

Said, A. A., Funk, N. C., and Kunkle, L. (2003). Cross-cultural conflict resolution. In N. N. Kittrie, R. Carazo and J. R. Mancham (Eds.), *The Future of Peace in the Twenty-First Century.* Durham, NC: Carolina Academic Press.

Sandford, J. L. (1989). *Why Some Christians Commit Adultery.* Tulsa, OK: Victor House,Inc.

Ting-Toomey, S. (2005). The matrix of face: An updated face-negotiation theory. In W. B. Gudykunst (Ed.), *Theorizing about Intercultural Communication.* Thousand Oaks, CA: Sage.

Chapter 12

Mediation–Arbitration in Dispute Resolution

Christine A. Coates

The increased use of alternative dispute resolution (ADR) in the United States in almost every type of conflict has resulted in the creative application of a variety of ADR models. Dispute systems designers and conflict management professionals have blended models, creating hybrids that contain the elements of two or more dispute-resolution processes. Parties and counsel have followed the admonition to "fit the forum to the fuss" (Sander and Goldberg, 1994), and sometimes the parties, counsel or conflict managers have designed a system that uses more than one model.

The most common hybrid, or blending of ADR models, is mediation-arbitration ("med-arb"). The purest form of med-arb involves selecting one neutral party to serve as both mediator and arbitrator (med-arbiter) in a dispute. The parties begin in mediation (facilitated negotiation) and failing settlement, the same-neutral third party acts as an arbitrator of the remaining unresolved issues and renders a binding decision. Some commentators have called this "same-neutral med-arb." (Phillips, 2005) A variation involves mediating with one neutral, and failing settlement, arbitrating with a different-neutral who issues a binding decision, ("different-neutral med-arb").

COMPATIBILITY OF MEDIATION AND ARBITRATION

Mediation and arbitration are both ADR processes that may be contractually agreed upon to avoid litigation and in which the parties can choose their neutrals. Sessions in both processes are generally closed to the public. The parties may contract to confidentiality of outcomes in both.

Mediation and arbitration, however, are fundamentally very different. Many mediators decry the combination of these two alternative dispute resolution processes into one as violating the basic principles of mediation. The roles of mediator and arbitrator may seem inconsistent when combined into one process. The following chart sets forth the major differences between mediation and arbitration:

MEDIATION:	ARBITRATION:
Goal is settlement	Goal is decision
Neutral is a third-party facilitator	Neutral is the fact-finder
Parties make decisions	Third party neutral(s) make decision
Parties must agree on decision	Parties do not have to agree upon the decision
Process is unlike litigation	Process resembles litigation
Generally less expensive than litigation	Can be as expensive as litigation
No "witnesses"	Witnesses
"Win-win"	"Win-lose"
Confidentiality of information presented during the session	Information presented may be included in findings of fact/rationale in the arbitration award

Self-determination, the hallmark of mediation, is missing in arbitration since the arbitrator makes decisions for the parties. Mediation purists assert that even "evaluative" mediation, in which the mediator offers opinions about the relative merits and weaknesses of each party's case and the possible litigated outcome, is a hybrid process, more like med-arb than mediation. (Shienvold, 2004). However, mediation-arbitration, as described herein, is a specific process that is agreed upon by the parties prior to entering into med-arb. It is not simply an agreement to mediate and then a later separate agreement to arbitrate the issues that were not resolved in mediation or, in reverse, an agreement to arbitrate preceded by an attempt by the arbitrator to help the parties negotiate the issues before the arbitration hearing begins. Informed consent to the med-arb process by the parties prior to beginning the mediation phase of the process is imperative.

Historical Development

Bartel (1991) states that the history of med-arb may have begun as early as 2500 B.C. but that its recent development has been through labor disputes. Labor arbitration developed when "management agreed to a grievance procedure culminating in binding arbitration of disputes in exchange for the union's agreement not to strike. In some instances the arbitrator would first attempt to help the union and management resolve their disputes through negotiation." (Bartel, 1991). Although this was not called med-arb, it did use a similar process of facilitated decision making followed by arbitration by the same-neutral. The soundness of this informal process was debated in the arbitration community as arbitrators felt that the roles of mediator and arbitrator were inconsistent and incompatible. Lon Fuller, a critic of mediation-arbitration (1962, as cited in Rau, et al., 2002) opined that "[M]ediation and arbitration have distinct purposes and hence distinct moralities. The morality of mediation lies in optimum settlement, a settlement in which each party gives up what he values less, in return for what he values more. The morality of arbitration lies in a decision according to the law of the contract." The separate hybrid process called mediation-arbitration arose somewhat later to clarify the role of the neutral. Some commentators (Henry, 1988; Bartel, 1991) credit Sam Kagel, a San Francisco attorney/arbitrator, as being the first to develop med-arb as a process which he employed in a 1970 San Francisco nurses' strike. It is unclear, however, if any one person or group can take credit for the name of the process.

The use of mediation-arbitration has proliferated. Mediation-arbitration in different forms has been used or suggested in labor disputes (Henry, 1988), shareholder conflicts (Kim, 2003), managed health care disputes (Grenig, 1998), end of life medical issues (Cohen, 2004), estate planning disputes (Phillips, Martinsen, & Dameron, 2006), family disputes (Shienvold, 2004; Coates, 1993; Baris, Coates, Duvall, Garrity, Johnson, & LaCrosse, 2001), community mediation—that is controversies between neighbors, landlord and tenants, former partners, merchant and client, etc. (Pruitt, 1995), real estate (American Arbitration Association, 2006), commercial disputes (Phillips, 2005), public-sector interest disputes (Rau, Sherman, & Peppit, 2002), and in many other types of disputes.

Mediation-arbitration provides the best of both processes, allowing the parties an opportunity to settle the dispute while guaranteeing a decision without going to court. The parties can tailor the timing and procedures to match their situation. They can agree to the date of a mediation session and then set the arbitration to occur after the mediation on a time-table that meets the parties' and counsel's needs. The mediation-arbitration agreement between the med-arbiter and the parties can contain particular rules of procedure, such as an agreement to follow rules for arbitrating certain types of disputes (American Arbitration Association,

2005) or an agreement to modify the procedures in particular ways to fit the needs of the parties.

Types of Disputes for Med-Arb

In situations in which the parties must have an ongoing relationship (for example as parents, co-workers, contractors, etc.) med-arb can help to preserve their relationship. Litigation is hard on relationships since it is public and emotionally and financially costly. Med-arb provides the parties a private means to discuss their needs and desires and to negotiate their issues with a trained mediator, and then to get an informed, impartial and judicious decision, if necessary. The parties may then return to their normal dealings with each other.

In the event that one party feels less powerful than the other, the ability to go from mediation to negotiation may keep the unempowered party from giving in or from being "steam-rollered" into a settlement against his or her best interests because there is an efficient back-up to the negotiations to get a decision. Such individuals are often fearful of litigation, but may have fewer qualms about the less formal arbitration phase of med-arb since it will be conducted by a neutral that the party knows and trusts. Conversely, the party who perceives him or herself as more powerful and able to control the other party may need to be more reasonable in mediation because of the belief that his/her behavior and positions could be held against him or her in the arbitration.

Even in situations where the parties will not have an ongoing relationship, med-arb allows disputants to be heard since "feeling conversations" are almost always a part of negotiations. (Cohen, 2004). While litigation and arbitration focus on facts and evidence and exclude feelings from the adjudication of the dispute, mediation recognizes the importance of emotions and offers the parties an opportunity to be heard, recognized, and acknowledged. Even if the parties are unable to settle, the process will have afforded them an opportunity to fully discuss the dispute from their individual points of view. The formality of arbitration and litigation with emphasis on procedure and evidence often leaves litigants feeling that they have not had an opportunity to be fully heard or understood.

In mediation, as opposed to the more litigation-like arbitration, the parties are allowed greater latitude and flexibility in the resolution of their dispute. The mediator facilitates the exploration of settlement options that might not be available to the arbitrator. The parties can be more creative in attempting to meet their needs as the process in focused on the parties' interests, rather than on their rights under a contract or the law. Mediation encourages disputants to think "outside of the box" and to do creative problem solving.

In mediation-arbitration, the parties may have a greater incentive to settle in the mediation phase since they know that the mediator will ultimately make the decision if they cannot. This psychological urging to resolve the issues without going to arbitration can give the mediator greater leverage when helping the parties develop and assess their options for resolution.

Dean Pruitt (1995) reports on a field study done in a community mediation center in New York which looked at the value of med-arb. In this study, cases that came to this center were randomly assigned to three different processes: straight mediation, same-neutral med-arb or different-neutral med-arb. The disputants were told about the type of process in which they would be engaged and were given an opportunity to opt out of the study. The mediation sessions were observed by researchers who were not told which process they were observing and who analyzed what was being said and the conduct of both the disputants and the mediator. They also rated the disputants' motivation to settle. The participants behaved more constructively and creatively during the same-neutral med-arb sessions and settled their disputes more often than in either the straight mediation or the different-neutral med-arb sessions. The parties were rated as more motivated to settle in the same-neutral med-arb process. Pruitt suggests that the participants may have had an increased motivation to settle in same-neutral med-arb because "the parties wanted to avoid loss of control over their destinies . . . and were particularly anxious to please the mediator." (Pruitt, 1995). The parties working with the same-neutral med-arbiter also perceived themselves as more involved in working toward settlement and perceived the mediator as less forceful than in either of the other two groups. The conclusion reached by this study was that med-arb was a valuable process that encouraged settlement in the mediation phase.

PROMOTION OF LESS EXPENSIVE AND MORE EFFICIENT PROCESS

Mediation-arbitration generally yields a decision at lower cost and higher speed than litigation. Even if the parties must arbitrate, there will be reduced discovery (information requesting and gathering from each side). The rules of evidence and procedure can be relaxed by agreement, allowing greater latitude in admitting evidence. The hearing itself is often less formal than a court hearing with parties sitting around a large conference table rather than in a courtroom. Unlike arbitration where the arbitration panel may consist of several arbitrators, med-arb is generally conducted by one neutral, although a co-med-arbiter process may be possible. The cost savings to the parties of having one neutral as opposed to three can be great.

Same-neutral med-arb is particularly appropriate and more expedient for certain types of limited issue disputes. If the case involves a conflict in which a limited number of exclusive options are to be selected, and neither party wants to give in to the other, med-arb assures a decision if they can't agree in mediation. For example, med-arb has been used in post-divorce parenting disputes when two parents with joint decision-making authority are disputing issues, such as which school a child will attend—the one in Mom's neighborhood or the one in Dad's neighborhood. When they both agree that no other option is viable for their child, a same-neutral med-arb process gives the parents an opportunity to resolve the dispute themselves, either by reaching an agreement together in mediation or by decision making by the med-arbiter, without going through the expensive, lengthy and disruptive process of litigation. (Coates, 1993). In some jurisdictions, same-neutral med-arb is commonly used by joint custodial parents to resolve disputes when the parents have failed to do so through their negotiations. (Backerman & Vick, 1996). Phillips (2005) states that same-neutral med-arb is "perfect" for a dispute where the parties agree that money is owed, but they can't agree on the amount of the debt. In this situation, med-arb would be used to help the parties work out a payment plan in mediation, while giving them a decision on the amount of the debt in arbitration.

THE CASE FOR MED-ARB

The role of the med-arbiter is a powerful one, since s/he may make decisions for the parties or even suggest possible resolutions in the mediation phase. Written informed consent by the parties is essential to ensure that the parties involved have selected this hybrid model purposefully and understand the implications of it. The med-arbiter must receive clear authority from the parties in advance of beginning this process to avoid the ethical problems of role confusion or dual roles. Since the roles are contradictory rather than complementary, the parties must understand the process and its limitations and benefits to them.

The conflicting parties may select the med-arb process and agree upon the neutral when the conflict is ripe for resolution. Often the selection of the med-arb process may have been inserted into a contract or other transaction document as the dispute resolution process of choice in the event of disputes. A simple mediation-arbitration clause in a transaction document or stipulation might be:

"Any and all disputes arising out of the Agreement between the Parties shall be resolved by mediation and then by arbitration. The arbitrator (who shall be ___) shall also serve as the mediator" (Phillips, 2005); however, the clause may call for mediation-arbitration without naming the neutral, but will include a process for selecting the med-arbiter in the future.

The med-arbiter will also want to have a written agreement between the med-arbiter and the parties which details the procedures that the med-arbiter will follow, expectations regarding fees, a description of the process, and other information that the parties need to give informed consent to the process.

INTEGRITY OF THE DECISION-MAKING ROLE

Lack of Candor in Mediation

In mediation, parties are encouraged to share information candidly and openly in order to help craft agreements that make sense and meet their needs. The guarantee of confidentiality of the information shared with the mediator helps insure that full disclosure of relevant information is being accomplished. Parties to med-arb may be reluctant to share information candidly, knowing that the information might be used by the med-arbiter in his/her decision-making deliberation. They may also purposefully and strategically craft how that information is shared, reserving particular information for use in the arbitration phase. Parties in a mediation session are not sworn in as they would be in arbitration or in a judicially litigated process. A risk exists that the parties in mediation might be untruthful in the mediation phase since they do not have the obligation imposed by the risk of perjury that sworn testimony provides. However, this risk exists in every mediation session. In the event that arbitration is needed, the med-arbiter will have the opportunity to swear in the parties and witnesses and will know if the evidence provided in the arbitration hearing matches the information shared in mediation. The med-arbiter must be skilled in creating trust with the parties in gathering information as well as in eliminating any prejudicial and/or extraneous information from use in making a decision. Judges are expected to rule out inadmissible information in making determinations; through experience and training, med-arbiters can also meet this standard of fair adjudication.

The Challenge of the Caucus

In litigation and arbitration, judges and arbitrators avoid receiving information privately from a party. They insist that all communications, whether written or oral, involve all parties or counsel. Counsel or parties must copy all parties on communication with a judge/arbitrator and must be involved in all discussions with the judge/arbitrator. Private communications with the adjudicator (judge or arbitrator) without notice to the other party(ies) or involvement by them are called *ex parte* communications and are forbidden in litigation and arbitration except in rare circumstances.

One of the tools of mediation is the private meeting or caucus in which the mediator meets individually with the parties to get information, to tease out the interests of the parties, to test possible settlement possibilities and to create trust between the mediator and the parties. Caucus sessions are generally described to the parties as confidential. For many mediators and lawyers in civil, commercial, or labor disputes, almost all of the mediation will be accomplished using caucuses in shuttle mediation. The mediator goes between the parties, carrying offers, counter-offers, information, etc. An ethical and practical issue arises from the use of the caucus in the mediation phase of med-arb: can the mediator effectively screen out irresponsible charges made by one party in a confidential caucus that the other party does not have the ability to rebut when serving as the arbitrator later in the med-arb process?

Some commentators, such as Lon Fuller (1962, as cited in Rau, et al., 2002) suggest that it is impossible and potentially unethical to have private sessions in med-arb. Others, such as Henry (1988), suggest that since the caucus is such an important tool for the mediator, that the med-arbiter should not abandon the use of the caucus. The mediator can obtain very useful, often candid information, which is essential to the success of settlement in mediation. The mediator uses the information that is disclosed by the parties to help move them closer to resolution. Most med-arbiters would prefer to enable the parties to settle in the mediation phase rather than to have to make decisions for the parties. However, parties may fear that the med-arbiter may also learn confidential information that is inappropriate, inaccurate, or inadmissible that could sway the med-arbiter in his decision-making role.

To help meet this challenge, med-arbiters could be trained to view the accusations that they hear in caucus as information about the speaker's views, but which should only be believed if the accused party has the opportunity to refute them. (Pruitt, 1996). An additional method of resolving this potential dilemma is to consider the use of the caucus or private meeting as part of informed consent prior to beginning the process. The use of the caucus and its advantages and disadvantages should be discussed with the parties and/or counsel in advance as one of the procedures that are possible in med-arb. The parties/counsel can agree to use the caucus or not, based upon informed consent to the possible consequences of its use or non-use. The written mediation-arbitration agreement signed by the parties would reflect their consent to their selection.

Directiveness of the Mediator

Another concern about med-arb is that the mediator will be more forceful in med-arb as opposed to mediation in pushing toward particular settlement options. In fact, Pruitt (1995) found in his study that mediators tended to use "heavy pressure tactics" when a same-neutral med-arbiter than as a straight mediator or different-neutral med-arbiter. However, this directiveness of the mediators was concentrated toward the end of the mediation phase, suggesting a "last ditch effort to rescue a failing mediation rather than a policy of forceful advocacy." (Pruitt, 1996). And interestingly, the parties viewed the mediator as *less* forceful in same-neutral mediation than did the parties in the different-neutral med-arb or straight mediation groups.

Conduct by the med-arbiter in mediation may be interpreted by the parties, rightly or wrongly, as a reflection of the decision that that the med-arbiter might be considering if called upon to arbitrate. A nod of the head, a lift of an eyebrow, a change in the med-arbiter's mood, or attention or lack thereof given to either party's statements, for example, are all ways that the parties' behavior might be shaped by the med-arbiter as they attempt to resolve the dispute. The med-arbiter may be totally unaware of these non-verbal cues that are being sent to the parties which may be providing direction to their negotiations. As in all mediation, however, the med-arbiter must be extremely aware of and strategic in behavior, comments, and non-verbal cues which might influence the direction of the parties' negotiations.

EXPERIENCE NEEDED TO CONDUCT MEDIATION-ARBITRATION

The med-arbiter should, of course, have comprehensive training in mediation, which at a minimum is generally forty hours of in-class training. The med-arbiter should also be trained in the process of arbitration. Arbitration organizations, such as the American Arbitration Association, offer this type of training. In order to effectively mediate-arbitrate, one must first be comfortable and competent in both processes individually. Therefore, the professional should also have extensive experience as both a mediator and an arbitrator in the "pure" processes.

Understanding of due-process issues in decision making and the ability to handle an arbitration hearing are prerequisites to arbitrating. The mediator must be able to shift from facilitator to decision maker and to be able to make up his/her mind when a decision is necessary. To make decisions, the neutral must be able to understand the positions of the parties, to apply the facts of the situation to the law or contract, and to make a decision in favor of one party and against others. This is often extremely difficult for a mediator to do because the mindset of a mediator is not one of fact-finding, but of creativity, understanding, and facilitation. Many very successful practitioners become mediators because they are able to see all sides of an issue and think globally rather than narrowly. And conversely, a competent arbitrator may approach the mediation from the outset attempting to determine which party is right and then may steer the parties toward a solution that the neutral feels is appropriate in the situation, based upon the law or contract. In med-arb, the neutral must be able to facilitate the mediation without leading the parties to a pre-conceived solution as well as make decisions in the arbitration phase when called upon to do so.

A reputation for integrity (Phillips, 2005) is important for the med-arbiter as are a commitment to objectivity and impartiality, patience, and strong conflict-management skills. The med-arbiter must have a firm grounding and belief in the importance of *process* itself—that is, the principled, yet creative adherence to a method of following steps and procedures that are necessary to accomplish the type of dispute resolution that has been selected. Since med-arb is a hybrid process of ADR and has few guidelines, rules, or regulations, the med-arbiter should be aware and follow standards of practice, rules of procedure, and statutes that pertain to both mediation and arbitration within the limits of these somewhat contradictory processes.

Arbitrators are often selected for their subject-matter expertise, and med-arbiters also will likely be selected based upon their knowledge of the subject of the dispute (for example, labor, family, health care, etc.). A combination of deep understanding of the mediation, arbitration, and med-arb processes combined with expertise in the subject of the dispute are the qualities that most enable the med-arbiter to function competently and effectively.

PREPARATION FOR MED-ARB

The med-arbiter or the scheduling staff will have some contact with the parties or their representatives in advance of the first med-arb session to set the date for the mediation session, and to discuss the process, rules, and fees. Because arbitration is possible, direct communication with individual parties or counsel is not suggested in order to avoid one side offering arguments designed to sway the med-arbiter. Phone conferences or e-mail communication are helpful in avoiding *ex parte* communication. The parties should always be able to have their legal counsel present, but the med-arbiter should direct the parties to notify the med-arbiter and other parties a certain period of time in advance if a party plans to bring counsel (for example, notification to occur at least three days in advance).

The med-arbiter should request pre-session statements, setting forth each party's view and history of the dispute, desires of outcome, legal authority, if appropriate, and special considerations. In the interest of due process and to avoid undue influence by *ex parte* communications, these statements should not be considered confidential and should be shared with all parties.

The med-arbiter should also provide a mediation-arbitration agreement to the parties in advance to be discussed at the first session. Included in the discussion should be an overview of the process and procedures, fee agreements, the decision about whether or not to use caucuses, time frames for entering arbitration awards, and other issues of importance to the process and which may be unique to the particular med-arbiter. The parties should decide whether the parties will engage in a mediation session followed by a separate arbitration hearing if the parties don't settle in mediation, or whether the med-arbiter is authorized to decide the unresolved issues based upon what was discussed in mediation. In the case of different-neutral med-arb, the professionals would propose their standard mediation or arbitration agreements and procedures.

CONCLUDING COMMENTS

Mediation-arbitration is a hybrid ADR process that brings the best of both of these dispute resolution worlds to parties seeking an efficient dispute resolution process.

The parties have an opportunity to solve the problem themselves and to reach settlement of their issues. If they reach impasse, however, they are guaranteed a decision in the arbitration phase of the med-arb process. Informed consent of the parties prior to beginning med-arb is essential so that the parties understand and agree to the procedures used in the med-arb process. Med-arb can be more efficient and less costly than arbitration while also providing the potential for self-determination of the parties. Finality results from med-arb because of the binding nature of the decision made in arbitration. Not without challenges, a thorough grounding by the med-arbiter in both mediation and arbitration allows the med-arb process to be applied to many different types of disputes. The dispute resolution professional who undertakes serving as a med-arbiter must be an experienced mediator and arbitrator with a firm commitment to self-determination, fairness, and following his or her set procedures.

Case Study: The Not-So-Neighborly Dispute

Herbie West and Jim Jones and their families lived next door to each other in the mountains outside of a university city. They became embroiled in a neighbor-to-neighbor dispute when Jim objected to Herbie's request from the county to build an addition onto his home. A series of incidents occurred after Herbie's request for a variance was denied by the county. Herbie planted a row of trees on his property that blocked the mountain view from Jim's deck. Jim cut off the tops of the trees and trimmed the branches that extended over into his property. Herbie installed floodlights on his home that shone into the windows of the Jones home. Jim's children were noisy in their outside play and trespassed on Herbie's property. When Herbie yelled and cursed at Jim's children, Jim filed an action in small claims court. Herbie counterclaimed, and they were referred to mediation. In discussions with the mediator about ADR processes, they learned about the process of med-arb and elected to use it instead of mediation and possible subsequent litigation if they were unable to resolve their dispute.

In the mediation phase, the med-arbiter helped the parties listen to each other's complaints and rationale for doing the things that they had done. Since Jim and Herbie had never discussed Herbie's request for a variance, Jim did not know that Herbie wanted to add on to his home to provide room for his elderly mother to live with him. Jim expressed concern for Herbie's situation, but also stated that the addition as proposed would have been too close to Jim's property for comfort. Herbie acknowledged Jim's need for privacy and a view of the mountains as important for both of their families. The men discussed different alternatives for the location and size of the addition. They decided that if Herbie could develop a proposal that did not block Jim's sight line of the mountains and would not encroach on his privacy, that Jim would not object to a subsequent request to the county for an addition. Jim and Herbie also discussed the reasons for the behavior that each man had deemed irrational and harassing in the other, and worked out ways of mitigating the damages that each had caused the other. When Jim found out that Herbie's wife had migraine headaches which were exacerbated by the noise of the children playing on the driveway, he agreed to have his children play inside or at least away from the West home when Jim knew that the headaches were occurring. Herbie offered to have his wife fly a small flag outside the front door when she was experiencing the headaches which would let Jim's family know that quiet was needed. Herbie also agreed to apologize to Jim's children for yelling at them. He agreed to talk to Jim if he had concerns in the future about the children's noise or behavior on his property. Herbie agreed to remove all of the floodlights except those at the rear of the home. He also agreed to have them installed with motion sensors so that they would only shine when something moved in the yard.

But Jim and Herbie were unable to agree upon what to do about the trees. Herbie had spent quite a bit of money on the trees, but Jim argued that they were partially inside of his property line and disturbed his view. They submitted this issue to arbitration, although they did not request a formal arbitration hearing. They asked the med-arbiter to make a decision based upon what the med-arbiter had learned during the mediation phase. The med-arbiter asked the parties some additional questions to clarify the facts, and then issued a decision. The med-arbiter decided that the trees would have to be either removed or replanted far enough inside Herbie's property line that no part of the branches intruded onto Jim's property. The med-arbiter also decided that Herbie must keep them trimmed to a height that did not obstruct Jim's view of the mountains from his deck. The med-arbiter awarded Jim the costs of filing the small claims court action, but awarded no other money damages. The written arbitration award was filed with the court in the small claims action and was confirmed as an order of the court.

QUESTIONS FOR DISCUSSION

1. Why might Jim and Herbie have selected med-arb over straight mediation?
2. Do you think that Jim and Herbie would have settled as much of the dispute as they did if they had been in straight mediation? Why or why not?
3. What were the advantages to each party of using med-arb? What did each party lose by using med-arb?
4. As the med-arbiter, would you have caucused with the parties during the mediation? Why or why not?
5. Do you see any possible problems with the settlement that the parties reached? What would you as the med-arbiter do to correct the problems?

Role Play: The Neighborhood Dispute

Jim Jones and Herbie West are neighbors whose mountain homes are unusually close to each other. Six months ago Herbie posted a notice in his yard of an intention to build an addition onto his property which was in variance with the property line setback ordinance. Jim protested to the planning board of the county, and the request for a variance was denied.

One month after the county's denial of the variance, Herbie put up a row of very expensive eight-foot evergreen trees between the two properties without any advance notification to Jim. Jim was concerned about the trees because the trees block his view of the mountains from his deck. He had the property line surveyed and found that the trees were planted two inches inside his property line so that the trunk of each tree was partially on his property. Jim then cut two feet off the top of the trees and all of the branches on his side of the trees which allowed him to once again see the mountains. Herbie then installed floodlights on his home to scare away mountain lions at nights. Jim claims that the lights shine directly into his bedroom and disturb his sleep.

Jim has three boys, ages 6, 8, and 10 who play basketball on their driveway. Several times, Herbie has yelled at the boys when the ball bounced into the West yard and the boys ran into the yard to retrieve the ball. After the last time that Herbie yelled at the boys, Jim filed a lawsuit in small claims court against Herbie asking for damages because of the property line encroachment and for emotional distress and outrageous conduct.

The parties have been referred to mediation by the small claims court magistrate. Both Jim and Herbie are prominent citizens and do not wish to have a public trial, but both believe that they have been harmed by the other man. After a discussion with the mediator about various ADR processes, they agreed that mediation-arbitration would best suit their needs since they want a decision without going to court.

INFORMATION FOR HERBIE WEST

You are neighbors with Jim Jones in a mountain home subdivision in which the homes are very close together. You have never really met the Joneses, but only have smiled and waved at Jim and his wife. Last year your mother became quite ill and it was decided that she would come live with you and your wife. However, to accommodate your mother's needs, you wanted to build a ground-floor bedroom for her. You engaged an architect who drew plans for a small addition which would meet your needs, but which would require a variance from the county. Your wife saw Jim's wife at the mailboxes and told her about the addition and that you would be glad to show them the plans if they were interested. You never received a request from Jim to view the plans. Six months ago you applied for a building permit and posted a notice in your yard of your intention to build the addition onto your property which was in variance with the property line setback ordinance. Jim protested to the county planning board, and the request for variance was denied. You were shocked that he didn't come to you first to talk about it to see if a compromise could be reached. Now you have had to place your mother in a nursing home and feel quite badly about not having her live with you.

Jim has three boys who play basketball on their driveway and ride their bikes up and down the driveway with their friends. They are quite noisy, and your main living area is right over their driveway. Your wife suffers from migraine headaches, and the noise of the children exacerbates her headaches. It seems that the only time that the boys come out to play is when you and your wife come home after a busy day at work. You are sure that the boys are encouraged to be especially noisy when you are home. You will admit that several times you have yelled at the boys when their ball bounced into your yard and the boys ran after it to retrieve the ball. However, in doing so, they trampled your flowerbeds and knocked over your potted plants that you displayed beside the walk. They also have worn a path through your back yard taking a "short cut" to go to their friends' houses down the street. You know that you behaved badly in cursing at them the last time that your prized begonia pot was overturned and broken, but they would not listen when you asked them to be more careful.

A month after the denial of the variance you put up a row of very expensive eight-foot evergreen trees between the two properties to help screen out the noise and to keep the children from running into the yard. Jim then cut two feet off the top of the trees and all of the branches on his side of the trees which negated the noise screening effect. Because of the recent sightings of mountain lions in the nearby mountains, two months after planting the trees, you installed floodlights on your home to scare away mountain lions at night. Your small dog had been chased one evening by a mountain lion when you took him out for his nightly walk. You feel a lot more secure with the lights on in the evening and have seen no more signs of mountain lions.

You were served with a small claims court complaint filed by Jim a month after installing the floodlights which complained about the lights, the trees, and "emotional distress." You immediately filed a noise complaint with the city and counterclaimed for damages to your trees. The court has ordered you into mediation. You think that the harassment allegations and property line issues are bogus and that you would prevail in a trial. However, you are a doctor with a busy practice and do not have the time to go to trial so you have agreed to mediation-arbitration. You also hate to have your dirty linen aired in a public setting. You insist that Jim pay you $2,000 for the cost of the damaged trees and the aggravation of it all.

INFORMATION FOR JIM JONES

You are neighbors with Herbie West in a mountain home subdivision that has very small lots. Six months ago, Herbie posted a notice in his yard of an intention to build an addition onto his property which was in variance with the property line setback ordinance. Because the lots are so small and the architectural drawings showed an addition that would loom over your property and block the sun, you protested to the planning board of the city and the request for a variance was denied. You had only had minimal contact with Herbie and his wife prior to the variance issue.

A month after the variance was denied, Herbie put up a row of very expensive eight-foot evergreen trees between the two properties without any advance notification to you. You were concerned about the trees because they blocked your view of the mountains from your deck. You had the property line surveyed and found that the trees were planted two inches inside your property line so that the trunks of each tree were partially on your property. You then cut two feet off the top of the trees and all of the branches on your side of the trees which allowed you to once again view the mountains.

Two months after planting the trees, Herbie installed floodlights on his home which shine directly into your bedroom and disturb your sleep each night. You have had to move a bookcase in front of your window to keep the light out of your bedroom.

You have three boys, ages 6, 8, and 10, who are lively and energetic. They play basketball on your driveway which is adjacent to the West home. Several times Herbie has yelled at the boys when the ball bounced into the West yard and the boys ran into the yard to retrieve the ball. After the last time that Herbie yelled at the boys and used profanity, you called your lawyer who advised you to sue him. You decided to sue in small claims court to save costs.

Because you are a prominent businessman in town, you prefer not to go to court on this complaint; however, you would like the harassment to stop. You are not willing to drop the lawsuit, however, but will enter into mediation-arbitration so that the decision can be filed with the court. You don't trust that Herbie will stop his harassing behavior. You are asking for $3,000 damages for Herbie's property line encroachment as well as for damages for emotional distress.

REFERENCES

American Arbitration Association. (2006). Arbitration rules for the real estate industry (including a mediation alternative, as amended and effective September, 15, 2005). *Practicing Law Institute/Real Estate Law and Practice Course Handbook Series, 529,* 175–190.

Baris, M. A., Coates, C. A., Duvall, B. B., Garrity, C. B., Johnson, E. T., and LaCrosse, E. R. (2001). *Working with High-Conflict Families of Divorce: A Practitioner's Guide.* New Jersey: Jason Aronson Inc.

Backerman, R., and Vick, M. (1996). Mediation/Arbitration: A Survey of Professionals and Clients. Unpublished manuscript.

Bartel, B. (1991). Med-Arb as a distinct method of dispute resolution: history, analysis, and potential. *Willamette Law Review, 27,* 661–691.

Coates, C. (1993, Fall). Using mediation-arbitration: it's time to settle the differences. *Association of Family and Conciliation Courts Newsletter, 12,* 3.

Cohen, G. (2004). Negotiating in the shadow of death. *Dispute Resolution Magazine, 11, No. 1,* 12–22.

Fuller, L. (1962). Proceedings, fifteenth annual meeting, national academy of arbitrators, 8, 29-33,37-48. In Rau, A. S., Sherman, E. F., and Peppet, S. R. (2002). *Arbitration* (2nd ed.). New York: Foundation Press. (pp. 298-303).

Grenig, J. E. (1998). Final report of commission on health care dispute resolution. *Alternative Dispute Resolution App.* N (3rd ed.) 2.

Henry, K. (1988). Med-Arb: An alternative to interest arbitration in the resolution of contract negotiation disputes. *Ohio State Journal of Dispute Resolution, 3,* 385-398.

Kim, S. M. (2003). The provisional director remedy for corporate deadlock: a proposed model statute. *Washington and Lee Law Review, 60,* 111–180.

Landry, S. (1996). Med-arb: mediation with a bite and an effective ADR model. *Defense Counsel Journal, 63,* 263–269.

Phillips, G. F. (2005). Same-neutral med-arb: what does the future hold? *Dispute Resolution Journal, 60-July,* 24–32.

Phillips, J. R., Martinsen, S. K., and Dameron, M. L.. (2006). Analyzing the potential for ADR in estate planning instruments. *Alternatives to the High Cost of Litigation, 24,* 1–9.

Pruitt, D. (1995, October). Process and outcome in community mediation. *Negotiation Journal,* 365-377.

Rau, A. S., Sherman, E. F., and Peppet, S. R. (2002). *Arbitration* (2nd ed). New York: Foundation Press.

Reich, J. B (2002). Attorney v. client: creating a mechanism to address competing process interests in lawyer-driven mediation. *Southern Illinois University Law Journal, 26,* 183-225.

Sander, F. E. A., and Goldberg, S. B. (1994). Fitting the forum to the fuss: a user-friendly guide to selecting an ADR procedure. *Negotiation Journal, 10,* 49-66. In Kovach, K. (2004). *Mediation: Principles and Practice* (3rd ed.). (pp 19-25). St. Paul, MN: West Publishing Co.

Shienvold, A. (2004). Hybrid Processes. In J. Folberg, A. L. Milne, and P. Salem (Eds.), *Divorce and Family Mediation.* New York: Guilford Press. (pp. 112–126).

Chapter 13

Transformative Mediation: Purpose Drives Practice

Lisa Blomgren Bingham
Cynthia J. Hallberlin
Denise A. Walker

Scholars have identified three models of mediation, including evaluative, facilitative, and transformative (Bush and Folger, 2004). Transformative mediation is a relatively new model of practice that requires mediators to engage in non-traditional strategies, tactics, and behaviors, for example, to avoid evaluation of the case methods or related reality testing techniques common in other models. Transformative mediation is applied primarily in employment, family, and community settings; it is less frequent in court-annexed and agency dispute resolution programs. Its proponents argue it is an appropriate model for all mediation practice.

The transformative model has received an extensive field test for complaints of discrimination at the United States Postal Service (Postal Service) in its REDRESS® program (Resolve Employment Disputes Reach Equitable Solutions Swiftly, www.Postal Service.com/redress). Over the course of a ten-year independent evaluation of this program by the Indiana Conflict Resolution Institute at Indiana

University's School of Public and Environmental Affairs, researchers found that 1) the program correlated with a 30-percent reduction in the number of formal complaints of discrimination filed by employees; 2) on average 90 percent of all employees and supervisors were satisfied or highly satisfied with the mediation process and the performance of their mediators; 3) employee representatives were as satisfied with the program as their clients; 4) program satisfaction data was stable for a six-year period; and 5) there is evidence of improved conflict-management skills in the workplace in that the rate at which the disputants settle their own disputes after a complaint is filed but before the mediation session has increased from 2 percent to 14 percent (Bingham, 2003). This chapter will focus upon the use of transformative mediation in employment disputes, using the United States Postal Service as a case study.

MEDIATION AND ORGANIZATIONAL DISPUTES

Machine bureaucracies are breeding grounds for conflict. A machine bureaucracy is a form of organization in which there is rigid hierarchy, command and control management, and routine, highly mechanized industrial work. The emphasis on control, enforcement, and getting work done prevents the open discussion of problems and cultivates an atmosphere of tension. At the Postal Service, program designers believed that employees struggling with conflict either suppressed it or were directed to file a formal complaint. Baxter (1996) identifies sources of conflict including: hiring freezes, barriers to promotion, mandatory overtime, part-time employment, and training constraints. Other changes in practices, technology, policies, demands, and work expectations result in disruptions for employees that may cause conflict. Poor interpersonal communication can exacerbate these organizational issues, causing conflict to escalate. In general, the foci of conflict in the Postal Service lies between craft employees (labor) and their supervisors (management) because it is at this point in the Postal Service where productivity pressures are the greatest.

Prior to the implementation of the REDRESS® program, the Postal Service had received negative publicity stemming from a 1991 workplace violence shooting incident in Royal Oak, Michigan that left four supervisors and an employee dead. Although the phrase "going postal" became common in the 1990s to describe people who become violent in response to stress, a study by Columbia University revealed that workplace violence was not statistically more common or frequent at the Postal Service; postal workers are no more likely to physically assault their coworkers than employees in the national workforce.

However, workplace stress levels at the Postal Service were clearly reflected in the rising numbers of grievance and EEO complaints. The Postal Service national grievance arbitration database shows that in 1994, a total of 65,062 grievances involving postal management and union officials at the office level were filed. In 1996, this number increased 38 percent to 89,931. The number of backlogged grievances, those awaiting arbitration, also increased approximately 90 percent from 36,669 in 1994 to 69,555 in 1996. The GAO estimated the cost of dealing with Postal Service grievances at well over $200 million. There was also a correspondingly high rate of complaints filed with the Equal Employment Opportunity (EEO). The federal EEO complaint process starts with an informal complaint, followed by 'counseling' in which a professional EEO counselor explores the basis for the complaint and may attempt an informal resolution. Counseling is followed by a formal investigation, which may result in a formal complaint and a full, formal adjudicatory hearing before an administrative law judge.

By 1994, informal EEO complaints at the Postal Service had doubled over the prior 7 years from 15,000 to nearly 30,000; there was no indication that this trend was slowing or reversing. In 1997, prior to REDRESS, Postal Service employees filed over 25,000 informal EEO complaints annually. At that point, Postal Service employees accounted for approximately 30 percent of all federal employees but contributed more than 50 percent of all federal employee EEO complaints (Bingham, 2003). However, over 95 percent of these cases were resolved in favor of the Postal Service.

The Postal Service in-house EEO complaint process was primarily a paper process, with some telephone contact with the parties. It was not uncommon for the two disputants not to meet face to face to discuss the underlying dispute until it reached a formal hearing. Later, during the mediation program, observers and mediators alike noted that complainants rarely used the term "discrimination" when they described the dispute. Instead, they would describe how their supervisor treated them, or was disrespectful or abusive. They might assert that their supervisor did not like them, and would then speculate on the reason, which could include the fact that they were female or black or Hispanic, or some other reason. The great majority of cases did not present a prima facie case of discrimination within the meaning of federal law. Instead, they concerned instances of poor management and communication in an environment of constant production pressure.

It was common knowledge that employees checked a box for some category of prohibited discrimination on an EEO complaint because it provided access to a procedure for addressing the perceived abuse and making it stop. In the Sun Belt and Southern states in particular, employees were less likely to resort to the union grievance procedure due to prevailing political views on collective bargaining. In some cases, a frustrated employee had been known to file as many as sixty EEO complaints a year.

DISPUTE SYSTEM DESIGN

Clearly, the existing Postal Service dispute system was not optimal for effectively addressing workplace conflict. The problems were systemic: conflicts emerged from the organization's mechanistic and hierarchical structure, and were exacerbated by a time-consuming rights-based dispute system design. In the past twenty years, the concept of dispute system design has emerged. Dispute system design (DSD) is a phrase coined by Professors William Ury, Jeanne Brett, and Stephen Goldberg (1988) to describe the purposeful creation of an ADR program in an organization. Dispute resolution processes can focus on interests, rights, or power. Lipsky, Seeber, and Fincher (2003) suggest that the rise of ADR in the workplace reflects a changing social contract between employers and employees.

There are substantial arguments for using the transformative model of mediation in institutional settings like employment where the employer is unilaterally designing, implementing, and paying for the mediation program. In these contexts, there is the risk that the mediation program will be perceived as biased toward management. Moreover, employers prevail on the majority of workplace complaints of discrimination.

In court-connected practice, it is common for mediators to use an evaluative model of practice, which is one in which they assess the strengths and weaknesses of a legal case and share this with the parties. When disputants are represented by counsel and have no continuing relationship, this may be a desirable service. However, in an employment mediation program run by the employer, this may lead to a situation where mediators (paid for by the employer) are (truthfully and objectively) telling employees in the vast majority of cases that they have no legitimate legal claim. Rather than hearing this as objective, third party mediator evaluation, employees may perceive it as mediator bias. To avoid this result, and to build conflict-management skills in the workplace, the Postal Service adopted a dispute system design requiring the transformative model of practice (see www.PostalService.com/redress; Bingham, 2003).

The mediation program had to be embedded in the EEO complaint process, because the Postal Service is the largest unionized employer in the world. It negotiates separate contracts with bargaining units of clerks, letter carriers, rural letter carriers, mail handlers, and others. To adopt mediation in the grievance procedures, the Postal Service would have to negotiate with each union independently. This would result in a variety of procedures, and in fact, the Postal Service has negotiated co-mediation and grievance mediation in certain contracts in the past.

However, the EEO complaint process is not subject to mandatory bargaining. Federal statutes provide employees with individual rights and protection against discrimination that is independent from the collective bargaining agreement. Under Supreme Court decisions, the Postal Service could adopt a single program for EEO complaints for all employees. Moreover, during the period that the Postal Service was implementing mediation, the EEOC adopted a regulation that required all federal employers to provide employees with dispute resolution as an option in the EEO complaint process. Thus, in order for an employee to get access to the mediation program, Postal Service employees needed to enter through the EEO complaint process. Some managers were concerned that this would cause an increase in complaint filing, and that employees would file both EEO complaints and union grievances on the same subject just to get access to mediation. They called this "getting two bites at the apple." However, over the life of the program, overall complaint filings dropped.

TRADITIONAL EVALUATIVE AND FACILITATIVE MEDIATION APPROACHES

The field has largely accepted that there are three different models of mediation: evaluative, facilitative, and transformative (Bush & Folger, 2004). Riskin (1996) developed a grid that describes what mediators "do" on one axis from evaluation to facilitation, and another from broad to narrow problem definition (Riskin, 1996). On the first axis, the evaluative mediator focuses on helping the parties understand the strengths and weaknesses of their case by providing assessment, prediction, and direction. An evaluative mediator generally asks the parties to make formal opening statements presenting their case and often conducts one or more caucuses with each side. The mediator focuses on collecting facts, identifying issues, and evaluating legal arguments to determine who is likely to win and how much they would probably recover. The mediator then strategically moves the parties toward settlement and may even propose a resolution.

In contrast, the successful facilitative mediator clarifies and enhances communication between the parties and helps them decide what to do (Riskin, 1996). Like an evaluative mediator, a facilitative mediator generally listens to opening statements and sometimes conducts caucuses; however, a facilitative mediator does not assess the legal merits of the dispute, but rather focuses on the parties' underlying needs and how an interest-based settlement could meet those needs. The facilitative mediator may engage in "reality-testing" to help the parties better understand their BATNA (their alternatives to a negotiated settlement) and helps them generate options for settlement.

The second axis in Riskin's grid is problem definition. Mediation issues range from narrowly construed (as in litigation) to broader community interests (e.g. environmental mediation).

In their controversial and influential book, *The Promise of Mediation: The Transformative Approach to Conflict* (2004 and its earlier edition), Bush and Folger distinguish between the "problem-solving" and "transformative" models of mediation practice. They argue that problem-solving mediators focus on achieving an agreement that resolves the issues in dispute by controlling the mediation process and discussion among parties, identifying and narrowing the problems and issues, and persuading the parties to accept a workable solution (Bush & Folger, 2004). Their view is that both evaluative and facilitative are problem-solving mediators.

In contrast to evaluative and facilitative models, transformative mediators are successful when something happens to change the way parties relate to each other and understand their respective situations (Bush & Folger, 2004; Bush & Pope, 2002). The goal of transformative mediation is to develop opportunities for empowerment and recognition—to give people control over resolving their own conflicts by fostering self-determination and responsiveness. Empowerment is analogous to self-determination; they define it as enabling the parties to describe their own issues and to seek their own solutions to problems. Parties who are empowered will become calm, confident, and more clear and decisive. In practice, this means that the mediator should try to identify opportunities to give parties greater clarity about their goals and support their decisions-making (Bush & Folger, 2004).

Recognition occurs when the parties see and understand the other person's point of view—when each understands how the other defines the problem and why he or she seeks the solution they do. Recognition is achieved when, given some degree of empowerment, parties expand their perspective to include an appreciation for another's situation (Bush & Folger, 2004). The transformative mediator identifies points in the mediation in which parties consider the other's point of view and supports their effort to get perspective (Bush & Folger, 2004). This transformative process often results in an agreement and settlement; however, these secondary effects are derivatives of the transformation in the parties' relationship. Empowerment and recognition allow the parties to achieve this change.

TRANSFORMATIVE MEDIATION

There is no single course of education that prepares a mediator for transformative practice. Mediators on the Postal Service panel are required to have both an undergraduate degree and a graduate degree in some professional or academic field, a standard 40-hour mediation training course, and at least ten cases in which they are the lead mediator. The roster is drawn from all areas of professional practice; they include lawyers, psychotherapists, clinical psychologists, social workers, and people with masters or doctoral degrees from the fields of communication, psychology, sociology, business, and others. Candidates for the Postal Service mediator roster then participate in additional intensive training in the transformative model. This training was developed by Professors Bush and Folger and consisted of three days. In addition to role plays, participants learned to identify critical moments in the conversation between disputants for purposes of highlighting moments of empowerment and recognition. This training is now offered through the Institute of Conflict Transformation (www.transformativemediation.org).

To ensure adherence to the transformative model of mediation, the Postal Service evaluated mediators during a mediation session to identify actual practices that were outside the transformative model. Examples of behaviors that were contrary to the model were mediators who attempted to push the parties to settlement.

The results of the face-to-face evaluation sessions were shared with the mediators, providing them with an opportunity to learn from the feedback. The evaluators were trained transformative mediators, and used a standard form. This process provided "hands on" training in the model.

The transformative mediator is not a passive observer, but pays attention to where the parties themselves take the conversation. Transformative mediators do not set ground rules for the parties; instead they ask the parties whether they feel they need ground rules. In transformative mediation, problem definition is left to the disputants. Some might argue that transformative mediators, as with all mediators, engage in selective facilitation (Greatbatch and Dingwall, 1989). In other words, they make choices about which critical points in the discussion represent opportunities for empowerment or recognition.

The ten hallmarks of transformative mediation (Figure 13.1: Bush & Folger, 1996) suggest that transformative mediation differs from other forms of mediation. For example, in transformative mediation sessions, problem solving, developing agreements, and crafting settlement terms for the parties are not acceptable mediator behaviors. A transformative mediator will not engage in integration to find a solution or common ground for the parties or pressure parties to reduce the set of non-agreement alternatives, nor compensate the parties to increase the set of

1. *"The opening statement says it all":* Describing the mediator's role and objectives in terms based on empowerment and recognition.
2. *"It's ultimately the parties choice":* Leaving responsibility for outcomes with the parties.
3. *"The parties know best":* Consciously refusing to be judgmental about the parties' views and decisions.
4. *"The parties have what it takes":* Taking an optimistic view of parties' competence and motives.
5. *"There are facts in feelings":* Allowing and being responsive to parties' expression of emotions.
6. *"Clarity emerges from confusion":* Allowing for and exploring parties' uncertainty.
7. *"The action is 'in the room'":* Remaining focused on the here and now of the conflict interaction.
8. *"Discussing the past has value to the present":* Being responsive to parties' statements about past events.
9. *"Conflict can be a long-term affair":* Viewing an intervention as one point in a larger sequence of conflict interaction.
10. *"Small steps count":* Feeling a sense of success when empowerment and recognition occur, even in small degrees (Bush & Folger, 1996)

Figure 13.1
The Ten Hallmarks of Transformative Mediation

agreement alternatives. Finally, although inaction appears to be an appropriate strategy in transformative mediation because it allows the disputants to handle the conflict themselves, a true transformative mediator would be active in identifying and highlighting opportunities for empowerment and recognition.

PREPARATION FOR TRANSFORMATIVE MEDIATION

Transformative mediation emphasizes micro-analysis of the disputants' conversation during the actual mediation session. Thus, typically, a transformative mediator does not request information on the merits of the claims in advance of the mediation session. In the Postal Service model for employment disputes, the mediator simply arrives for the session, which averages four hours in duration. Bush and Pope (2002) describe the essential steps of a transformative mediation as listen, reflect, summarize, check in, and let go. The mediator is listening with the goal of supporting the parties in their interaction and identifying opportunities for empowerment and recognition. This requires the mediator to stay in the moment and listen to the parties' own conversation cues. A mediator uses reflection by summarizing, in the party's own words, the emotion or content that he or she hears. Summarizing happens when there is a natural break in the conversation.

Mediators check in with questions like "Where do you want to go from here?" or "Is there something more you want to say about that?" Occasionally, they may ask, "Is this helpful?" A period of silence may be powerful and appropriate. Mediators avoid taking control and telling the parties what to do, or imposing their own views about goals on the parties, for example with statements like "Let's stay on track" or "The real, serious issues are these."

Competent transformative practice entails orienting the parties to a constructive conversation, orienting the parties to their own agency, orienting the parties to each other; supporting the parties in "conflict talk"; and supporting the parties' decision-making process (Della Noce, Antes, & Saul, 2004). For example, a transformative mediator would describe the process in terms of assisting the parties in having a discussion or conversation, talking about differences, and assisting them with understanding their own goals and needs and those of the other person. The mediator would use "you" or the person's name in reflection of their statements to emphasize agency. The mediator would talk about "both of you" or "all of you" when checking in about the conversation to orient the parties to each other. They support the parties' conflict talk with words of encouragement. They would check in by asking the parties questions, "Are these the things you want to talk about?" The mediator would de-emphasize their role with "I don't know" or a series of choices for the parties to make (Della Noce, Antes, & Saul, 2004). In sum, unlike other models of mediation, the transformative model entails less preparation in advance of the mediation and more concentration on the micro-level communications of the parties during their conversation.

In the Postal Service context, transformative mediators are able to provide a safe space in which parties can have a meaningful conversation about the communication issues that have given rise to the complaint. One of the most surprising results from the program is the prevalence and persistence of apology as an outcome. Both employees and their supervisors report that supervisors apologize to employees in almost a third of all cases. Moreover, it is precisely an apology and respectful treatment that employees seek. The median settlement value of most cases is zero in monetary terms.

Issues and Problems with Transformative Mediation

Critics suggest that transformative mediation is inefficient and will take substantially longer than facilitative mediation because of the focus on communication analysis between the parties. The Postal Service mediations average about four hours in duration, as contrasted with 30 to 45 minutes for facilitative or evaluative mediation models in small claims courts. In cases where the parties do not know each other or have any continuing relationship—for example, an auto accident—they may have no interest in changing the nature of their relationship; there will be no future communication.

Another issue is that transformative practice does not follow the recipe that is accepted facilitative mediation practice. One state suggested that a transformative mediator's training would not be certified because the trainer failed to include the "stages of the process," but that concept does not apply in this model.

Transformative mediators do not set ground rules. They follow the parties' lead in what they want to talk about and when. They must be much more comfortable with high emotions. They allow parties to remain together in the room and have heated exchanges rather than take control through use of caucus. They do not enforce turn-taking in the conversation or time limits on how long someone may speak. They do not soften, reframe, or try to de-emphasize the emotional content of someone's statements.

As a result, there are issues with efforts to regulate and assure the quality of mediation practice. For example, in some quality assurance initiatives from state courts such as Florida, the initial definitions of competent mediation excluded transformative practice (Della Noce, Bush, and Folger, 2002).

Moreover, it is challenging to determine success in the transformative model, because it is not defined as settlement. Mediators attempt to foster empowerment and recognition, while the parties (or their lawyers) may just want to get the deal done. As a result of these differences, some have suggested that transformative mediators need to do more disclosure up front with disputants.

CONCLUSION

Transformative mediation can be the right choice for certain kinds of cases and in the context of institutional dispute system designs where one party has control over the key design choices. Within a given case, it puts control over both process and outcome in the hands of the disputants, helps them have meaningful conversations about the nature and circumstances of the conflict, and can help change the nature of an interaction from destructive to constructive. In cases where the parties must have continuing contact and maintain a relationship, this transformation of their interaction may help reduce future conflict. Proponents argue that even in cases in which there will be no continuing relationship, the transformative model can help the parties achieve moral growth through a better understanding of their own capacity to handle conflict and recognition of the needs and perspectives of others. The model has great potential and represents an important alternative skill set for aspiring mediators.

Case Study: The Route Number Case

The Postal Service's goal for its mediation program was to improve the communication skills of employees and supervisors, and to provide an effective avenue to address the thousands of disputes that found their way into the EEO complaint process. The following case study was used extensively in the Postal Service training program. It illustrates how transformative mediation can be used for the most common kinds of workplace disputes.

A female letter carrier has filed an informal complaint of sexual harassment and sex discrimination with the Postal Service. She is petite, thirty-four years old, and very attractive. Her supervisor is a male in his mid-forties who is responsible for overseeing all the letter carriers in the geographical area covered by this zip code. In her complaint, she alleges that her male supervisor has created an offensive working environment. There are no other details regarding the allegations in the complaint itself. The supervisor is at a loss to understand the basis for the complaint. He has never, to his knowledge, made a sexual advance or untoward suggestive remark to this employee.

During the mediation session several weeks later, the two disputants have a long conversation in the presence of the mediator. She explains to her supervisor that he addresses her by her route number, which is 328, rather than her name. This happens several times each day. She finds this demeaning and dehumanizing. As a woman, she feels like she is invisible and that her supervisor has not even learned her name.

He responds that this was not his intention and he had no idea she found it offensive; he addresses all letter carriers, male and female alike, by their route numbers. He apologizes and volunteers never to call her by her route number again. She agrees to this settlement and withdraws the complaint.

Questions for Discussion

1. Why would an employee file an EEO complaint on these facts rather than approach the supervisor directly with her concerns?
2. What would an evaluative mediator do in this case?
3. How would a facilitative mediator handle this case?
4. Imagine a conversation between the disputants in a transformative mediation of this case. How would it differ from a conversation in an evaluative or facilitative mediation?
5. Why would the employee file an EEO complaint rather than a grievance under the collective bargaining agreement?
6. What are the advantages and disadvantages for the employer in offering mediation for cases such as these?

Role Play: The Claim of Sexual Harassment

The following information provides a case simulation. It can be used for evaluative, facilitative, or transformative mediation practice. One variant of the exercise is to have student groups use different mediation models and then compare the conversations when they debrief.

General Information

Letter carrier Alice Brown is a petite, attractive, 30-year old letter carrier who was transferred to this district three months ago. She has been with the Postal Service for five years and has an excellent record. She was assigned a delivery route in accordance with standard practice, Route No. 328. She has been making her deliveries on time and there are no problems with her performance. Several weeks ago, Alice filed a complaint of sexual harassment and sex discrimination with the Equal Employment Opportunity Commission (EEOC), alleging that her supervisor has created an intolerable working environment.

Alice's supervisor, Jim Smith, is in his late 40s and has been with the Postal Service since he left the Army after the Gulf War. He was an officer in the Army, and is accustomed to running a tight, well-disciplined operation. He has a good performance record and has twice been promoted by the Postal Service. While there have been the usual grievances and complaints filed by employees (for example, protesting discipline) under his supervision, he has never been the subject of a sexual harassment complaint before.

INSTRUCTIONS TO MEDIATORS

In this case, use transformative mediation practice. Introduce yourself; explain that you are there to help the parties have a conversation, and then ask them how they wish to proceed. Ask them if they wish to have any ground rules and whom they would like to speak first. Tell them this is their process and their conversation. Then, follow the parties where they take the process. Periodically, ask them if this is helpful; ask them how they wish to proceed. Periodically, paraphrase what you hear back to the parties. If you hear one party getting clearer about his or her own concerns and interests, paraphrase that back to them. If you hear one party acknowledge the legitimacy of the other's views, perspective, concerns, or interests, take a moment to paraphrase that back to both of the parties. If the parties start to speak to you, ask them to speak to each other, since this is their conversation; you are not going to decide anything or do anything but assist them in having this discussion. Do not separate the parties unless they ask you to.

INFORMATION FOR ALICE BROWN

You were recently transferred to this district. You have two children, an 11-year old daughter and a 5-year old son and you are a single parent. You value your job with the Postal Service because it is secure, well paying employment with excellent benefits that allow you to support your children. You have been here about three months. You like your new delivery route; it is reasonable, and you have been able to make your deliveries on schedule for the most part. However, over the past several weeks, you have found circumstances at work increasingly oppressive. Your supervisor, who is responsible for overseeing all letter carriers in this zip code, refers to you as "328," instead of using your name. You find this demeaning and dehumanizing. You know he calls all employees by their route numbers; however, as a woman, you feel like you are invisible and that your supervisor has not even learned your name. You have filed an informal complaint of sexual harassment and sex discrimination. You are willing to try mediation; your last experience with the complaint process ended up in an adversarial hearing before an administrative law judge, and even though the Postal Service ultimately disciplined that supervisor, the stress of the whole process almost made you quit your job.

INFORMATION FOR JIM SMITH

You are at a loss to understand the basis for the complaint. Neither you nor your boss has any more information about the reason for it. You are a happily married man with three daughters and have been utterly faithful to your spouse; the idea that you would hit on someone under your supervision is both ludicrous and deeply offensive to you. In your former career as an Army officer, you severely disciplined enlisted men under your supervision if they failed to treat female soldiers with the appropriate dignity and respect. You have heard through the grapevine that Ms. Brown filed a complaint at her previous job assignment in a nearby town, and you wonder whether you have a troublemaker on your hands. You are surprised; her performance has met your demanding standards and you have been very pleased with it.

In the past, after a complaint like this is filed he hears nothing further for a period of months or years because of case backlogs. However, the Postal Service has a new mediation program, and Ms. Brown has agreed to mediation. Although there is no requirement that he reach an agreement in mediation, he must attend and participate in good faith under Postal Service rules. In the EEO complaint process, the Postal Service is the respondent or defendant, and the supervisor its agent. For that reason, the Postal Service requires that managers and supervisors like Jim attend the mediation session. This is different from many mediation programs, in which even participation in the mediation session is voluntary for both participants. While he resents the fact that a complaint was filed, he is willing to attend the mediation because he wants to find out the imagined basis for it.

REFERENCES

Antes, J. R., Folger, J. P., and Della Noce, D. J. (2001). Transforming conflict interactions in the workplace: Documented effects of the POSTAL SERVICE REDRESS™ Program. *Hofstra Labor and Employment Law Journal, 18*(2), 429-468.

Baxter, V. (1994). *Labor and Politics in the U.S. Postal Service.* Cambridge, MA: Plenum Press.

Bingham, L. B. (2003). *Mediation at Work: Transforming Workplace Conflict at the United States Postal Service.* Arlington, VA: IBM Center for the Business of Government.

Bush R. A. B., and Folger, J. P. (1996). Transformative mediation and third-party intervention: Ten hallmarks of a transformative approach to practice. *Mediation Quarterly, 13,* 263-78.

Bush R. A .B., and Folger, J. (2004). *The Promise of Mediation: The Transformative Approach to Conflict.* San Francisco: Jossey-Bass.

Bush, R. A. B., and Pope, S. G. (2002). Changing the quality of conflict interaction: The principles and practice of transformative mediation. *Pepperdine Dispute Resolution Law Journal, 67* (3), 67-96.

Hallberlin, C. J. (2001). Transforming workplace culture through mediation: Lessons learned from swimming upstream. *Hofstra Labor and Employment Law Journal, 18:,* 75-383.

Lipsky, D., Seeber, R., and Fincher, R. (2003). *Emerging Systems for Managing Workplace Conflict: Lessons from American Corporations for Managers and Dispute Resolution Professionals.* San Francisco, CA: Jossey-Bass.

Moore, C. (1996). *The Mediation Process: Practical Strategies for Resolving Conflict.* San Francisco: Jossey-Bass.

Pope, S. G. (1996). Inviting fortuitous events in mediation: The role of empowerment and recognition. *Hofstra Labor and Employment Law Journal, 18*(2), 287-294.

Riskin, L. L. (1996). Understanding mediator orientations, strategies and techniques: A grid for the perplexed. *Harvard Negotiation Law Review, 1,* 7-51.

Ury, W. L., Brett, J. M., and Goldberg, S. B. (1988). *Getting Disputes Resolved: Designing Systems to Cut the Cost of Conflict.* San Francisco, CA: Jossey-Bass.

Chapter 14

Conclusion

Jerry Bagnell
Bruce C. McKinney

During years of teaching mediation in the classroom as well as presenting a number of programs throughout the United States, we have been unable to find a source we could refer students to that would answer many of their basic questions about mediation. There are many books containing specific guidance on subjects from the effective use of a caucus to empowering participants, but none that merely stimulate interest in mediation in general with some insight about various settings in which mediators practice their profession.

We hope that you have found *Readings and Case Studies in Mediation* to be a source of information about much more basic questions such as, "What is it like working with couples going through a divorce?" or "Can you really mediate with gangs?" Our focus was on "What's it all about?" rather than how to perform specific tasks in mediation. We are certain that experienced practitioners will find some of the contributing authors' comments to be very basic but are equally certain they will acknowledge that they have provided those same answers to students and other interested persons throughout the years they have practiced.

The authors have always enjoyed and welcomed the curiosity of people who bring enthusiasm and an open mind to our classrooms and trainings. As you have read each of the chapters of this book, we hope your experience has been much like someone wandering the aisles of a store containing lots of interesting items.

Some of you may have just been looking. Others may have had a specific item you were searching for, and we hope that you may have found it in this book.

Whether you just wanted to find out how mediation differed from arbitration, or you wanted to see if there was a better way to handle conflict at work, our contributing authors were pleased to show off their wares and not be too concerned about a scholarly analysis of their opinions. However, as you may have noticed, some of the chapters present more research than others. This is intentional—we wanted both scholars and practitioners to contribute to this book, and we think it is a nice blend of experiential and academic information about mediation. The term "practice wisdom" is often used to describe the lessons learned by seasoned practitioners. If those who seek such wisdom have spent some time as practitioners, what they learn will have some relevance. On the other hand, those who may seek the answer to some academic question about mediation will find plenty of answers in this text. Those who are merely curious and want to decide whether to become practitioners or consumers of mediation services often hesitate to ask what they are afraid might be perceived as naïve questions. This book is an attempt to help those people as well.

We hope that you recognized that our authors anticipated even the most basic questions and answered them in a manner that was easy to understand and inspired you to look even further into the profession of mediation. If we have aroused your interest—if we have even tickled your curiosity—we have succeeded in accomplishing our goal for producing this text.

Certainly, there are many more questions to be answered and many more books available to peruse for those answers. You have had an opportunity to wander the aisles and look at what was on the shelves. Our authors invite your questions and comments. All are professionals who realize that the seasoned practitioner who is truly wise knows that his or her ultimate task is to step aside so that new practitioners can get by on the road to success. We hope that by sharing our insights and opinions, you have been inspired to begin your journey down that road.